Canada - India
Partners in Progress

Canada - India
Partners in Progress

Prem K Budhwar

Foreword by

K. Natwar Singh

Vij Books India Pvt Ltd
New Delhi (India)

Indian Council of World Affairs
Sapru House, New Delhi

Canada-India: Partners in Progress
First Published in India in 2016

Published by

Vij Books India Pvt Ltd
(Publishers, Distributors & Importers)
2/19, Ansari Road
Delhi – 110 002
Phones: 91-11-43596460, 91-11-47340674
Fax: 91-11-47340674
e-mail: vijbooks@rediffmail.com
web : www.vijbooks.com

ISBN: 978-93-84464-88-2 (Hardback)
ISBN: 978-93-84464-89-9 (ebook)

Contents

Foreword

This book was waiting to be written. The right person has produced it at the right time. I have known the author, Prem Budhwar, for several decades. He was one of our ablest diplomats. He served India well. His major contribution was to deepen, widen and constructively expand our relations with Canada. Indo-Canadian cordiality began with Jawaharlal Nehru's first visit to Canada in 1949. He established friendly relationships with Prime Minister Louis St. Laurent.

Indo-Canadian bilateral relations are time tested and we value this friendship with one of the great democracies in the world. Inevitably, there were one or two hiccups, the most striking one was in May, 1998 when India became a nuclear weapons power. The setback was short lived.

Written in two parts, part one is an in-depth survey of Canada covering its various aspects. Part two is devoted entirely to India- Canada relations, including their ups and downs and the reasons thereof. The author had the satisfaction of participating in and witnessing the new beginning of an upswing in these relations during his tenure in Canada.

Prem Budhwar was the longest serving High Commissioner to so important and influential a country. The author's style is lively and lucid. Packed with details and sound analysis the book is eminently readable and absorbing. It deserves a long shelf life.

– K. Natwar Singh

November, 2015

Preface

When, at the beginning of 2013, I was formally asked by the Indian Council of World Affairs (ICWA) to do a comprehensive volume on Canada, I agreed to do so readily and without any hesitation. The time limit prescribed for this project was two years, which too was acceptable and reasonable. It would, I felt, keep the desirable pressure on me to finish the project on schedule and, at the same time, give me enough space to read a lot, collect various relevant materials, absorb them and put them in a readable form and lace them copiously with my own comments and observations. At the end of the day, I am happy to achieve all these objectives and deliver on schedule.

I undertook this project enthusiastically for a variety of reasons. I had lived and worked in Canada for nearly five years as India's High Commissioner from 1992 to 1997. The end of my term coincided with my superannuation from the Foreign Service, a very satisfying career spanning a little over three and a half decades. Happily, Canada turned out to be the longest single posting in my career and by the time I left Ottawa, I had the distinction of having served the longest in the post of the High Commissioner of India to that country. I do not think that record has been broken yet by any of my successors, at least not so far.

Apart from the length of stay, I enjoyed my Canadian assignment for more reasons than one. Canada is not only a vast country, the second largest in the world in size, but also a beautiful country with friendly and helpful people. Given the opportunities for travel within the country and my fondness for travel, I made full use of them. Professionally, I felt it was desirable, in fact, essential if one had to truly understand this huge country and its people. I enjoyed and benefitted a lot from interacting with the Canadian people, from different walks of life and with different backgrounds; not the least, the huge Indian Diaspora spread all over, quite literally, the entire country. To understand and appreciate the enormous variety and beauty of Canada, even its vastness and emptiness, the circumstances of my official position enabled me to traverse across the full length and breadth of the country, from the Arctic region and the magnetic North Pole to the border with the USA and from the eastern most point jutting out into the Atlantic Ocean to the western most point on the Pacific coast. I visited all the ten provinces, some several times, and crossed the Arctic Circle a few times in the course of my forays into the Yukon and the huge North-West Territories. I was even fortunate enough to see the spectacular Aurora Borealis, the northern lights.

My attitude, over the years, has been that before going to any place, be it in India or abroad, whether on a visit or for living there for a certain period, read as much as possible about it. This attitude has paid off well and I continue to do so even in retirement when my quest for travelling has not diminished. This approach, what I often like to call doing your home-work before going to a new place, has paid off well. Thus equipped, you look at things differently, you have queries, you are looking for answers, you are more perceptive; altogether you get much more satisfaction out of the effort being put in by you.

But in a Foreign Service career, very often, you do not get enough notice before a country on the world map becomes your home for the next few years. Once your posting is formally made known to you, you get caught up in several other things, winding up your current establishment, the farewell visits and calls, the inevitable spate of farewell parties, to mention a few only. And yet, mentally, increasingly you are already elsewhere, the new country of your posting. Yes, you try and eke out some time, in the midst of these happenings, to read and know more about your next assignment. But the constraint of time, at least that was my experience, does not allow you to delve into great details. And, what happens when you finally reach the new place? This time, a round of welcome parties, meeting people, settling down both with your work and at home, sorting out various personal matters. It is action from day one. It is like being thrown into battle from the moment you land. True, it is very exciting, interesting, even challenging, but finding time for in-depth study and analysis remains a daunting task.

This is what I experienced, when, in about two months, I was told to proceed to Canada from Brazil, where I was serving as the Ambassador. Since the Ottawa post was already lying vacant and the government did not favour leaving it so for too long, I was asked to reach there directly from Brasilia. This meant a direct overnight flight from Brasilia to New York and on to Ottawa after a change of flights. It was the very beginning of November.

Brasilia, being in the southern hemisphere, was warm and balmy. Ottawa was already below zero and covered in snow.

I have often maintained that in a Foreign Service career, getting posted to interesting places is one thing, but being at the right place at the right time is quite another thing and it can make a big difference. I have been singularly fortunate in this respect, be it my three postings in Moscow (while still the Capital of the Soviet Union) or Hong Kong or Hanoi, or Hamburg, Bonn and Berlin, or Addis Ababa or Brasilia, with New Delhi in between. The five years that I was in Ottawa proved to be no exception in this respect. For the last several years, since 1974 (India's first nuclear test) to be precise, India's relations with Canada had remained normal at the best and indifferent at their worst. The dramatic change occurred in the aftermath of India's economic reforms from 1991 onwards that coincided with the change of government in Canada and a new mind set. India's economic and commercial attraction increasingly came into focus and Canada was keen, once again, to do business with India. My five years in Canada overlapped with this phase, climaxing in January, 1996 with Prime Minister Jean Chretien's "Team Canada" visit to India. It was after a quarter century that a visit from Canada to India took place at that level. The visit went off extremely well with several concrete outcomes. My biggest satisfaction was to be in the thick of all these unfolding positive developments. India was once again the flavour of the month, so to say, in Canada.

I not only immensely enjoyed working on this volume, but, at the end of the exercise, I had a certain sense of satisfaction. If I may be allowed to be a little immodest, I felt that only if I had such a convenient access to all this information and analysis at the start of my assignment to Canada, things would have been a lot better for me, at least in the early stages. The rest I leave to the readers to judge and this would hopefully include not just diplomats, but business executives, journalists, academics, research scholars, public figures; in short, any one seriously interested in Canada and what it should mean to India and, indeed, to the rest of the world.

— **Prem K. Budhwar**

Acknowledgements

First and foremost, my sincere thanks are due to the Indian Council of World Affairs (ICWA) for commissioning me to write this book. This resulted from the initiative of its Director General, Ambassador Rajiv Bhatia, to fill certain obvious knowledge gaps, hence a comprehensive volume on Canada and its relations with India was conceptualised. The cooperation extended by numerous colleagues, retired and serving, in the Ministry of External Affairs, the High Commission of India in Canada and the High Commission of Canada in India deserves to be very much placed on record. My interactions with them provided useful inputs. Sincere thanks are also due to various friends and scholars, who I was privileged to know while serving in Canada. Their views and the materials provided by them, carefully saved by me, came in most handy. My thanks are also due to the two referees to whom the manuscript was referred to by the ICWA. Quite understandably, their identity was never made known to me. But I was encouraged by their appreciation of what I had written and also benefitted from their valuable views and suggestions that I have endeavoured to incorporate as much as possible. I would also like to acknowledge the most helpful and constructive role played, notably towards the final stages of this project, by Dr. Pankaj Jha, Director (Research) of the ICWA.

Finally, I owe a big thanks to my wife, Kusum. Her computer skill was a huge help to someone like me who has yet to go beyond the stage of typing on the computer. At times it was a taxing job for her but she always did it with a smile. Thank you my dear.

I would also very much like to express my grateful thanks to Sh. K. Natwar Singh, himself an author of repute and former Minister of External Affairs, for agreeing to write the Foreword.

List of Abbreviations

AANDC	Aboriginal Affairs and Northern Development Canada
ADB	Asian Development Bank
APEC	Asia-Pacific Economic Cooperation
ASEAN	Association of Southeast Asian Nations
BARC	Bhabha Atomic Research Center
BQ	Bloc Quebecois
CARICOM	Caribbean Community
CBC	Canadian Broadcasting Corporation
CEPA	Comprehensive Economic Partnership Agreement
CFDC	Canadian Films Development Corporation
CIBC	Canada-India Business Council
CIDA	Canadian International Development Agency
CIRUS	Canadian-Indian Reactor, US
CPPIB	Canadian Pension Plan Investment Board
CTBT	Comprehensive Test Ban Treaty
DFAIT	(Canadian) Department of Foreign Affairs and International Trade
FAO	Food and Agriculture Organization
FDI	Foreign Direct Investment
FIPPA	Freedom of Information and Protection of Privacy Act
FTA	Free Trade Agreement
FTAA	Free Trade Area of the Americas
GDP	Gross Domestic Product
IAEA	International Atomic Energy Agency
IATA	International Air Transport Association

IBRD	International Bank for Reconstruction and Development
ICAO	International Civil Aviation Organization
ICCC	India-Canada Chamber of Commerce
ICOBC	India-Canada Ottawa Business Council
ILO	International Labour Organization
IMF	International Monetary fund
INAC	Indian and Northern Affairs Canada
INTERPOL	International Criminal Police Organization
IPU	Inter Parliamentary Union
LNG	Liquefied Natural Gas
NAFTA	North American Free Trade Agreement
NATO	North Atlantic Treaty Organization
NDP	National Democratic Party
NFB	National Film Board of Canada
NORAD	North American Aerospace Defense Command
NPT	Non-Proliferation Treaty
NSR	Northern Shipping Route
OAS	Organization of American States
OCI	Overseas Citizen of India
OECD	Organization for Economic Co-operation and Development
PC	Conservative Party
PEI	Prince Edward Island
PIO	Person of Indian Origin
PNE	Peaceful Nuclear Explosion
POW	Prisoner of War
RCMP	Royal Canadian Mounted Police
TFO	Trade Facilitation Office
UN-CLCS	UN Commission on Limitation of Continental Shelf
UNCLOS	United Nations Convention on the Law of the Sea

UNESCO	United Nations Educational, Scientific and Cultural Organization
UNO	United Nations Organization
UNRRA	United Nations Relief and Rehabilitation Agency
USSR	Union of Soviet Socialist Republics
WHO	World Health Organization
WTO	World Trade Organization

PART – I

CANADA

Chapter One – History

The story of the vast territorial expanse that is today's Canada is, in many ways, a saga of the human spirit of adventure and survival in the face of extreme adversity, the quest for discovery propelled both by necessity and curiosity, lure of money and profit, the grit and courage to confront the unknown and to take on the extreme harshness of nature, weather, the elements and wilderness.

The beginning of this story takes one back by several centuries, much before the European explorers discovered this vast territory straddling across North America. Wandering nomads crossing over from Siberia, across the frozen Bering Straits to the icy wilderness of Northern Alaska and Yukon, were possibly the first known inhabitants of Canada and probably some twenty to forty thousand years ago. Some even opine that the first human occupants of Canada arrived during the last ice age, which began around 80,000 years ago and ended around 12,000 years ago. A recent study conducted by the Natural History Museum of Denmark's Centre for Geo Genetics also suggests that the first North Americans came directly from Siberia. This was based on results from a DNA study by a researcher of Indian origin, Maanasa Raghavan, of a young boy's skeletal remains believed to have died 24,000 years ago. According to Raghavan and her colleagues at the above Centre, the study proved that the ancestors of Native Americans migrated to the Americas from Siberia and not directly from Europe as some have suggested (As reported in the *Times of India*, New Delhi edition, November 22, 2013).

Finds along the Old Crow basin in the northern Yukon have indicated the presence of hunting populations in the periods 25,000 to 30,000 years ago. But these objects have been found in re-deposited sediments and there is a possibility that many of them may have been made by agencies other than man. The archaeological site of the earliest accepted occupation made by man is Blue Fish Caves in northern Yukon. Three small caves overlooking a wide basin have been found to contain chipped stone artefacts; carbon dating indicates their age as *at least 10,000 to 13,000 years and possibly 15,000 to 18,000 years.

Either unable to return from where they had originated their journey (the frozen narrow strip of the Bering Strait linking eastern most Siberia with the western most tip of Alaska would have melted away in summer – historically, Alaska was part of Russia till it was sold to the USA in the 19th century) or curious to proceed further and explore more, they were to become the first known inhabitants of what was much later to be known as Canada. They were, no doubt, courageous and tough people or else they would not have survived the extremely harsh and brutal climatic conditions. Innovation combined with intelligence and the capacity to adapt in order to survive characterised the ancient lifestyle and civilization of these extremely hardy people, now commonly referred to as the Inuit (the only people), who had discovered the vast frozen northern expanse of the American continent.

The culture of the Arctic Inuit is rightly referred to as the "Stone Age" culture. Living way beyond the tree line, the only materials available to these people were stones, chunks of ice, ivory (tusks of walrus), bones of animals and fish besides, of course, animal furs. This would explain their snow huts or igloos, their bows and arrows made with tips of flint, ivory or bone, their cooking utensils, their clothing and hunting techniques adapted to the very long winter and very short summer conditions. Their diet consisted essentially of meat and fish, consumed raw. When natural food supplies dwindled in one area, whole families would move to another area either on foot or on sleds made of frozen fish or hides that could also be eaten if there was no other food available. In a way, precursors to the modern day fancy survival kits so well-known now to the present day explorers.

Going down further the history lane of Canada, one comes across people, who migrated to and discovered other parts of Canada; this time, more hospitable and environment friendly. It is thus that one finds signs of a rich and varied culture and civilization of the Indians that ultimately fell victim to the arrival of European explorers and settlers.

Starting with the west coast, along the Pacific Ocean, where climatic conditions, when compared to the extreme North, were much more mild and friendly, one comes across various Indian groups and tribes. Prominent among these were the Haidas, the Tlingit, Bella Coola, Nootka and the Kwakiutl. Their settlements being along the Pacific coast, they found abundant supplies of various natural resources. The dense forest not only provided timber for their huts to live in, canoes to cross rivers, but also wild life like deer, beaver and bear both for food and furs and skins. The rivers and the sea were a rich source of cod, halibut and salmon. All this ensured a relatively comfortable and secure life style that generally provided time and encouragement for the pursuit of culture and the arts. Animals, mythical creatures, human forms depicting unusual shapes and features were popular with artists. Evidence of this form of art can be come across even today on totem poles, canoes and wooden bowls. These motifs can also be associated with the lineage, rank, wealth and status within each group and tribe. Some of the tribes focussed more on particular items; Haidas on ceremonial canoes, while Nootkas developed an expertise in whale products. Thus, slowly developed the practice of exchanging gifts amongst different tribes or even barter trade.

The wide expanse of Canada attracted Indian settlements in other parts as well. Commonly referred to as the Plains Indians, the main tribes were the Assiniboine, the Blackfoot and the Sarcee. Though distinct from each other in many ways, including language, a common factor was the heavy dependence on the buffalo on the part of the Plains Indians. Buffalo hunting on foot was both a sport as well as a necessity. With the arrival of the horse in the 18th century, hunting on foot gradually gave way to this swifter mode. The Plains Indians went where the buffalo herds were to be found, thus, bringing about a nomadic life style. Different tribes generally co-existed in peace and harmony; there was plenty for everyone, their needs were limited, life style simple, and the tribal chiefs sorted out mutual differences, if any. The Plains Indians enjoyed their cultural pursuits including the famous Sun Dance festival held every few years when offerings of food and various decorated items were made to the Great Spirit in whose honour a sacred pole was erected with different bands (groups) dancing around it.

Besides the West Coast Indians and the Plains Indians, another well known category was the Woodland Indians, who inhabited Canada's eastern woodlands. These semi nomadic tribes struck roots in eastern Canada almost as far back as 1000 BC. The Algonquian, the Hurons and the Iroquois were the main tribes amongst the Woodland Indians. They lived in harmony with their environment, made full use of it, and also took to horticulture and agriculture, thus, gradually getting out of a nomadic life style. This pattern of life made them look for sites for habitation that ensured plenty of water, a rich soil and proximity to forest for both timber and hunting.

Compared to the other Woodland Indians, the Iroquois were much more fierce and warlike. Also, they were the only Indians, who believed in the concept of two Great Spirits, the good and evil, constantly at clash with each other, thus giving rise to various myths and beliefs woven around this concept. Being more aggressive and assertive, the Iroquois even sought to unite, through dominance, other tribes by way of a rudimentary confederacy of several tribes. This was, broadly speaking, the Canadian scene till the arrival and settling down of Europeans, a development that was to ultimately transform things almost beyond recognition.

But there was to be a long gap between Europeans travelling to at least some peripheral parts of Canada and serious and, ultimately, successful attempts towards establishing European settlements on this vast and unexplored part of North America. The first Europeans to have a glimpse of Canada, and that too accidentally, were the Vikings, the great seafaring adventurers of northern Europe. Having already traversed the area between Norway and Iceland, their spirit of adventure gradually took them further West till the well known Viking hero, Eric the Red, discovered and settled in Greenland. In the course of a voyage between Iceland and Greenland, a sailor by the name of Bjarni Herjolfsson got caught in a heavy sea storm and was blown off course. It was during this unplanned voyage that he had a glimpse of the North American coast, thus spreading the story of an unknown land upon returning home. It was around 1000 AD that another Viking explorer, Leif (son of Eric the Red) set out to discover the new continent that had been sighted earlier. It is generally believed, glorified in Viking sagas of adventure, that Leif on his voyage of discovery, found Helluland (now known as Baffin Island), the eastern most part of Canada in the Arctic region), Markland (Labrador) and Vinland (probably the present day Newfoundland). Possibly, while a few more such exploratory voyages took place in subsequent years, there is little hard evidence to suggest that the Vikings tried to set up any settlements on these newly discovered lands. Or, even if they did try, they were probably discouraged and prevented from doing so by earlier inhabitants already there, the Inuit in the extreme north or the Indians. Viking tales do mention the Skraelings, the dark skinned people, who, some anthropologists believe, may have been the Algonquian Indians. At the most, some of these Norse people either stayed on or were forced by circumstances to do so and, subsequently, even interbred with the Inuit of Baffin Island. The term 'Copper Eskimos' coined by the explorer Stefansson in 1910 to describe the tall, blonde Inuit of Baffin Island, very likely, inspired this suggestion.

The 15th century truly marked the beginning of more serious and determined voyages of discovery by the Europeans in the direction of

Canada. Accounts of the fabulous riches of the Orient, jewels, spices and silks, were regularly reaching Europe. Exploring the Atlantic Ocean, the 'Sea of Darkness' as it was often referred to, was beginning to excite adventurers and explorers. Their hope and expectation being that beyond this vast expanse of water possibly lay a route that would ultimately lead to the riches of the Orient. Ship building in the sea faring countries of Europe had also been progressively improving, resulting in larger, better and safer ships. John Cabot, an Italian navigator from Genoa in the service of King Henry VII of England, persuaded him to sponsor a voyage of discovery to be led by John Cabot. The king obliged and on May 02, 1497 began the voyage of 'The Matthew' for the Americas with a crew of eighteen under the Captaincy of John Cabot. Braving rough seas and storms for 52 days, Cabot and his crew finally sighted Cape Breton Island where Cabot landed on June 24, 1497, planted the English flag and laid claim to the country to be under the sovereignty of King Henry VII of England.

John Cabot found the soil to be fertile and being mid-summer with the weather warm and balmy, he convinced himself that he had landed on the north coast of Asia. But disappointment was soon to set in since there was no fabled gold, silks or spices to be found. Only lots of fish, spectacular scenery and thick forest with promise of lots of timber (Cabot's Trail, on Cape Breton Island, today, is a popular tourist destination in Canada). A somewhat disappointed John Cabot returned to England to an equally unenthusiastic sovereign. Nevertheless, Cabot's main satisfaction was that he was formally, in subsequent years, credited with having 'discovered' Canada. To emphasise the historic importance of this voyage of discovery by John Cabot in 1497, exactly five centuries later, in the summer of 1997, a replica of The Matthew, but naturally equipped with modern navigational aids and this time under the command of a British captain, repeated the voyage of The Mathew to welcome ceremonies held at various Canadian ports wherever it dropped anchor (The author and his wife attended one such ceremony, when they were welcomed on board The Mathew by its Captain, shown around and signed in the ship's log book). Despite the far less than expected outcome of the first voyage, John Cabot repeated his performance the very next year, 1498, this time to discover the Baffin Island and Newfoundland. Cabot died young in England at the age of 48.

This pioneering effort by John Cabot was to inspire many more explorers in subsequent years to undertake this voyage fraught with risks. However, it was not till 1534 when the French explorer Jacques Cartier, commissioned by King Francis I of France, discovered the Gulf of St. Lawrence and, thus also triggering off the rivalry between England and France for the control and exploitation of North America.

Virtually, the next three centuries were a struggle to explore and discover what is today Canada. Alongside the quest for discovering a route to the Orient was the relentless effort to find a North-West passage to the West Coast and the Pacific. This constant challenge to the European explorers was to produce endless sagas of adventure, often ending in tragedies, but ultimately, determination and fortitude and relentless pursuit yielded the desired results.

The North American coast line had already been officially discovered in 1497 by John Cabot. However, it was Jacques Cartier of France, who first ventured into the interior and in 1534, explored the Gulf of St. Lawrence. The following year, in 1535, he sailed nearly 500 miles up the St. Lawrence River. But the man, who in many ways, pioneered the discovery of Canada was Samuel de Champlain, a French man, who not only penetrated deep into the interior, but went about exploring in a systematic and scientific manner and steadfastly held the view that with peace and justice, the Europeans could co-exist with local Indians and to mutual benefit. Deservedly known as the Chief architect of 'New France' or French Canada, he started this process by founding Quebec in 1608. What is now a thriving Quebec City, had, in that year, a modest beginning in three small two-storey buildings and a store house below the famous cliffs of Quebec City. Earlier, in 1604, Champlain had established on behalf of the French monarchy, the first French colony in North America in Acadia (Nova Scotia).

While Champlain was busy establishing French colonies and settlements, other settlers from Europe, mostly French, began to arrive in Canada. They were mostly people doing menial jobs back home and leading a life of drudgery. They were hardy people willing to take on hardships of a life in Canada in the hope that things could only improve for them. Champlain's approach of living in peace with the Indians paid off dividends. He even encouraged the Indians to take young French boys to live with them and learn the techniques of surviving in the wilderness. Ultimately, these boys were to become well known Coureurs De Bois (forest runners) and spear head the French exploration of North America. To raise funds and resources for his quest for further discoveries, Champlain was attracted by the already

History

flourishing fur trade. But this gradually sucked him into the inter tribal rivalry between the Indians. Having already established friendly links with the Hurons, he attracted the hostility of the Iroquois. Clashes with the latter began, often involving casualties on both sides, making the French trading posts a particular target of the Iroquois.

As part of his colonization strategy, Champlain's focus was twofold. Apart from regularizing the increasingly lucrative fur trade (mostly beavers that were proving to be a hit with the hat makers in Europe), the second task he took upon himself was the Christianization of the native population. First the Franciscan priests and later the Jesuits were encouraged to join in this process. However, the cultural gap and the very different lifestyles of the Indians proved too formidable to bridge and the French priests met with very limited success only. Mutual suspicions grew turning, at times, into open violence against these priests. Failing to make much headway with the Indians, the French priests turned their attention to setting up hospitals, schools, even a Jesuit college in 1636 to satisfy the needs and demands of the growing number of French settlers for whom the lure of fur trade and good cultivable land available for the asking were a big draw. By 1685, according to one estimate, the population of New France had already touched about 10,000 from a modest beginning of just a few hundred a couple of decades ago. From tiny little hamlets, Montreal and Quebec, the former sites of Iroquois Indian villages of Hochelaga and Stadacona, respectively, had transformed themselves into thriving decent sized towns.

Further exploration and discovery remained a principal feature of European focus on this vast and unknown stretch of North America during the 17th century and beyond. The efforts of John Cabot and Jacques Cartier in the 15th and 16th centuries have already been mentioned. Samuel de Champlain, in early 17th century, had played a pioneering role in the establishment of French Canada. Some other names worthy of mention in this context are Henry Hudson, who, in 1610, discovered the huge bay, which still bears his name. But it was Luke Foxe, who finally chartered the western coast of the Hudson Bay. However, the real target before Hudson and Foxe was the discovery of the Northwest passage to Asia. The search for this passage was to continue over the next three centuries, with several unsuccessful attempts, till this was accomplished in 1903-1906 by the Norwegian Roald Amundsen. While it was Sir Alexander Mackenzie, who first achieved the overland crossing to the Pacific, it was England's Captain

Cook, who was to be the first European to land on Canada's Pacific coast in 1778.

Drawing a rough parallel, what spices did to European rivalry in the Orient, the highly lucrative fur trade did in the case of Canada. The rivalry and tension between England and France in Europe was, quite naturally, to find its echo in Canada, where, ultimately, these two countries were emerging as the two principal actors struggling for influence and space. It was thus in 1627 that the notorious English adventurers, the Kirk brothers, who had supported the Huguenot (The Protestantism, which spread in France, was the most clear cut and radical kind, namely Calvinism, which preached at kings, attacked bishops, smashed religious idols and desecrated churches. The Huguenots, as the French Calvinist were called, though always a minority, were neither a small one nor modest in their demands) effort in France, succeeded in blocking the St. Lawrence River for three years and wresting the fur trade from the French. Another dispute arose in Acadia, which was claimed by Sir William Alexander for King James VI of Scotland. Differences of this nature continued to simmer till 1632 when Canada and Acadia were restored to France under the Treaty of Saint-Germain-en-Laye, thus resuming normal trade.

But a sense of unease continued to prevail in New France or French Canada spurring a growing demand on the part of the French settlers for a strong centralized authority to manage the affairs of French Canada. It was in response to this demand that, in 1647, a council comprising of the Governor of Montreal, and the head of the Jesuit Order was formed, essentially to regulate and monitor economic activities. Encouraged by this experiment, New France or French Canada was officially designated a ward of the Crown (under Louis XIV of France) in 1663. Under this arrangement, the two names deserving special mention were Jean Baptiste Colbert, a finance minister, who sought to regulate France's colonial role with a new administrative system and Governor Comte de Frontenac, who was largely instrumental in successfully defending French interests against frequent Indian raids. For a while, these factors gave a good push to French interests in North America. A large number of French colonists poured in, most of them settling down in towns of Quebec, Montreal, and Trois Rivieres. However, quite a few amongst these new arrivals from France ventured beyond the St. Lawrence region, travelled inland, often marrying Indian women, thus giving rise to the Metis, people of half French and half Indian blood.

The flag following trade has been the most common factor with European colonialism. Canada was no exception and the growing attraction of fur trade was already being acknowledged in Europe, notably in France and England, the two most active European actors on the fast unfolding Canadian scene. But, interestingly, the final push that England got in this direction was provided by two French disgruntled dissidents. In the 1660s, two French coureur de bois or voyagers, Medard Des Groseilliers and Pierre Radisson, felt that they had had enough of the high costs of transporting furs back to Quebec as per the orders of the colonial government and, on top of it, the exceptionally high tax they had to pay on fur pelts. These two voyagers fled and sought refuge in the English dominated areas from where they were helped to go to England. While in London, Groseilliers and Radisson managed to win over a few prominent English merchants, ultimately convincing them to take control of the highly profitable fur trade in Central Canada by setting up the Hudson Bay Company with claim to trading rights in all territories draining into the Hudson Bay. The French, thus, almost felt cornered and squeezed – in the South by the English supported by Iroquois and to the Northwest by the fast expanding Hudson Bay Company. The stage was, thus, being set for armed clashes between the English and the French.

By the beginning of the 18th century, hostilities between the French and the English were a common and a regular feature. While the Hudson Bay Company was spearheading English commercial and political interests in the West, the newly arriving English farmers were increasingly eyeing Acadia because of its fertile soil. These tensions and clashes were to continue till the Peace Treaty of Utrecht was signed in 1713 with North America being parcelled out among European powers. The French were possibly the biggest losers with both Acadia and the Hudson Bay being ceded to the English. This Treaty also recognised English sovereignty over the Iroquois Indians and additionally acknowledged their right to trade with Western Indian, something that had traditionally been a French prerogative.

While there was relative peace for a few decades, the undercurrent of French unhappiness was often visible. The vigorous pursuit by the English of their trade interests only kept adding to this tension between the two European powers until active hostilities began between the two in 1744, escalating further to ultimately become part of a larger conflict between the English and the French in Europe – the Seven Years War (1756-1763). Before even the end of this conflict in Europe, the fate of the French in

North America was sealed in 1759. Quebec City, in many ways the pride and symbol of French power in North America, witnessed an open clash between the French and the English forces. The English, under the command of General James Wolfe, took on the French under the command of Marquis de Montcalm. Though the French were on higher ground atop the cliffs of Quebec, on September 12, 1759, the English crossed the St. Lawrence River under the cover of darkness to gain the cliffs, to the surprise of the French. The ensuing clash between the two sides claimed heavy casualties on both sides with General Wolfe getting killed in action and Montcalm, the French commander, getting mortally wounded. But, ultimately, the English prevailed and with this defeat, the French hopes of a French North America also faded away, ironically in the same place where on July 03, 1608, Champlain had given birth to the dream of French Canada by founding the small hamlet of Quebec. The fate of the rest of New France or French Canada was just a matter of time. The Treaty of Paris of 1763 that put an end to the Seven Years War between England and France in Europe also sealed the fate of the rest of New France, with all the French lands in Canada going to England.

The transition following these dramatic developments was not easy. The French Canadians felt betrayed, abandoned and let down by France. In France, there was more relief than regret over the loss of New France or French Canada or possibly it was a case of making virtue out of necessity. The French philosopher, Voltaire derisively dubbed New France as a "few acres of snow". The British, on the other hand, while happy and satisfied with the outcome, faced problems of a different kind. The control over the highly lucrative fur trade shifting from the French to the British brought in its obvious economic gains and rewards. But upsetting from the English point of view was the fact that an overwhelming majority of its newly acquired colony of Canada was of foreign, mostly French origin. Having emerged as a victor, the natural urge was to convert Quebec into an English settlement with the English language, ways and lifestyle of the English and to increase dramatically the number of English inhabitants. The prospects of such a cultural defeat only added to the unease of the French inhabitants. But Britain's attempts at converting Quebec to English ways, even on the religious front from Catholicism to Anglicanism was not at all going to be smooth or easy. By now, the British rule south of Canada was already experiencing the early rumblings of protest. The American War of Independence increasingly looked like a possibility. Britain was in no position or mood to take on an insurrection on a wider scale. Taking an overall realistic view the British thought of securing the support if not outright loyalty of French Canadians. Compromise rather than confront. The British Governor Sir Guy Carleton played a leading role in projecting this approach on the part of the British in Canada. The outcome was the Quebec Act of 1774, which in effect gave the French Canadians freedom to practice their religion, and also retain their language, laws (civil as distinct from criminal) and customs. There was also to be no discrimination against French Canadians holding public office. While the Quebec Act of 1774 considerably pacified the French Canadians, the British subjects felt that their government had given in too much. In a way, this was to mark the beginning of a sentiment that one still comes across in Canada, viz., Quebec is pampered too much and invariably ends up getting more than it deserves.

The American Revolution or War of Independence of 1776 against the British rule had its inevitable fall out for Canada. British North America was still mostly a territory inhabited by people of French origin. France briefly intervening on the side of the American revolutionaries raised the hopes of the people of Quebec or the Quebecois. The minority English still held a grudge that British policies favoured the Quebecois too much. However, the arrival of the British regular troops in 1776 apparently convinced both the French and the English in North American, that to side with England would serve their interests better in the long run.

In a way, thanks to the American War of Independence, the concept of a distinct Canadian identity (or Canadianism) began to emerge and take shape. This process was helped further by the influx into Canada of nearly 60,000 United Empire Loyalists, elements who did not support the cause of the Americans or view their grievances with any sympathy. Most of these were British Loyalists from the New York region and they were welcomed into Canada besides being granted indemnity and land. These Loyalists brought with them values dear to them – loyalty to Britain and a fondness for an aristocratic society of privilege besides, of course, a rejection of Americans and the United States. This influx of Loyalists into Canada was to continue for quite a few years. Adding to their numbers were even a fairly large number of Americans, who either did not feel particularly excited by the cause of their fellow Americans or just thought that by moving to Canada, they would be ensuring a better life for themselves.

All these migrants into Canada from America were to open up Upper Canada, present day Ontario province and even areas beyond. But even more significantly, this influx was to alter the demographic face of Canada. The overall population began to tilt in favour of the English speaking Anglo-Protestants, slowly creating a cultural dualism and even strengthening the feeling among the British that the people of French origin, the Quebecois, were being favoured too much and getting more than their due. Gradually, this divide within Canada only gained momentum with the Loyalists pitching their demands for a representative government, something denied to them under the Quebec Act of 1774. A delicate situation was indeed evolving till it was sought to be rectified by the Constitutional Act of 1791. The colony was to have an elected assembly exercising legislative authority in conjunction with a legislative council appointed by the King. But of greater significance was that under this Act of 1791, the St. Lawrence valley (the province of Quebec) was divided into two colonies – Upper Canada (Ontario) and Lower Canada (Quebec). This was also to mark the beginning of Anglo-French rivalry in British North America, something that even present day Canada has not been able to entirely overcome.

In the meanwhile, the continuing influx of Americans into Canada was acquiring a character of its own. According to one estimate, by 1812 more than 80 per cent of Upper Canada's population comprised of people of American birth or descent with only a quarter of it Loyalists. But these American Canadians were happy with their new home, that is, Canada, leading a good life and their affinity towards their fellow Americans to the South was already considerably diminished. However, the Americans misread the situation and under the Presidency of James Madison launched an attack on Canada seriously hoping that the large number of American Canadians would support them. But this was not to be with the American Canadians showing little or no sympathy for what they derisively labelled as 'Mr. Madison's War'. The outcome shocked the Americans, when English colonists under Britain's Sir Isaac Brock defeated the larger American force imposing surrender on it at Detroit. Again to the disappointment of the Americans, French and English colonists joined to defeat the Americans at Lake Champlain. These momentous events of 1812 were to be a proud moment in Canadian history in the context of Canada's relations with its big neighbour to the South. Good humouredly, the Canadians still enjoy reminding their American friends of the events of 1812 whenever the latter appear to be getting a little pushy. The Canadian suspicion, if not hatred, of American intentions owes its origin to 1812 as also the big boost it gave to the now much cherished concept and sentiment of 'Canadianism' as distinct from Americanism. The war of 1812 also formalised British North America's right to remain British.

The events of 1812 instilled a high level of self-confidence and pride amongst the inhabitants of Canada. It considerably strengthened their resolve to project an identity of their own. They were North Americans, but not Americans. This self-confidence received a further boost from the fact that, particularly in Upper Canada (Ontario), the economy was doing well even though the picture was not so bright in Lower Canada (Quebec), resulting in criticism of the British among the French Canadians.

The cumulative effect of these factors was a growing tendency to criticise the British colonial rule and express unhappiness with their colonial political structure. The Assembly set up under the Constitutional Act of 1791 was an elected body, but a Council appointed by the King of England not only wielded executive power, but often overruled the decisions of the elected Assembly or the legislature. In Quebec, opposition to the role of the Council was growing till it became a demand for its abolition. This movement was led by the firebrand politician, Louis Joseph Papineau, founder of the *Patriote Party*. Matters came to a head when in October 1837, the '*Patriotes*' demonstrated in public and clashed with British troops stationed in Quebec. The uprising became somewhat messy and bloody, but, ultimately, it was put down with Papineau fleeing to the United States. Upper Canada (Ontario) was not to be left behind with the demand for a *Responsible Government* being led by a hot-headed Scotsman, William Lyon Mackenzie. But here too, the uprising, a bit scattered in any case, came to an end after a brief clash with the police in Toronto's Yonge Street and with Mackenzie seeking refuge in the United States.

Though taking a dim view of these two unsuccessful uprisings, Britain nevertheless began to see the writing on the wall by way of accepting the need for changing and reforming the outmoded colonial political structure of Canada. What Britain obviously was also conscious of was that in the aftermath of the American independence in 1776, the political scene south of Canada served as a good constant source of inspiration for the Canadians. The United States, on its part, showed little restraint towards the political events in Canada and certainly provided a safe haven for Canadian dissidents, even rebels. The uprisings of 1837, led by Papineau and Mackenzie, though ending in failure, did serve the purpose of at least alerting the British to the risks of continuing to ignore the legitimate demand for responsible government in Canada.

The result was the setting up in 1839, under Governor General Lord Durham, of a royal commission to examine the political problems raising their head in British North America. Besides acknowledging the economic stagnation of British North America, significantly the Durham Report also stressed that in order to exist next to the rapidly changing political scene in the United States, Canada would have to do much better, both politically and economically. The solution was – unite the two parts of Canada under a joint legislature, each part equally represented. Consequently, the Union Act of 1840 joined Upper and Lower Canada under a single government. By 1848, this United Canada had won the right to self or responsible government and in 1849, the legislature set up an administrator for the Province of Canada, thus marking the birth of Responsible Government for Canada.

Stepping into the 1850's Canada was gripped by another feeling, namely, the good old dictum: in unity lies strength. Ever fearful of America being increasingly resentful of British domination, Canada's protection and prosperity demanded that the colonies unite instead of remaining separate geographic units. This political concept understandably needed time to strike a firm root and take hold of the popular mind. The 1850's and early 1860's were to witness the germination, discussion and spread of this idea- the concept of a confederation. With the ongoing American Civil War to the south of the border, the idea of unification gained further strength. Both in the Maritimes and in the Atlantic Provinces discussions were already afoot based upon a platform of Confederation.

Rough terms for setting up a Confederation were drawn up (politicians like John A. Macdonald, George Brown and a few others playing the lead role). With the ratification of these terms at the Quebec Conference the basis was laid. Finally, with the passage of the British North America Act, confederated Canada became a reality on July 01, 1867. The Act divided the British Province of Canada into Ontario and Quebec (hitherto, Upper and Lower Canada) and united them with New Brunswick and Nova Scotia with the new nation being officially designated as the Dominion of Canada. In 1849, Vancouver Island became a British colony with British Columbia following in 1858. In 1866, Vancouver Island and British Columbia united as one entity, that is, British Columbia. July 01, continues to be observed as Canada Day or National Day till today.

With the proclamation of the Dominion of Canada, the country was truly on its way to nationhood. The process, though not always smooth had begun. Sir John A Macdonald, Scottish by birth who, along with his parents, had migrated to Kingston, Ontario, as a small boy, became the first Prime Minister of Canada and, thus, in-charge of guiding the country in the initial stages. His wit and sense of humour, perceptive approach and sharp intelligence made him a popular public figure. This despite some personal failings and problems, like an over fondness for alcohol, an unhappy family life, an ailing wife and a mentally handicapped child from his second marriage, following the death of his first wife. On his way to building up the new Confederation, the first road block that Macdonald hit was in 1869/70 when Canada bought, for Pounds 300,000, St. Rupert Island and North West Territories from the Hudson Bay Company. However, this transaction overlooked and ignored the feelings and views of the indigenous population, the Metis, half French half Indians, the result of inter marriages between the French explorers and the local Indians, who the British derisively labelled as "half breeds". The Metis, who viewed themselves as a distinct identity, neither Indian nor French, and zealously guarded their autonomy, were highly resentful of their lands being thus taken over without them being consulted, much less consent. Under the leadership of Louis Riel, the Metis rose in revolt and seized Fort Garry, a British outpost. Matters threatened to take an ugly turn when Thomas Scott, a resident of Ontario captured by the Metis, was executed on the orders of Riel on charges of assault (on Riel himself) and gross misconduct. The incident threatened to spin out of control by acquiring the larger dimension of Ontario (Scott) versus Quebec (Riel) and a Protestant (Scott) being executed on the orders of a Catholic (Riel). With things heating up, Louis Riel fled to the United States and matters finally resolved with the Metis revolt fizzling out and Manitoba joining the Confederation in 1870 as the fifth province. Things moved fast when in 1871, British Columbia joined as the sixth province with Prince Edward Island entering the Dominion of Canada in 1873 as the seventh province. The Prairies and the Pacific coast had been added to the Confederation.

Despite various controversies surrounding him, including his unorthodox ways of raising election funds when new elections were due in 1872, it is to Macdonald that the credit goes for conceiving the Pacific Railway project. With the Confederation fast expanding, developing and maintaining links among the far flung territories, touching the Pacific by 1871, was quite naturally a major election issue in 1872. The task of building the Canadian Pacific Railway was entrusted to a prominent Montreal shipping magnate, Sir Hugh Allan. But Macdonald was exposed for asking Hugh Allan for election funds, in return giving him the huge railway project, with this political scam costing Macdonald his Prime Ministership and being made to quit office in disgrace. However, work on the railway continued. The year 1885 was to witness a few major developments. Work on the Canadian Pacific Railway was completed, thus realizing Macdonald's dream of spanning a major link across the continent, with Prime Minister Alexander Mackenzie at the helm of affairs. Though, not an entirely ungrateful nation accepted Macdonald later on as Prime Minister again and for over a decade. The year 1885 witnessed another land mark development, the arrival of the telegraph in Canada. On a somewhat jarring note, Louis Riel returned from his refuge in the United States in 1885 to lead the second Metis revolt. But this time, he was not only defeated, but captured and executed. Though, the three decades since the birth of the Confederation of Canada had seen many major developments, some positive and some not so positive, this new nation was, over all, stepping into the twentieth century full of hope, vigour and determination to go ahead.

Sir Wilfred Laurier, the first French Canadian Prime Minister of the country (1896-1911) had confidently predicted that "the twentieth century belongs to Canada". Subsequent developments were to prove that this was not going to be an empty boastful claim. And things were to move at a fairly rapid pace. In 1905, Alberta and Saskatchewan joined the Confederation as eighth and ninth provinces, respectively. With Manitoba (1870) and British Columbia (1871) having already done so, Canada now was one continuous land entity all the way up to the Pacific. By 1914, Canada had a railway link (the Canadian Pacific) that extended from coast to coast. Inspired by these developments and its growing profile, the urge to forge direct links with the rest of the world was natural and understandable. But the colonial masters sitting in London controlled and organized this aspect for Canada. Gradual resentment was, therefore, to be expected. Even in matters of law, the final Court of Appeal for the Canadians was the British Privy Council. The outbreak of World War I in 1914 further brought out how Canada followed where Britain led. Canada being at war too was taken for granted by the British and Canada indeed responded to the call without questioning. But this cruel exposure to the world outside, so to say, slowly but surely resulted in a Canadian awakening. The Canadians began to appreciate their unique identity. They were from North America, but not Americans. Despite the initial British disdain for their fighting capability and professionalism as soldiers, they gave an excellent account of themselves, grudgingly accepted and even appreciated by the British commanders in the field. Disproportionate to their small population (still well under ten million), they suffered as many casualties in combat as the United States, their heroics being confirmed by the fact that by the end of the War, the Canadians had won as many as seventy Victoria Crosses. All this naturally instilled a sense of unique pride and identity amongst the Canadians, who were no longer willing to stand in awe of London and their British cousins, or as mere side-kicks of the Empire. No wonder, as the War ended in 1918, Canada insisted on its right to sign the peace treaty and, shortly thereafter, applied for separate membership of the League of Nations. As further assertion of its growing self-confidence and keenness to project its distinct identity, in 1919, Canada became the first British Dominion to refuse to allow its citizens to accept British titles (earldoms, knighthoods, etc.). In 1922, the British sought to put down the Turks at Chanak in the Dardanelles international zone. They ordered their colonial governments to contribute troops. Mackenzie King, the then Canadian Prime Minister, was quick to announce that before Canada agreed to send any troops, it had to consult its Parliament. The message was not lost on London and Canada had taken a significant first step towards asserting its right to manage its own affairs rather than be a silent and unquestioning participant in British imperial policy.

Another factor contributing significantly to this new found Canadian confidence was its rapid economic growth. World War I gave a big boost to its industrial production. The Trans Canada rail link was fast opening up the country and also uncovering its hidden wealth. A fall out of the extensive excavations in connection with the laying of the railway line was the discovery of substantial deposits of silver, gold, copper, zinc and other non-ferrous metals. Foreign investments, mostly British and American, in mining and related industry were not far behind. Agriculture was another promising area. The Prairie Provinces offered virtually limitless land for cultivation. American farmers were already pouring in from across the border. Somewhat weary of too much American influx, Canada opened up to immigrants from other parts of Europe (British immigrants were not coming in large enough numbers), resulting in a massive influx of Ukrainians, Slovaks, Poles, Czechs, Hungarians and Serbs to the vast lands of Alberta and Saskatchewan. For a meagre $10 as registration fee and willingness to work on land, these newcomers were given 160 acres of land for free. These early migrants, no doubt, had to work hard, but in the process, they were to transform Canada as not only agriculturally rich, but a virtual bread basket for Europe. The Canadian Pacific Railway greatly facilitating the movement of grain and other products. The fisheries industry also developed impressively with the introduction of canning and refrigeration. Canada was indeed reaping in full the benefits of its fast changing circumstances.

The growing Canadian self-confidence made it more assertive and demanding in its dealings with the mother country, Britain. The Governor General as the representative of the British Crown could, at times, cross swords with the popularly elected Prime Minister. Showing realism, the British Parliament passed in 1931 the Statute of Westminster granting Canada the status of an autonomous dominion within the Commonwealth. The principle was also established by this statute that any Canadian legislation, in case it conflicted with the legislation passed by the British Parliament, would no longer be null and void, as had hitherto been the position. Carrying this process further, in 1935, Britain's Privy Council relinquished its power as the final court of appeal in Canadian criminal cases.

By the time World War II started, Canada was already in a different frame of mind. Unlike in 1914, when in 1939 Britain declared war on Germany, Canada was not automatically a participant on the side of Britain. It took a whole week to debate and to decide and finally with pledges against conscription and many reservations, it went into war only on September 10, 1939.

As in World War I, once again, Canada covered itself with glory. The Canadians served in virtually all theatres of operations. They fought gallantly and suffered heavy casualties in proportion to their numbers. By the time the War ended in 1945, Canada had attained new levels of power and prestige. The war effort had given a tremendous boost to its economy and industry. It had played the role of the arsenal to the Allied Powers. Its steel production had doubled and aluminium production had jumped six fold. Forest products and fisheries showed equally impressive growth, while the generation of hydro-electric power had increased by over forty per cent. Days of economic boom were definitely there. Oil was discovered in the West, iron ore in Labrador and uranium in Ontario. Jobs went a begging. A nation of as yet just about fourteen million, its skill, manufacturing capacity and high productivity were widely acclaimed and accepted. Even the huge neighbour to the South, the United States, began to show respect for Canadian talent, skills and distinctiveness. They were no longer push-overs of the British nor a satellite of the USA. In the post World War II scenario, Canada had indeed arrived on the world stage. With Germany, Italy and Japan defeated, with

France recovering from the trauma of war and with Britain, though victorious, utterly exhausted and getting ready to see the beginning of the end of the once great British Empire, Canada, along with the United States, became one of the leading Western countries, possessing both economic and political clout. It was indeed an hour of glory for Canada. With the British colony of Newfoundland joining the Canadian Confederation in 1949 as the tenth province, the political map of Canada, as we see it today, was complete. Other symbols of independent nationhood were to gradually follow. In 1962, the trans-Canada highway was completed. The same year, Canada's first nuclear power plant became operational. In 1952, Canada got its first native born (Vincent Massey) Governor General. Hitherto, the post, the highest in the land as the official representative of the British Crown, was largely viewed as a reward for either a well connected member of the British nobility or an over aged General. Vincent Massey was Governor General from 1952 till 1959, when he was succeeded by a French Canadian, General George P. Vanier. In 1959, another long cherished dream was realized when the St. Lawrence seaway, jointly built by Canada and the United States, was inaugurated by Queen Elizabeth II and President Eisenhower, thus linking, through inland locks and channels, the Great Lakes and the US and Canadian Middle West with the Atlantic Ocean. In the fitness of things, Canada adopted its new flag, the red maple leaf on a white background in 1965 as also its own national anthem. Having joined the NATO upon its inception in 1949, Canada implemented, for its largely uninhabited northern territories, a sophisticated air defence system called NORAD. In a further de-linking with Britain, in the 1980s, the British North America Act of 1867 was replaced (during Prime Minister Pierre Trudeau's time) by a new Constitution that included a Bill of Rights. This document was made into law by Queen Elizabeth II in Ottawa on April 17, 1982.

Flushed with growing prosperity and self-confidence, in the years following World War II, Canada was to play an active role on the international stage. It was an important founder member of the UN serving competently on several committees. Its diplomats, known for their professionalism and negotiating skills, were sought after by various international bodies. It participated in the Korean War. After the 1954 Geneva Conference on Indo-China, it served as a member, representing the West, on the three International Control Commissions set up for Vietnam, Laos and Cambodia. Poland was the member representing the Communist Block and India, as a founder member of the non-aligned group of countries, the Chairman.

The Suez crisis of 1956 was a testing time for Canada and its diplomacy. It was a blatant attempt by Britain to regain its status as a great power. It expected the senior "white" dominions to support its decision to, along with France, invade Egypt in protest against its nationalization of the Suez Canal. While Australia and New Zealand backed Britain, Canada backed the United Nations. Canada's Prime Minister, Louis St. Laurent, was more in sync with the thinking of India's Nehru, who had deplored such colonial actions by the Great Powers. A resolution drafted by Canada's Foreign Minister, Lester B. Pearson, brought UN forces to intervene in the threatened area, defeated the British-French power bid and ended the crisis that otherwise had threatened Western unity and the nascent UN itself. The positive and constructive role played by Canada was internationally acclaimed and, a year later, won for Mr. Pearson and Canada the Nobel Peace Prize. But perhaps even more importantly, by backing the UN (and incidentally siding with the US too) Canada had openly defied and opposed the mother country, Britain. Canada had, so to say, arrived on the world stage as an independent and influential voice.

Having thus traced the history of Canada, from the dawn of antiquity to the second half of the twentieth century, it is time to wrap up things before one enters the realm of current affairs, too recent to qualify as history. However, a few general observations would be neither out of place nor inappropriate.

As would be clear from what has been said so far, to reach where it is today, Canada has been a story of immense hardships, struggle against nature and the elements, grit and determination, resourcefulness, innovativeness and, ultimately, success and a sense of tremendous achievement. All this and more accounts for the Canada of today, a highly developed country known for its skills, a country that has weathered successfully various challenges, a country that, despite its vastness and harsh weather, through its excellent infrastructure, has, in many ways, converted what were at a time obvious disadvantages into challenges and opportunities. It is today a country that is an attractive destination for many, a magnet for immigrants from the world over, providing a quality of life to its people that would be the envy of many and deservedly continuing to rank in the top bracket of countries considered as the best places to live in.

Of course, Canada has its problems, some unemployment and a few pockets of poverty. Particularly, several places in its Northern Territories, not without reason, are called the Third World of Canada. Its handling of the indigenous population, the Inuit and the Indians, still attracts criticism and the concern of the human rights activists. From time to time, it is beset with political controversies, occasional scandals and even alleged financial scams. But that only means that it is a normal country with normal people. It is proud of its multiculturalism, inspired very much by its historical past, current realities and the keenness to strive for the co-existence of its Anglo-French past and present. The problem of Quebec has been a part of its history and is not likely to go away any time soon. The Canadians have, or, at least, they try to learn to live with it. Whether Quebec will separate one day remains a question that will continue to defy a clear answer. One can only hope, above all for Canada's sake, that it will never again acquire the ugly face that it did for a while in the 1970s when Pierre Trudeau, himself a French Canadian, was the Prime Minister. That is when riots broke out in Montreal and Quebec City, the British Trade Commissioner, James Cross, in Montreal was kidnapped by the FLQ, the McGill University in Montreal was stormed by angry students demanding that all classes be held in French and the Quebec Minister of Labour, Pierre Laporte, kidnapped and later assassinated. All this prompting Prime Minister Trudeau to invoke on October 16, 1970, to the horror and surprise of most Canadians, the War Measures Act and 10,000 troops poured out into the streets of Montreal. It is not something that the Canadians are proud to recall, but it is part of their recent history that they can neither deny nor easily forget. In fact, the separatist sentiment in Quebec still keeps raising its head from time to time and is very likely to continue to bedevil Canada. At times, it even raises serious questions about its future as a country and a nation.

In the midst of all this, Canada remains committed to multiculturalism and its bilingual official language policy, English and French. An expensive commitment that finds few serious takers in the country outside the provinces of Quebec and Ontario and hardly exists by the time one reaches the West Coast. Even the choice of By Town, renamed as Ottawa in 1857 by Queen Victoria, as the nation's Capital was part of this syndrome. Despite some other strong claimants, notably Kingston, the choice ultimately was Ottawa because of its location. Though in Ontario, it was right on the edge with just the Ottawa River separating it from Quebec and the virtual twin city of Hull. In the Ottawa of today, one has just to cross a bridge and you are in Quebec. Unlike Washington or Brasilia, architecturally, Ottawa does not follow geometrical straight lines. Instead, it is woven around its natural beauty, landscape, greenery and the Ottawa River with the Gatineau Hills (in Quebec) providing an impressive backdrop.

This is Canada, despite its problems, faults and shortcomings, a proud and a happy country. Blessed with a sound economy (currently, March 2013, the only country besides Germany enjoying a triple A rating in terms of its economy), a relatively smooth running system, inhabited by disciplined, hardworking and skilled people, possessing an excellent system of education, health care and a security net that many others will aspire for.

Chapter Two – Geography

According to the Cambridge Gazetteer of the United States and Canada (pg. 99) the name Canada is derived from a local term for the village of STADACONA, founded in the 1530s on the site of present day Quebec City. This was gradually applied to a larger and larger territory and in 1791, with the Constitutional (or Canada) Act, was first given officially to Upper and Lower Canada.

Geographically, in terms of the size of its territory, Canada is the largest country on the entire American Continent and the second largest in the world, next only to Russia. While it is roughly three fourths the size of Russia, it is larger than the USA and China combined. Its total land area is 9,976,140 sq. kilometres. In the North it is bordered by the Arctic Ocean, in the West by the Pacific Ocean, the Atlantic, Davis Strait and Baffin Bay on the East and by the USA in the South with which it shares an 8,892 kilometre long land boundary. In 1846 the Oregon Treaty determined that the international boundary between the USA and Canada should follow the 49th parallel, but that Vancouver Island should remain British. The other neighbours of Canada are Russia, which faces Canada across the North Pole and the Arctic Ocean, and Greenland (Denmark). Canada has a vast maritime terrain, with the world's longest coastline of 202,080 kilometres.

The Canadian Shield, studded with hundreds of lakes, big and small, stretches across nearly half of Canada. The Shield has some of the world's oldest rocks, geologically speaking. The southern portions of the Shield are covered with boreal forests, while the northern parts are tundra as it is too far north for trees to grow. A few hours flight northwards from the nation's Capital, Ottawa, and you are beyond the tree line. West of the Canadian Shield are the Central plains or the prairies. The southern plains are mostly grass and the north is forested. Farther west, rising from the western edge of the prairies are the scenic and famous Rocky Mountains. The rugged mountains reach a high point of 19,524 ft. (5,951 meters) in Mt. Logan, Canada's highest, in the St. Elias mountain range of the Yukon. Along its border to the South with the

USA are located four of the Great Lakes—Lake Superior, Lake Huron, Lake Erie, Lake Ontario—and the St. Lawrence River lowlands. Along the Western edge of the Canadian Shield are the Great Slave Lake and the Great Bear Lake, besides hundreds of other. These lakes have been caused by depressions in land due to the last glaciation. The largest lake of Canada is the Great Bear Lake with an expanse of 31,153 sq. kilometres. With most parts of the Shield being rocky and with cold temperatures, agriculture is difficult. But this is more than compensated by the huge hydroelectric potential and resources besides rich mineral deposits like gold, iron ore, lead, zinc, copper, to name a few. The Laurentian Plateau or Shield is the oldest and largest covering about five million square kilometres and lies roughly half in Canada and the rest in Greenland. According to geologists, this Shield was formed some 3.75 to 500 million years ago. The Laurentian mountains in Quebec and visible from Ottawa are actually upturned escarpments on the edges of this Shield.

Climatically, Canada is temperate in the south to arctic in the north. Winters in most of Canada are long and harsh. It is often said, and rightly so, that where the coldest parts of the USA end, the warmest parts of Canada begin. Ottawa ranks as one of the coldest Capitals in the world and in several parts of Canada, peak minimum winter temperatures dropping to forty, or even, below zero is not uncommon. The population of Canada (November 2012 figure) stands at about 35 million (34, 980,000 to be precise). Seventy two per cent of the total population is concentrated within 150 kilometres of the border with the USA and 79 per cent of the population lives in urban areas. The US-Canada border, stretching over 8,893 kilometres, is the world's longest undefended border. With a population density of 3.5 per sq. kilometre, Canada is one of the most sparsely populated countries in the world.

The country comprises of ten Provinces and three Territories. Moving from east to west, the ten Provinces are: 1. Newfoundland (St. John's), 2. Nova Scotia (Halifax), 3. Prince Edward Island (Charlottetown), 4. New Brunswick (Fredericton), 5. Quebec (Quebec City), 6. Ontario (Toronto), 7. Manitoba (Winnipeg), 8. Saskatchewan (Regina), 9. Alberta (Edmonton), 10. British Columbia (Victoria). The names within brackets are those of the provincial capitals. Ottawa is the national capital. Some other big and important cities that might be mentioned are Dalhousie, Montreal, Kingston, Saskatoon, Calgary and Vancouver. Prince Edward Island is the smallest of the ten provinces and Ontario is the largest.

The vast area north of the 60ᵗʰ parallel that comprises 40 per cent of Canada's land mass is the Canadian Arctic or Canada North. The Canadian Arctic stretches 4,256 kilometres from the east coast of Baffin Island to the Yukon/Alaska border and 2,520 kilometres from the 60ᵗʰ parallel to the northern tip of Ellesmere Island. And yet, this vast swathe of territory is inhabited by barely 70,000 Canadians, the rough break up being about 20 per cent Inuit, 16 per cent Indian, 10 per cent Metis and the rest being from different parts of Canada. It is an area known for its very sparse population, emptiness and wilderness in the true sense of the word. This is accentuated by the fact that most of the population is to be found in towns like Whitehorse, Dawson City, Inuvik, Yellowknife, Fort Chimo and Iqaluit. This is that part of Canada where coming across small communities in places like Pangnirtung (Baffin Island), Resolute and Old Crow on the Porcupine River is not uncommon with the total population in most places being under a thousand. This entire vast expanse of territory consists of Yukon in the west bordering on Alaska and with Whitehorse as its capital. Till the 1990s, the rest was called the North West Territories with Yellowknife on the Great Slave Lake as the capital. However since 1999, for reasons essentially of administrative convenience, the North West Territory has been split roughly into two halves with the eastern part known as Nunavut as a separate Territory with Iqaluit as its capital.

Chapter Three – The People

When it comes to the people, who inhabit Canada, it is only fair and historically correct to start with the earliest on the scene – the Inuit and the Indians.

The Inuit are mostly to be found beyond the Arctic Circle, the 60th Parallel and further on and their number is small – roughly 20 per cent of the total of about 70,000 people, who inhabit the North West territories and Nunavut areas of Canada. Though very much in Canada and part of it, the modernity and impressive growth visible in ample measure elsewhere in Canada does not seem as yet to have reached or touched the Inuit. Spread out mostly over this vast northern stretch of Canada, 40 per cent of the country's total land mass, they are to be found in small groups or communities in far flung places like Pangnirtung on Baffin Island, Resolute towards the North-West or Old Crow on the Porcupine River in the Yukon. The population of these places is just about a thousand inhabitants each, if not even less. Based on the author's personal experience of having visited these places, this is what the Canadians themselves admit to be the Third World of Canada. Dust roads, poor infrastructure, inadequate medical facilities, limited education, high unemployment and generally a life of hardship, accentuated by the severe weather conditions and long spells of sub – zero temperatures. Modern influence has touched them in a negative sense by upsetting their traditional pattern of life. With bans on hunting and fur trade, these people have been slow to switch to other occupations. Alcoholism is a problem, depression level not surprisingly high and suicide rate higher than the national average. Canada is rightly proud of its impressive achievements in many fields. But it needs to look after better its first inhabitants—the Inuit.

Indians, the term commonly used by Europeans and the Whites of North America to identify the aboriginal people of the Americas, is believed to have originated with Columbus, who thought he had reached Asia when, in fact, he had arrived in the Caribbean.

In Canada, the legal definition of Indian is contained in the Indian Act, legislation first passed in 1876, but stemming from similar pre-Confederation laws. People legally defined as Indians are called Status Indians. Non-status Indians are of Indian ancestry, but through inter- marriage with Whites or by abandoning their status rights, they have lost their legal status while retaining their Indian identity. Among Status Indians, there are two groups: Treaty Indians and registered Indians outside treaty areas. METIS, an old French word meaning "mixed" is used in a general sense to describe people of dual Indian-White ancestry.

Roughly 20 per cent of the Yukon inhabitants are native people, including Metis. In the North West Territory and Nunavut, the native population including Metis and Inuit constitute about 60 per cent of the population. The 2006 Census puts the number of aboriginal people in Canada at 1,72,790.

All across Canada, there are about six hundred Indian settlements or Bands, a little over thirty being in the Yukon, NWT and Nunavut. These Bands are somewhat like municipalities with powers of self-administration. They may levy property taxes, manage businesses and operate on Reserves without paying taxes. Speaking generally, Bands derive from the original village or unit living in a cultural area. Members of the same Band, therefore, usually share a common linguistic and cultural background. This category of Canada's inhabitants has integrated much more with the mainstream of life in Canada. Their settlements too are located close to inhabited and developed areas, with some of them even becoming something of an attraction for visitors and tourists with small restaurants and souvenir shops thrown in. But the Indians remain conscious of their rights and unique identity and are somewhat resentful of their traditional life style being encroached upon and often seek to attract the attention of the protagonists of human rights.

With a total population of about 34 million (2012 figure) Canada can rank as a mid-sized country in this respect. Of the total figure of 34 million, the rough break up would be 80 per cent Whites, six per cent Orientals (those from China, Korea, Japan Vietnam and the Philippines) five per cent Natives, four per cent Asians (those from India, Pakistan, Bangladesh and Sri Lanka), also sometimes referred to as Indo-Canadians, or East Indians or South Asians and about four to five per cent Blacks, Latinos and from the Middle East. This is at best an approximate break up due to some overlapping in the racial mix. But the thing to note is that everyone living in Canada today, except for the small number of aboriginals, is an immigrant or a descendant of an immigrant. The "sons of the soil", if one may use that term, constitute only a microscopic minority.

Historically, the first immigrants to Canada were from France and England. These two countries constituted the origin of much of Canada's white majority. Immigrants from other parts of Europe were to flow in much later. Canadians of English descent, known as Anglos, have traditionally formed the majority in all provinces except perhaps in Quebec. This would also explain the urge to maintain close links with the mother country, Britain, and the British monarchy, even if this sentiment is now slowly on the wane, partly due also to the changing demographic character of the country. This change of popular attitude towards the British monarchy has been in evidence for over fifty years now, though very gradually only. In 1939, George VI became the first reigning British monarch to visit Canada. The country was awash with Union Jacks and the playing of "God Save the King" by military bands with visibly instilled patriotic joy on the faces of the Canadians. But eighteen years down the line, there was already a perceptible change in the popular mood. In 1957, when King George's daughter, Queen Elizabeth II, visited Canada to open the Canadian Parliament, gallop polls across the country revealed that 63 per cent of the Canadians polled were either indifferent or even openly critical of the visit. Keeping Canada British though still remains a factor not easy to ignore. In fact, till not too long ago, 1976 to be precise, the Canadian law favoured immigrants from Britain quite explicitly by observing no legal difference between "a Canadian" and "a British subject". If you were the latter and could afford the cost of travel, you had just to pack your bags and come and start living in Canada.

French Canadians or Francophones constitute the second largest ethno-demographic group in Canada, though confined mostly in the province of Quebec. The separatist sentiment continues to simmer amongst this group occasionally even erupting into political drama, something likely to continue. In appreciable numbers, French immigrants to Canada ended in late 18th century coinciding with the end of the French empire in North America. Consequently, most French Canadians today trace their roots to the small French community left behind by France in Quebec. Intermarriages between these colonial families became the norm and their number kept growing, helped by the high Catholic birth rate factor. Small pockets of French communities are to be found outside Quebec in other parts of Canada and they benefit considerably from Canada's "mosaic culture", liberal policy and the protective approach of the government.

But overall, the Canadian demographic and ethnic content has been undergoing significant changes over the years, notably in the post World War II period. Till 1962, Canada's immigration policy was very much influenced by the stand taken by its late Prime Minister, Mackenzie King as World War II ended, namely, that "the people of Canada do not wish, as a result of mass immigration, to make a fundamental alteration in the character of our population". In terms of official policy, this implied Canada's distinct preference for immigrants from Britain, France, the USA, Ireland, New Zealand, South Africa and Australia. Immigrants from other countries were accepted only if the Citizenship and Immigration authorities considered them "desirable future citizens not likely to give rise to social and economic problems." Even Commonwealth citizens were not welcome if they were coloured British West Indians or Asians. In fact, till 1962, the Department of Immigration reigned supreme in this respect and nobody questioned its authority. In the post war period, nearly a quarter of a million Germans were allowed into Canada without any fear of a demographic imbalance resulting. In 1952, as many as 7,709 Poles were admitted with the number drastically dropping to 2,870 in the following year (1953). In the two years following the Hungarian uprising of 1956, waving all screening regulations, Canada took in 37,566 Hungarian refugees, a number larger than that admitted by any other country, earning Canada plaudits in the eyes of the Western world. To be fair to Canada, faced with the possibility of a large inflow of would be immigrants, most other white countries around the world were following highly restrictive policies as well in the period following World War II. However, this obvious racial prejudice was not allowed to shut the door to Canada in the case of perceived persecuted religious groups like Mennonites, Hutterites, Doukhobors and Jews. Their presence in Canada only added to religious diversity in the country without conflicting with its otherwise racially inspired restrictive immigration policy.

The situation for the visible minorities changed substantially only in the period after World War II, essentially in the 60s, 70s and 80s. Till then, the visible minorities were not favoured except for cheap labour as in the case of the Chinese at the time of the construction of the Trans Canada Railway. Otherwise, till the 1960s, Canada was essentially a white country with people of British and French origin dominating the scene, but with a fair sprinkling of other European origin people, like the Irish, Germans, Italians and East Europeans, notably from Poland, Ukraine and Hungary.

The big change came in 1962 when a new regulation removed all racial and ethnic quotas from the Canadian Immigration Act, did away with the hitherto system of preferred countries and brought in a policy that laid " primary stress on education, training and skills as the main conditions of admissibility, regardless of the country of origin of the applicant." The newly acquired confidence in the post World War II period made Canada realise that it was no longer a wild west frontier country desperately looking for brute labour and hardy settlers, but people with skills, qualifications and talent. This major shift in policy required that the immigration net be thrown far and wide, rather than be restricted to the whites only policy of the past.

Today, Canada has over five million non-white people accounting for about 16 per cent of the total population or roughly one in every six inhabitants of the country. And, this trend continues with over 80 per cent of the new immigrants being non-white. Canada now welcomes more immigrants per capita than any other country in the world, roughly 2,30,000 a year. Canada's demographics are indeed changing rapidly with all this being a sea change considering that as late as 1981, Canada's population was 99 per cent white. But that is not so any more.

But this growing racial diversity is yet not so visible everywhere in Canada; instead, it depends on where in the country you happen to be. Six out of every ten non-whites live in Vancouver or Toronto, while the rural parts of Canada still remain essentially white. A walk down Vancouver's Panjabi Market or Toronto's Gerard Street will put you in a nearly total Indian or South Asian ambience. Asian Canadians broadly fall into two categories: "Orientals" or those originating from China, Japan, Korea, Vietnam and the Philippines. Whereas' the term "Asians" is used to refer to people from India, Pakistan, Sri Lanka and Bangladesh. This category also, very often, gets referred to as Indo-Canadians, East Indians or South Asians. The Chinese today constitute the largest minority group, nearly four per cent of the total population. Most of them are in British Columbia, where Richmond City now has a Chinese majority.

During the American Revolution, England promised freedom to some of America's "slaves" for supporting the British cause. The British Empire had outlawed slavery in 1833, much before America. Some descendants of these "Black Loyalists" are still to be found in Canada's Maritime Provinces. However, of late, Black immigrants have come into Canada mostly from Africa or the Caribbean. But a few "African Americans" are still there and they claim that their roots go much further. Altogether, Blacks today constitute nearly three per cent of Canada's total population.

Against this backdrop of Canada's growing racial and ethnic mix, it is possible to understand and appreciate its policy of multiculturalism or the mosaic culture policy as opposed to the melting pot approach adopted by the United States of America just south of the border. In a way, the origins of Canada's multicultural approach can be traced to the Treaty of Paris of 1763 that brought to an end the Seven Year War between England and France in Europe and also sealed the fate of the rest of New France with all the French lands in Canada going to England. The oddity of the resultant situation was the fact that the overwhelming majority of its newly acquired colony of Canada was of foreign, mostly French, origin. As the victor, England could have tried to impose its language, culture and life style on the majority people of French origin. But realising the complexities involved and taking a more practical view, it chose the path of reconciliation. The people of French origin were already feeling abandoned and let down by the mother country, France. Their feelings and sentiments were rather raw. A policy of confrontation and imposition of English values and life style would have alienated the Quebecois even more. It was time for healing and reconciliation, the English colonial masters realised. All the more so when just to the south, their American colony was already showing signs of strong resentment, even protest, leading ultimately to the events of 1776 and American independence from British rule.

If this background provided the beginnings of multiculturalism or as it has come to be known, over the years, as Canada's mosaic culture policy, then the big question is: has it worked? In pursuit of this policy, Canada officially not only accepts and tolerates the various strands of culture that its mixed bag of immigrants have been bringing along as they move to Canada to make it their new home, but it even encourages the preservation of original identities, even extending financial support, at least in a limited way – a policy of not imposing too much burden on immigrants to assimilate. If one is looking for symbolic signs of success of this policy, then they are there in plenty. Starting with the French Canadians, they have held high offices like the Governor General and the Prime Minister. They are to be seen in substantial numbers in the nation's armed forces and the elite police force, the Royal Canadian Mounted Police (RCMP). They are to be seen occupying posts, both at junior and senior levels, in virtually all departments of the federal government. They are there, at all levels, in business, and as doctors, lawyers, accountants and what not. And yet, the big poser remains: has it really reconciled the Quebecois? Has it truly and finally made Quebec accept itself to be an integral part of Canada despite its being in Canada for well over two centuries now? Has the separatist sentiment fizzled out? Is the threat of Quebec one day breaking away from Canada really dissipated or does it continue to lurk in the shadows? Speaking honestly, the answer to all these questions is not yet a categorical 'No'! This does give rise to resentment, if not open protest, on the part of other Canadians, Anglophiles, other whites and even the coloured, particularly by those living and working in Quebec and often becoming victims of discrimination, if not open hostility, at the hands of the Quebecois. It is not surprising that the view is often expressed, in non-French Canadian quarters, that Canadians of French origin are a pampered lot, that they often get more than they deserve, and yet remain an unhappy lot. Even the wisdom of the mosaic culture policy comes under severe strain and gets seriously questioned. Is Canada's multiculturalism a happy reality or an illusion, is a question that will possibly always defy a clear cut answer.

In terms of symbols, other minorities in Canada have not either done badly at all. Those of Chinese origin are visible, often with a high profile, in virtually all walks of life. In the one province, British Columbia, where the Chinese origin Canadians are to be seen the most, a Hong Kong born Chinese, Adrienne Clarkson, was appointed the Governor of the province in 1999. Raymond Chan, another high profile Chinese origin figure from British Columbia was one of the Deputy Foreign Ministers at the federal level in the 1990s.

The prominent community of Indo-Canadians too has impressively made its mark in virtually all fields. In the 1980s, Baltej Singh Dhillon became the first turban wearing officer in the RCMP, prompting some critics to even ask if this was not going a bit far. Following the general election of 1993, the lower House of the Canadian Parliament, the House of Commons, saw for the first time in its history a turbaned Sikh, Gurbax Singh Malhi from Toronto, as one of its members, along with two more of Indian origin. Indo-Canadians are to be come across in prominent positions elsewhere in Canada too including as federal ministers. The 1990s also saw Ujjwal Singh

Dosanj becoming the first ever Indian born Premier of the British Columbia province. These are just a few illustrative examples.

Canada deservedly is proud of all such examples and instances. But the critics of multiculturalism are still there and continue to raise objections. In 1993, a nationwide opinion poll was commissioned by the Canadian Council of Christians and Jews and conducted by Decima Research. The results surprised, if not shocked many. Nearly 72 per cent of the respondents were of the view that Canada as a nation of communities, each preserving its ethnic and racial identity with the help of government policy must give way to the US style and concept of cultural absorption. Growing intolerance towards the demands of the ethnic groups was attributed to many Canadians, who expressed frustration over "the lack of conformity" in Canadian society.

"CANADIANS WANT MOSAIC TO MELT, SURVEY FINDS"

This is how one of Canada's leading dailies, *The Globe and Mail*, reported on December 14, 1993.

The Montreal Gazette of the same day, while reporting on this poll, gave it a racial twist and interpretation with the headline:

CANADIANS HARBOR 'LATENTLY RACIST' ATTITUDES: POLL

Comparisons with Canada's big neighbour to the south, the USA, also very much a country of immigrants, are inevitable and support expressed for its "melting pot" approach as opposed to Canada's "mosaic culture" policy. The "melting pot" policy of the USA implies that those immigrating to that country should, as far as possible, leave the baggage of the past behind and merge with the mainstream of life in their new home. There is no pressure to do so, but nor is there any official help, financial included, extended to retain and develop the past links. Of course, it has to be accepted and recognized that the total wiping out of your past is neither possible, nor perhaps even desirable. You can adopt the American life style, even habits, but you cannot change the colour of your skin, nor your looks. In the case of inter marriages involving the whites, this may happen up to a point. But you still carry the label of the country of your origin. But this reality is not allowed to come in the way of your progressing in life. If the USA is often referred to as the land of opportunity, it is not without reason. People with different ethnic and racial backgrounds have and continue to thrive. Many amongst them have made it to the top in various walks of life, including in the political field, except that those from this category cannot aspire to be the President of the country since it is Constitutionally required that one should be a natural born (not naturalised) citizen of the USA. But otherwise, this "melting pot" approach has not come in the way of people with different ethnic, racial or religious backgrounds pursuing their respective cultures. This is more than adequately reflected in the hundreds of different places of worship, cultural centres, super markets specialising in certain types of foods and ingredients, restaurants and what not all over the country. If anything, it only adds to the rich variety and diversity that the USA offers in its own way. Conformity to local laws is understandably insisted upon, but nobody views it as a curb. As against all this, if you have talent and the will to work hard and move ahead in life, the system does not put hurdles in your way. All this is there within the parameters of the "melting pot" policy. In fact, with the passage of time, the original identity itself begins to slowly give way to what may be called the American way of life. This happens gradually even to the first generation of immigrants, but much more to their children, born and brought up in the USA, and even more so with subsequent generations. A stage very often is ultimately reached where the country of origin only reminds you of your roots in the distant past and even a visit there is more of a sentimental journey than for any pressing family reasons. Your family is now with you and where your home is. Very often, a few generations down the line, beyond how you look, it is difficult to identify with the country of your origin. You perhaps do not even speak any more the language of that country.

Canada's mosaic culture policy ensures more or less the same except that under it you are, in however small way, officially encouraged or at least assisted to preserve and promote your original identity. The two approaches, mosaic versus melting pot, do overlap a lot and, ultimately, it is more perhaps a difference in nomenclature than substance. Perhaps, Canada prefers it that way since it once again brings out the point that they are different from the USA, they are North Americans without being Americans and that they have a distinct identity of their own, which they are keen to preserve and promote and remain proud of.

In the evolution of the people, a few generations, perhaps even centuries, is not enough. It is a very slow process involving a gradual change of mind set and attitude. An average Canadian still, while introducing or describing himself or herself, often tends to bring out the country of his or her origin. He/she is an Anglophone or a French Canadian, a Scottish Canadian, an Irish

Canadian, a German Canadian, an Indo-Canadian or a Chinese Canadian. The link with the country of origin is still a fresh memory and, therefore, very often mentioned. But given a few more generations, this tendency to link yourself with another country, just because you or your forefathers originated from there, will very likely weaken to a point where it will get dropped as an unnecessary and meaningless appellation with the term "Canadian" alone sufficing. It will happen with the passage of time and no one seems to be in a rush or hurry to telescope centuries into years. Canada is a new country inhabited by new people. In time, their distinct identity will get firmly established.

Chapter Four – The Economic Scene

Today, Canada is the eleventh largest economy in the world (in US dollar terms) and is one of the world's richest nations. But it has not always been like this. Instead, for Canada, it has been a long and hard journey to reach this level of development and prosperity.

A quick survey of the historical background takes one back by several centuries to the days of the First Nation people, the INUIT and Indians. Life in those days was simple, living conditions extremely harsh and demands few in keeping with the then existing realities. Life was essentially nomadic, hunting the main occupation and the main products were furs, simple tools made of stone or bone and occasional decorative items whenever "leisure" permitted. It was often a struggle to survive against the brutal elements. Trade, if any, was carried out on a barter basis.

Then the European discoverers arrived. To begin with, their main focus was on the exploitation of Canada's immense natural resources – furs (mostly beaver pelts) to begin with and later on, as communications improved, timber and fish and other marine products. The guiding principle for developing the Canadian economy, during the colonial times, was mercantilism; the quest being, to derive the maximum material benefit from the colony, with minimum investment. It was sheer economic exploitation so very typical of the then European colonial powers, no matter where they went in search of new lands and attractive commercial possibilities.

In New France (Canada), under a Royal Charter, the French established a number of corporate trading monopolies like La Compagnie Des Marchands from 1613 to 1621; Compagnie De Montmorency from 1621 to 1627 to be replaced by the French King, Louis XIII, in 1643 by the Communaute Des Habitants. In what is now Canada, these were the first commercial corporations to operate.

Fur trade played a crucial role in the development of interior Canada. It very much involved the native people because of their intimate knowledge of and familiarity with the land coupled with their expertise in hunting. Beaver furs were in great demand with the Europeans, readily bought by them from the natives, who were happy to get in exchange items like guns, textiles and luxury items, like mirrors and beads.

In the early stages, the French dominated the fur trade in Canada. But the English were not to be left far behind. A major step in this direction was the setting up of the Hudson Bay Company with its elaborate net-work of trading posts and forts. However, a negative side effect of this fur trade was that it led to a nomadic way of life rather than resulting in permanent settlements. People followed the animals and kept moving to wherever there was more to hunt. This contrasted with the American agricultural settlements that gave people a somewhat stable life and even time to multiply and raise families. This would explain why Canada's population remained so low, virtually stuck at a few thousand till the 1660s.

By early 19th century, Canada's vast timber resources began to attract the Europeans, notably the English. Because of the industrial revolution, the forest cover was dwindling rapidly in Britain. It is interesting to note how, in history, events in one part of the world can influence things elsewhere, however remote. The Napoleonic wars in Europe and the continental blockade virtually cut off or drastically reduced the supply of timber to Britain from the Baltic region, otherwise a traditional source. This resulted in a spurt of timber imports from Canada, overcoming the difficulties caused by distance and transportation. The main supply points were naturally along Canada's eastern coast, the closest part of Canada to Europe. It was from money made from timber exports that the Bank of Montreal was founded in 1817.

This increase in timber exports to England had an interesting side effect to Canada's advantage. It caused a spurt in English immigration to North America. Ships laden with timber from Canada had little cargo to carry back from England, beyond perhaps salt and a few other items. The enterprising shipping companies, in order to fill up their ships, started offering extremely cheap passages to those wanting to emigrate to Canada and, therefore, crossing the Atlantic. These were no luxury liners and travel conditions were quite tough and miserable. But for many, looking for new lands and opportunities, the plunge was still worth it, more so when it cost so little as to make it within the reach of most. Once they reached Canada, even if it meant a lot of hard work, there was at least the hope of a better tomorrow. In any case, few ever wanted to go back to England by repeating the miserable travel experience that they had been through to reach Canada. Also, many of these immigrants had very little to look forward to even if they somehow got back to England. They had burnt their boats, so to say. Canada was their new home now and with determination and hard work came the opportunities and, subsequently, a much better quality of life. Talking of the growing influx of immigrants from Britain and other parts of Europe, soon fifteen thousand Irish loggers were employed in the Gatineau region alone of eastern Canada. This swelling population was soon to be a visible reality. Canada's population that was in thousands only in the 17th and a better part of the 18th century touched one million by 1820 and was ten million in 1920. By 2001, the figure stood at thirty million and is now (2013) at 35 million. The first ever Census was conducted in 1851.

Growth and development constituted the dominant philosophy behind Canada's economy. The changing scene understandably ushered in the banking and insurance sectors. Possibly the first bank in Canada's history was established in 1792, the Canada Banking Company. Encouraged by the fast growing scope for banking business others were not far behind, such as the Bank of Montreal (1817), the Bank of New Brunswick (1820) and the Bank of Upper Canada (1821). By 1886, as many as thirty six banks had been chartered, logically resulting in the Bank Act of 1871 by the newly formed government of Canada following the birth of the Confederation in 1867.

Almost running parallel to the growth of banking business was the coming up of insurance companies. In the 1860s and 70s, the big names to emerge were: Sun Life (1865), Mutual Life (1870), Confederation Life (1871), and London Life (1874).

In the aftermath of the establishment of the Canadian Confederation in 1867, the country's first Prime Minister, John A. Macdonald, recognizing the future trends and immense possibilities of growth enunciated the broad outlines of Canada's economic programme that was to be at the core of the nation's policy for decades to follow. It was realised that it was time for Canada to step beyond the exploitation and export of its natural resources. It was necessary to enter the next stage of economic growth, namely manufacturing, thus adding more job opportunities and also adding value to its vast natural resources. Accordingly, the concept of protective tariffs was introduced to encourage Canada's manufacturing industry. Further, equally important was the development of infrastructure by way of railways and canals to make the movement of goods and people easier and cheaper and also to facilitate more trade with its American neighbour to the south. The Grand Trunk Railway of Canada had already linked Toronto and Montreal in 1853. Subsequently, with lines opened to Portland, Michigan and Chicago by 1870, it became the longest rail link in the world. In 1876, the Maritimes were linked by rail to Quebec and Ontario. In the meanwhile, work was going ahead on the Canadian Pacific Railway running almost parallel to the US border. As this ambitious project progressed, it encouraged settlement in the vast Prairie Provinces that were to be ultimately Canada's bread basket and granary. The completion of this rail link connected Canada from coast to coast, the Atlantic in the West and the Pacific in the East. An incidental positive outcome of the construction of this massive project was that thanks to extensive digging and excavation work, a large number of metal and mineral deposits were also discovered paving the way for their exploitation on a commercial scale in the future. As part of this growing focus on economic growth and development, work on various canals was going on apace inter-linking different parts of the country, besides creating more job opportunities and stimulating the economy. Rideau Canal was one of the first such projects in Upper Canada (Ontario) to be followed by other such major projects like the Rideau Welland and Trent-Severn Waterway. The overall picture was almost one of feverish economic activity and growth.

The world-wide depression of the last quarter of the 19th century inevitably hit Canada too. The job market shrank and immigration dropped. However, this set back was temporary only and in the period 1896 till 1914, Canada made a remarkable recovery to become the world's fastest growing economy. Population grew and the western parts of the country were experiencing rapid settlement, thanks to the improved transport links. The growth of agriculture was making rapid strides in the prairies, wheat notably. Soya too was introduced though it caught the fancy of the farmers somewhat slowly.

World War I (1914-18) was in many ways a turning point for Canada. It not only played an important role in the war effort of the allies by contributing significantly in terms of combatants, but also became a major supplier of food and arms and ammunition, thanks to its fast developing agriculture and manufacturing sectors. Both the prairies and the maritime provinces experienced something of a boom. The former due to their healthy agricultural growth and the latter because of the increased manufacturing capacity. Despite a short period of depression immediately after the War, due to a sudden fall in demand for the aforementioned major supplies from Canada, the country recovered fast and the economic boom lasted till 1929, resulting in the coining of the phrase "the roaring twenties".

The Great Depression of the 1930s hit Canada hard. By 1933, relief camps had to be set up for the unemployed. By that year, nearly 30 per cent of the labour force was out of work. Wages fell as did prices. The gross national expenditure declined by 42 per cent. In the prairies, 2/3rd of the total population was on relief. Canada's depression, which was running almost parallel to that in the neighbouring USA, lasted till 1939.

But the outbreak of World War II in September, 1939 rapidly changed the scene again. With mass recruitment, unemployment virtually disappeared. Both the agriculture and manufacturing sectors picked up substantially due to increased demand because of the war effort. For the first time, Canada was in the unusual position of financially helping the British economy through its equivalent of the US Lend Lease. This time, the economic upturn was to last far beyond the end of the War. In fact, the period 1945-1970 witnessed an impressive expansion of the Canadian economy. Record high war time production was diverted to the manufacture of a wide range of consumer goods. Unemployment was a record low. This continuing growth encouraged Canada to establish itself as a welfare State after the pattern of most other developed nations. The health care system was publicly funded. A pension plan and similar other welfare programmes were started. This period also witnessed the development of closer links between the economies of Canada and the USA, a trend that continues to be very visible till today.

However, the economic recession in the 1980s and early 90s once again brought back some economic woes like huge government deficits, high unemployment and general disaffection. The Progressive Conservative Party under Brian Mulroney paid the price in the 1993 general election by being rejected by the people and the Liberals under Jean Chretien came to office. A brief recovery in 1994 was followed again by a slump in 1995-96. But Canada managed to come out of it again and since then, its economy, by and large, has improved markedly.

Today, Canada is a model of fiscal stability. From 1996 to 2008, the government posted a surplus every year, not a small achievement. This time, when an economic downturn hit the US economy, Canada was touched only mildly. It has been one of the very few times that Canada has managed to avoid following the US into recession. Several factors account for this. Though the US is still a major economic and commercial partner and is most likely to remain so in the future, Canada has been consciously and gradually spreading out into other fast growing regions of the world, notably Asia and Latin America. Domestically, it has been concentrating its economic growth in sectors like petroleum, real estate and income trust. As a developed economy, it has now graduated from the primary products stage, to manufacturing to now the service sector. The following Table 1 provides a tell-tale picture of its GDP growth pattern in the first decade of the 21st century.

Table 1: Canadian GDP Growth Pattern during 2000-2012

Sr. No.	Year	Change
1	2000	+5.2%
2	2001	+1.8%
3	2002	+2.9%
4	2003	+1.9%
5	2004	+3.1%
6	2005	+ 3.0%
7	2006	+2.8%
8	2007	+2.2%
9	2008	+0.5%
10	2009	-2.5%
11	2010	+3.2%
12	2011	+2.2%
13	2012	+1.7%

Source: https://en.wikipedia.org/wiki/Economic_history_of_Canada

Except for the year 2009, when the economy went into the negative because of the global slowdown, notably in the US and the EU, for a highly developed economy, Canada has been showing a consistent and robust growth.

Against the back drop of this quick run through the history of the Canadian economy, it is time to take in some basic data of the present day scene. As mentioned at the very start of this chapter, the Canadian economy today ranks as the eleventh largest in the world, making it one of the wealthiest nations. Its currency, the Canadian Dollar, is a shade stronger than the US dollar. Its fiscal year runs from April to March. Its GDP stands at $ 1. 839 trillion with an annual growth rate of about two per cent. In the last decade, in some years, its growth rate has been well above that figure, highest at 5.2 per cent in 2000 and showing negative growth only once so far in 2009. The sectoral break-up of the GDP is agriculture: 1.9 per cent, industry: 27.1 per cent and services 71 per cent. Inflation is low at 1.2 per cent and in relative terms, going by the high Canadian standard, 10.8 per cent of the total population of 35 million is below the poverty line. Canada's labour force of 18.67 million, little over half of the total population, is deployed as follows in terms of occupation: Agriculture - two per cent; Manufacturing - 13 per cent; Construction - six per cent and Services - 76 per cent. Clearly, as a highly developed economy, it has moved up from the primary stage to manufacturing to services now. Unemployment stands at seven per cent. The country's main industries are: transportation and communication equipment, chemicals, processed and unprocessed minerals, food products, wood and paper products, petroleum and natural gas. Its relatively smooth and efficient system earns the country the 17th rank in the world in terms of ease of doing business with. Talking of public finances, in Canadian Dollars (CAD), its public debt is $ 582.2 billion, federal budget deficit about 34 billion, federal revenues $237 billion, expenses 270 billion, and Canada annually disburses, as a donor, economic aid worth about $ 4 billion. According to Standard and Poor, the country enjoys an all-round rating of triple A. Canada's foreign reserves stand at around $ 66 billion. All these figures relate to 2012-13.

Foreign trade plays a major role in the Canadian economy with exports at around $463 billion and imports at about $461 billion. The major exports of Canada are: motor vehicles and parts, industrial machinery, aircraft, telecommunications equipment, chemicals, plastics, fertilizers, wood pulp, timber, crude petroleum, natural gas, electricity and aluminium. The US at about 74 per cent and the UK at around five per cent are the two major destinations for Canadian exports. The country's principal imports are: machinery and equipment, motor vehicles and parts, crude oil, chemicals, electricity and durable consumer goods. The main sources for these imports are the US 60 per cent, China 11 per cent and Mexico six per cent. All these are approximate and round figures. As already emphasized, international trade constitutes a major component of the Canadian economy, specially of its natural resources. Agriculture, energy, forestry and mining exports account for nearly 60 per cent of its total exports. While machinery, equipment, automotive products and other manufactures cover the balance nearly 40 per cent. Canada's exports account for nearly 30 per cent of its GDP. Taking its overall exports and imports into account, the country ranks in the top ten trading countries of the world.

With a strong and stable economy, Canada, understandably, is a major player on the world economic stage as a member of the Organization for Economic Co-operation and Development (OECD) and the Group of Eight (G8). In the mould of other developed economies, service industry dominates the Canadian economy, employing about three quarters of the country's work force. But the continuing importance of the primary sector distinguishes Canada from the other developed nations. Logging and oil industries are two of Canada's most important components of the primary sector. Its manufacturing sector, notably the automobile and aircraft industries are heavily concentrated in central Canada. With the world's largest coastline of 202,080 kilometres, Canada has the 8th largest commercial fishing and sea-food industry in the world.

Canada is fortunate in terms of possessing abundant natural resources and that too spread across its vast and varied regions. This generous distribution of nature's bounty has also determined the economic growth pattern and the nature of industries in different parts of Canada. Thus, if it is forestry in British Columbia, it is oil and gas in Alberta, Saskatchewan, Newfoundland and Labrador. Northern Ontario is the home of mining industry, while the Atlantic Provinces have traditionally been known for fishing. Canada has sizeable mineral resources of coal, copper, iron ore and gold. However, due to the rapid growth of manufacturing and service sectors, primary industries are gradually dwindling in importance to Canada's overall economic scene. Only about four per cent of the country's labour force is today employed in the primary sector, which contributes just over six per cent to the nation's GDP. Increasing use of latest techniques and modern equipment would also explain the declining need for human labour. But as one keeps moving towards the northern parts of the country, where agriculture becomes increasingly difficult due to climatic conditions, many small towns and settlements primarily exist because of mining or timber. In what is possibly an extreme case, there is the world's highest (87 degrees North) Polaris mine in Canada North mining copper and zinc in extremely harsh climatic conditions, necessitating a very special package of working conditions by way of much higher wages and other perks. Canada is the world leader in the production of many natural resources, such as gold, nickel, uranium, diamonds and lead. Some of the country's largest manufacturing industries are directly linked to and dependent on primary ones, paper and pulp, for instance, on logging. Reliance on the widespread natural resources does have some side effects on the Canadian economy. It determines differing development in each region and province; creates a sense of regionalism but also results in varying shades of growth. Thus, while the national unemployment figure is about seven per cent, it is the highest in Newfoundland and Labrador at nearly 13.5 per cent and around five per cent in agriculture rich prairie provinces and possibly even a shade lower in oil and gas rich Alberta. Since most of the natural resources are exported, it has the effect of closely integrating Canada into the international economy. Fear is sometimes expressed as to for how long can this dependence on natural resources be sustained, the fear of its depletion. But this really poses no serious threat in the foreseeable future. New and substantial discoveries continue to be made. The vast known natural resources and deposits of the extreme north are waiting to be exploited as soon as more modern technologies are developed and the exercise becomes commercially more viable. Given its rich experience in the mining sector, Canada is active in this field in Latin America, Africa and South-East Asia where these natural resources are in plenty and wages much lower.

Turning next to Canada's key industries, the choice logically would be the service sector that is vast, varied and employing almost three fourths of Canada's work force and contributing 78 per cent to the GDP. The largest employer is the retail sector employing close to 12 per cent of Canadians. This is followed by the business services sector employing nearly the same high percentage as the retail sector. This would include financial services, real estate and communications industries. It is one of the fast growing sectors concentrated, for obvious reasons, in major urban centres like Toronto, Montreal and Vancouver. Education and health sectors occupy an important and a large place in the category of services, but with considerable government control. Canada's health care industry is the third largest in the country. Likewise, its important high tech industry plays a significant role in the service sector as does its growing entertainment industry. Tourism, something highly developed and helped by the country's vastness, stunning natural beauty, excellent infrastructure, too plays an important role in Canada's burgeoning service sector. Though a large number of tourists are from the United States, other countries, notably the fast growing economies of Asia, are increasingly getting attracted by Canada as a tourist destination.

Typical of the economic growth story of advanced and developed countries, Canada too has followed the same path, primary to manufacturing to the service sector. During World War II, its manufacturing sector registered rapid growth accounting for, when the War ended, 29 per cent of the GDP. The role of manufacturing started declining somewhat from the 1960s. But while this decline in relative percentage terms of the GDP was noticeable (24 per cent in 1960 to 16 per cent by 2005), manufacturing volumes kept pace with the overall growth in the volume index of GDP. The years 2007-10 were bad for the manufacturing sector, because of the global financial crisis. Things have stabilised now with this sector accounting for around 14 per cent of the GDP.

Canada continues to be a popular destination for the location of branch plants of many US major manufacturers. In southern Ontario, London and Windsor particularly, there is a heavy presence of major US automobile manufacturers and also of GE's electric locomotives. Canada's highly educated work force, lower labour costs without compromising on quality and its publicly funded efficient health care system have all contributed to the attraction of Canada in this respect. Canada's health care system exempts companies from high health insurance costs. The only downside of this pattern is that branch plants create essentially mid and junior level jobs with R and D and senior executive positions remaining in the US. However, Canada does not seem to mind this as long as it adds to its manufacturing capacity and creates more jobs. Of course, Canada has its own industrial giants like Bombardier Inc. with an international reputation and reach. Some other big names include EnCana, Cameco, Goldcorp, Barrick Gold and Alcan.

Energy is a major industry in Canada. In fact, Canada is one of the few developed countries that is also a net exporter of energy almost accounting for three per cent of the GDP. Oil and gas resources are in the lead including its vast oil bearing sand deposits (ATHABASCA OIL SANDS) that put Canada in the third place in the world, after Saudi Arabia and Venezuela, in terms of reserves of oil. Hydroelectric power is yet another considerable source of energy, inexpensive in the long run and relatively environmentally friendly and widely spread over in British Columbia, Quebec, Ontario, Saskatchewan, Manitoba and Labrador. Thanks to this nature's bounty and its efficient use, Canada is one of the world's highest per capita consumers of energy. Easy availability of power at an affordable price has also attracted high energy consumption and important industry like the manufacture of aluminium. However, the Ontario province, otherwise with a high concentration of industry, has relatively few local sources of power. The gap is sought to be filled significantly by the use of nuclear power, a field in which Canada is one of the world leaders, possessing rich uranium deposits.

Agriculture is another area in which Canada has and continues to do well, making it today one of the world's largest suppliers of agricultural products, notably to the next door USA and Asia. Exports particularly include wheat and other grains. As with other developed economies, agriculture in Canada is the beneficiary of significant government subsidies and support.

While examining the Canadian economic scene, its relations with the USA are indeed a very crucial factor. The USA is by far the largest trading partner of Canada with nearly 73 per cent of its exports going to the US market and with imports from the US at about 63 per cent of its total global imports. In the reverse, trade with Canada accounts for about 23 per cent of US total exports and 17 per cent of its imports. This unique relationship is beyond just a border state phenomenon. Canada is the leading export market for as many as 35 of US states and is also the largest foreign supplier of energy to the US, including oil, natural gas and hydroelectric power with the national electricity grids of the two neighbouring countries linked. The commodity sector is the largest component of this burgeoning bi-lateral trade. The US is Canada's largest agricultural market, accounting for nearly half of Canadian exports in this category. The position is even more impressive in some other sectors. Almost two-thirds of Canada's forest products, including paper, pulp and newsprint are exported to the US. The US is also Canada's largest foreign investor with the principal focus being on sectors like mining and smelting, petroleum, chemicals, machinery and transportation equipment and finance. Reciprocally, Canadian foreign investments find the US the most popular destination with main focus being on manufacturing, wholesale trade, real estate, petroleum, finance, insurance and other services.

Given this huge economic and commercial relationship between Canada and the US, occasional disputes and glitches are inevitable, but over the years, these two mature nations have evolved various bi-lateral mechanisms to resolve all such problems whenever they arise. The occasional areas where there is scope for clash of interests include agriculture and cultural fields, fisheries, lumber, etc. If bi-lateral talks fail, then the two sides can take resort to other means by common agreement. For instance, they took their Gulf of Maine boundary dispute to the International Court of Justice in 1981. Both sides accepted the Court's verdict that demarcated the territorial sea boundary between Canada and the US. While both Canada and the US generally remain happy and satisfied over this highly important aspect of their relationship, Canada does feel, at times at least, a little uncomfortable with what some view as over-dependence on just one market. By way of remedial steps, Canada has been, for some time now, very active in other emerging markets in Asia, Africa and Latin America. This approach has helped it to at least somewhat reduce its dependence on its otherwise very useful and important neighbour to the South.

Canada's impressive economic and commercial profile gets reflected internationally in many ways. Apart from being a member of the OECD and G8, it is a party to several free trade agreements. These include the Canada-US Free Trade Agreement (1989) later superseded by NAFTA (North American Free Trade Agreement) involving Canada, the US and Mexico and effective since 1994, Canada-Israel Free Trade Agreement (1997), Canada-Chile Free Trade Agreement (1997), Canada-Costa Rica Free Trade Agreement (2002), Canada-European Union Free Trade Agreement (2009), Canada-Peru Free Trade Agreement (2009), Canada-Jordan Free Trade Agreement (2009) and Canada-Panama Free Trade Agreement (2010). In addition to all this, Canada is negotiating bilateral FTAs with Ukraine, Morocco, India, South Korea, the Dominican Republic, Singapore, CARICOM (Caribbean Community), Andean Community, with negotiations already concluded with Peru, EU, Japan and China. Canada is also involved in negotiations to create regional trade blocks like Canada-Central American Free Trade Agreement and the Free Trade Area of the Americas (FTAA). All this is indicative of the vigour with which Canada pursues its economic and commercial interests abroad.

By way of concluding this review of the Canadian economic scene, it may be said that overall the position remains optimistic and the potential for growth steady. However, there is no room for complacency and as the country stepped into 2013, some alarm bells were already beginning to ring. Without sounding alarmist, the disturbing reality is that austerity measures and other growth stifling policies in effect in large countries and economies around the world have the potential to hit the Canadian economy, somewhat at least. A country so active on the international scene cannot insulate itself completely against the difficult times that others are going through. A recent IMF report has already forecast a growth of 1.8 per cent for Canada in 2013, down from two per cent that it had projected earlier.

On the domestic economic scene, some areas of concern stand out visibly. Though the national unemployment figure at seven per cent looks manageable, critics point out that permanent, well-paying jobs are slowing down and correspondingly, thanks to recession, temporary jobs are on the increase. While the latter category grew by 14.3 per cent between 2009-2012, the latter (permanent well-paying jobs) increased by only 3.8 per cent. A recent (early 2013) survey by McMaster University and the United Way brought out the disturbing picture that 40 per cent of the work force in the Greater Toronto and Hamilton region (in many ways, the economic hub of the country) find themselves in temporary work with no security or benefits and constantly at the mercy of an unstable job market. This changing pattern of the job market, unless arrested and reversed, potentially can and, in some cases, has already left many Canadians economically vulnerable and will gradually increase the burden on provincial welfare systems.

One serious fall out of this changing job market scene has been the growing concern over consumer debt. The tendency to live beyond one's means is now coming home to roost with its negative consequences. For nearly a decade, if not more, average household spending in Canada has exceeded disposable income. Realising that this cannot go on, financial authorities, both at the central and provincial levels, are tightening the screws on risky borrowers to get mortgages or negotiate with them at much lower interest rates. An increase in unemployment from the present level (7%) or a rise in interest rates on borrowings and mortgages could have the unpleasant effect of pushing, some households at least, over the cliff and into the abyss of bankruptcy. This could, in turn, hit the real estate market, otherwise a growing sector. Some analysts have noted that house prices, though still rising everywhere, except Vancouver, disturbingly housing sales and housing starts have dropped. There is clearly a case for a rebound in business investment and an increase in exports. This also explains Canada's growing appetite for expansion abroad, both in terms of investments and exports. With the US economy still not in the happiest of situations, Canada's heavy dependence on this market will have to give place to its spreading its net far and wide. In fact, in the second decade of the current century and beyond this, change in Canada's outlook should be more and more noticeable. Changing circumstances will propel it in that direction.

Even the sales of oil and gas, Canada's biggest single export and very much tied up to the huge next door US market, could face a fall in prices, if not in actual demand, because of the boom in shale gas and oil in the US Midwest. Canada can ill afford to ignore such developments. Mid-course corrections and changes will be required in the interest of preserving and further increasing the level of comfort and affluence that this otherwise happy and fortunate country has, over the years, got so used to.

Chapter Five – The Political Scene

The Canadians are very particular about maintaining that while they are North Americans, they are not Americans. They are ever keen, to the point of being sensitive, about asserting how different they are from their big neighbour to the South, the United States of America. And, to be fair to the Canadians, they are indeed different from the Americans and that too in many ways.

In the context of this chapter on the Canadian political scene, the focus of this difference will be on how these two countries, Canada and the USA, together comprising North America, the former (Canada) far outstripping the latter (the USA) in size of territory though not in population, despite certain commonalities, are also very different from each other. Both are acknowledged democracies with federal structures. Both are today amongst the richest nations in the world and highly developed. But both have reached their present political scene and status following very different paths. Though both, at one time, were under British colonial rule, the USA had to fight a War of Independence to put an end to British rule and emerge as an independent country in 1776. A little under a century later, the Americans had to go through a bloody Civil War to hold the country together. In sharp contrast to all this, Canada never had to fight a "War of Independence", nor did it ever, despite the simmering issue of Quebec, have to suffer the pangs of a civil war to hold itself together. On the contrary, Canada very much threw off the colonial yoke and achieved its independence through a process of political evolution, avoiding all the rancour and bitterness that a violent struggle would inevitably entail, as it happened in the case of the United States. Interestingly, both countries today have the friendliest possible relations with the one-time mother country, Britain. But here again, while the USA is a republic with its own elected President as its Head of State, Canada still retains its link with Britain as a dominion and continues to accept the British monarch as its monarch too, thereby making it till today a Constitutional Monarchy.

In the historical context, the huge land mass today known as Canada had no unified national government till the dawn of the era of European settlements. During the time of the First Nation people, the Inuit and the Indians, local and even regional political arrangements, more like understandings, did arise through treaties amongst the different sects and tribes comprising the First Nations. But for all practical purposes, individual tribe leaders were effectively the local and indeed the only government. In other words, the concept of a unified national government had not yet occurred, leave aside materialised. One might even add here that this was nothing unusual. The concept of a nation state was to be a product of a much later period in history, even in respect of those parts of the world that otherwise have a stronger claim to antiquity. In the present or modern day context, things began to take shape only with the arrival of European settlers when Canada became a series of colonies. The process started with the French in what came to be called "New France" with the British not too far behind in "Upper Canada". Even the Spanish, with their hold over most of Latin America except for Brazil (Portuguese) and even the West Coast of what is now the USA, made brief forays into what is now the Canadian West Coast.

The era of European settlers and colonies has already been covered in detail in the chapter on the history of Canada. Therefore, coming straight to the political scene, the turning point and the defining moment as regards the birth of Canada was the British North America Act of 1867. This important British legislation not only sought to accommodate regional interests, but also enabled Britain to have a single unified administration for the area. This Act of 1867, though still serving as Canada's Constitution (along with the changes made in 1982), its stated mandate was not to bring independence, democracy or freedom, as with the American Constitution in the aftermath of 1776, but "Peace, Order and Good Government".

The Confederation of Canada, born in 1867, started off with four provinces. These were Upper Canada (now Ontario), Lower Canada (now Quebec), Nova Scotia and New Brunswick. The terms of the Confederation clearly defined the separation of powers between the provinces and the national government. There was to be an elected legislative body in each province with a British appointed Lieutenant Governor. The provinces were to have single chamber legislatures only (unicameral system). But at the national level, the legislature was to be bicameral, an elected National Legislature and a British appointed Senate. The overall control was through a British appointed Governor General. The bulk of the power remained with the British exercised through the Governor General at the national level and through the Lieutenant Governors in the provinces.

In the aftermath of the British North America Act of 1867 that initially brought together four provinces, six other provinces joined the Confederation, these being Prince Edward Island, Manitoba, Saskatchewan, Alberta, British Columbia, and Newfoundland. The last one, that is, Newfoundland joined as late as in 1949 following a referendum in which a majority opted to join Canada. Thus, the present day map or the boundary of Canada was completed only in 1949 so as to constitute ten provinces and three territories, namely; Yukon (capital Whitehorse), North West Territories (capital Yellowknife) and Nunavut (capital Iqaluit), the last one being carved out of NWT in the 1990s only, essentially for reasons of administrative convenience. Territories have their own local governments similar to provincial governments. The manner in which the overall borders of Canada, as of now, have emerged, gradually and through consent, between 1867 and 1949, again, contrasts with the present day USA, which has been through outright conquest and annexation (Texas 1845, New Mexico 1846, California 1847 and Arizona 1853—purchased. Ultimately, by the time the Mexican-US War ended in 1848, under the Treaty of Guadalupe Hidalgo, Mexico had lost to the US California, Nevada, Arizona, Utah and parts of Colorado and New Mexico) or purchase (Louisiana from France in 1803 for $ 11,250,000 and Alaska from Russia in 1867 for $ 7.2 million). The USA tried its hand at annexing some parts of Upper Canada or Ontario in early 19th century, but failed and the Canadians still like to recall this as a proud moment in their history. Thus, while the present day map of the USA was complete before the 19th century ended (Hawaii being the last territory acquired in 1900), that of Canada did so only by 1949 with Newfoundland joining it voluntarily following a referendum, a true evolutionary process indeed. The USA and Canada have been, over several decades, not only co-existing peacefully, but with a very high level of cooperation in virtually all fields. The border between the USA and Canada, easily one of the most peaceful in the world today, roughly runs along the 49th parallel. Initially, there were a few border disputes, but they were amicably resolved through negotiations. Thus, unlike the boundary of Manitoba, Saskatchewan and Alberta, that of British Columbia along the west coast is not strictly defined along the 49th parallel. In fact, some parts of British Columbia, Vancouver Island for instance, dip below the 49th parallel, whereas the "Alaskan Pan Handle" secured a significant amount of coastline for Alaska, where more of British Columbia lies to its east. But all these territorial adjustments between Canada and the USA were achieved peacefully and through negotiations.

This evolution of what politically is Canada today is a unique feature indeed. With the passage of time since the British North America Act of 1867, British control and power gradually kept getting diluted. Especially in the period after World War II, Canada's status and power as a nation became very clear. The Constitution of 1982, which introduced further amendments to the original Act of 1867 further sealed this process, and all this without any rancour or controversy with Britain. Thus, today Senators are appointed by the Prime Minister of Canada and not by London. Similar is the case with the appointment of Lieutenant Governors in the provinces. All their powers have shifted to the Legislature and the Cabinet. Likewise, though technically and officially the British monarch (the Queen or the Governor General acting on her behalf) is Canada's Head of State, their power is strictly symbolic. Like in any other parliamentary form of government, the real power in Canada today rests with the popularly elected Prime Minister. But, formally speaking, Canada's form of government still remains a constitutional monarchy.

The Executive

As just mentioned, Canada is a Constitutional Monarchy with the British Monarch, acting through the Governor General, as the Head of State. In her individual capacity, the British Queen is today the Head of State of fifteen countries, all in the Commonwealth with Dominion status. For conventional and technical use, the term "Dominion of Canada" still remains legal though in actual practice, it is rarely used.

The Governor General, acting on behalf of the Queen, though Canada's Head of State, his powers are strictly symbolic. These include signing a "Bill" into "Law", officially dissolving and opening the Parliament, meeting with Heads of State, officiating at awards ceremonies like the conferring of the prestigious "Order of Canada". Foreign envoys accredited to Canada officially present their papers to the Governor General even though they are addressed by the sending Head of State to the Queen. Even the agreement for a foreign envoy to Canada is sought by the sending government from Ottawa and not London. All this might sound as a set of legal fictions, but in practice, it is well established and accepted. The fact remains that the Governor General is ultimately responsible to the Prime Minister and would not defy or ignore any "requests" or "advise" given by the Prime Minister. Even his appointment in the first place, though technically made by the Queen as her representative, is actually the decision of the Prime Minister. The Governor General's office is, thus, purely symbolic. While the monarchy is hereditary, the Governor General, though appointed for a non-specific term, traditionally, it is generally for five years.

The somewhat complex legal pattern pertaining to Canada perhaps needs some elaboration. The Constitution Act of 1867 declared Canada as a constitutional monarchy with the role of the reigning sovereign as both legal and practical, but not political. The Crown is regarded as a corporation with the monarch, vested as she is with all powers of state, at the centre of a construct in which the power of the whole is shared by multiple institutions of government acting under the sovereign's authority. The crown, thus, becomes the underlying principle of Canada's institutional unity. Hence, the Executive is formally called the Queen-in-Council, the legislature the Queen-in-Parliament and the courts the Queen-on-the-Bench. Quite naturally, the word Queen would get replaced by King if the next monarch is a King.

In continuation of this legal and technical pattern, the present (2013) monarch, Elizabeth II, becomes the Queen of Canada, wearing the sovereign's insignia of the Order of Canada and the Order of Military Merit. As a point of further emphasis and clarification, Elizabeth II is the Queen of Canada, "truly Canadian" and "totally independent from that of the Queen of the United Kingdom" and other Commonwealth realms. As already mentioned, as an individual, Elizabeth II is (2013) also the Head of State of fifteen other countries in the Commonwealth of Nations. As the Queen of Canada, she appoints a vice-regal representative, the Governor General, who since 1947, has been permitted to exercise almost all the sovereign's "Royal Prerogative", though some powers remain with the Queen alone. In practice, of course, the monarch as well as the Governor General follow the near binding advice of their ministers of the Crown in Cabinet. But the important thing to note is that the Royal Prerogative belongs to the Crown and not to any of the ministers, who rule "in trust" for the monarch and upon losing the confidence of the elected House of Commons, must relinquish the Crown's power back to it, whereupon a new government, which enjoys the lower chamber's confidence, is installed by the Governor General. The public, at large, may not always be very clear about the complexity of this relationship between the monarch, the Governor General, ministers and parliament. They remain happy in the knowledge that Canada has a robust, mature and fully functional parliamentary democracy with a popularly elected Prime Minister as the main executive in reality and in practice.

As per the Constitution, the government is defined as the Queen acting on the advice of her Privy Council. This body, the Privy Council, consists mostly of former Members of Parliament, Chief Justices of the Supreme Court and other elder statesmen. But this body rarely meets in full because the cardinal principle of responsible government requires that those, who directly advice the monarch and the governor general on how to exercise the Royal Prerogative, must be accountable to the popularly elected House of Commons. Consequently, the day to day working of the government is guided only by a sub-group of the Privy Council made up of those only, who hold seats in the Parliament. This group, known as the Ministers of the Crown, is the Cabinet.

A principal duty of the Crown is to "ensure that a democratically elected government is always in place", which implies appointing a Prime Minister to head the Cabinet. The convention requires that the Governor General must appoint as Prime Minister the person, who holds the confidence of the House of Commons. This refers to the leader of the political party that holds more seats than any other party in that Chamber. In the event that no single party enjoys a majority in the House of Commons, then the leader of the party, either with the most seats or one supported by other parties, will be invited by the Governor General to form a government. But in such a situation, it will be known as a minority government. Once sworn in by the Governor General, the Prime Minister continues to hold office till such time as he or she resigns or is removed by the Governor General, after either a motion of no-confidence in the House of Commons or his or her party's defeat in a general election. So far, Canada has had only one woman Prime Minister, Kim Campbell, in 1993, who did not last long. In fact, both she and her party, the Progressive Conservatives, lost very heavily in the 1993 general election.

The size of the Cabinet, headed by the Prime Minister, is generally around thirty ministers. They are chosen by the Prime Minister and then appointed by the Governor General. The endeavour is to respect the principle of regional representation. Normally, ministers will be from the leader's (PM's) own party. But this is not a legal or a constitutional requirement and if special reasons require, the Prime Minister is free to appoint a Cabinet Minister from another party.

The Prime Minister and his Cabinet colleagues head various departments or ministries of the government. The public service in Canada is operated by the Canadian government through various departments and smaller agencies. The main departments being: Finance, Revenue, Human Resources and Skills Development, National Defence, Public Safety and Emergency Preparedness and Foreign Affairs/International Trade. Talking of departments, there are two types. There are central agencies, such as Finance, Privy Council Office and Treasury Board Secretariat with an organizing and oversight role for the entire public service. As against this, line departments are those responsible for specific areas or fields, such as Foreign Affairs and International Trade, Defence, Agriculture and Environment. It is common for cabinet rank ministers to be assisted by junior ministers (Ministers of State), who are also elected members of the House of Commons.

The federal government also has a number of smaller agencies like Commissions, Tribunals and Boards as well as Crown Corporations. Some of the main ones are: Canadian Broadcasting Corporation (CBC), Via Rail, Elections Canada, Canada Council, Canada Post and Export Development Canada. They all function as autonomous bodies.

The Legislature

The Parliament of Canada is the chief legislative organ of the country, located in a Gothic style building on the right bank of the Ottawa River that flows through the national Capital, Ottawa. It is a bicameral body (the legislatures in the provinces are all unicameral, that is, a single House only) comprising of the monarch or presently the Queen (represented by the Governor General), an appointed Senate (Upper House) and the popularly elected House of Commons (Lower House). The Senate presently (2013) numbering 105 Senators, who are all summoned and appointed by the Governor General on the advice of the Prime Minister. Once appointed, a Senator serves till the age of seventy five. To begin with, the Senate was formed with equal representation from each of Ontario, Quebec, the Maritime region and the Western Provinces, in deference to the principle of providing "regional" representation. But in practice, this principle, over the years, has been bent several times so that currently the Senate is a product of various exceptions, additions and compromises. Consequently, both the concepts of regional equality and representation-by-population are not strictly reflected in its present composition. The normal number of Senators can be exceeded by the monarch on the advice of the Prime Minister subject to the additional Senators being distributed equally with regard to region and provided that the total number of additional Senators does not exceed eight. So far, this power of appointing additional Senators has been used only once when Prime Minister Brian Mulroney, in the 1980s, petitioned the Queen to add eight seats to the Senate so as to ensure the passage of the Goods and Services Tax legislation. But true to the principle of a parliamentary form of government, the Senate can at best discuss and delay legislation. The true and final authority in this context rests with the House of Commons, the popularly and directly elected lower House of the national parliament.

The House of Commons currently (2013) has 308 members elected in single member districts in a plurality voting system (first past the post), meaning that members must attain only a plurality (the most votes of any candidate) rather than a majority (50% plus one). The electoral districts are also known as ridings, historically an area conveniently coverable in a day on horseback. Canada has universal suffrage and any Canadian citizen aged 18 years or older is eligible to vote. There are only two exceptions to this rule, that is, only two Canadian citizens cannot vote, namely, the Chief Electoral Officer and the Deputy Chief Electoral Officer. This is to preserve the principle of impartiality. Technically, the Governor General is eligible to vote, but, following a well established constitutional convention, he abstains. The mandate of the House of Commons cannot exceed five years. Thus, a general election must be held by the end of this period. So far, this fixed mandate has been exceeded only once, when Prime Minister Robert Borden rightly felt the need to do so while there was a war on, World War I. The size of the House and the allotment of seats to each province are revised after every Census, held every five years. This apportionment of seats takes into account population changes and seeks to follow the principle of representation-by-population.

Leaders of various political parties are elected by party members before the general elections. These elections are held as run-off elections to ensure that the ultimate winner bags more than 50 per cent of the votes, in other words, a clear winner. These elected party leaders then contest as candidates for the posts of MPs. The election of a local MP naturally determines which of the several political parties in the fray has won the seat from that constituency or riding. The party getting the most seats forms the government with its leader becoming the Prime Minister. Technically speaking, therefore, the Prime Minister is not the direct choice of the general population. He is only directly elected as an MP within his or her constituency. But the leader of the party getting the most seats across the nation becomes the normal and logical choice for the post of the Prime Minister. Very often, a party might very well project one of its elected leaders as its Prime Ministerial candidate even before the general elections. This enables the voters across the broad spectrum to decide on who they would like to have as the leader of the government. This is a common practice in parliamentary form of government across the world.

In the event one party wins majority of the seats in the House of Commons, then that party is in a position to form a "majority government". The leader of that party, though elected from one particular constituency or riding, becomes the Prime Minister. Party discipline ensures that he enjoys considerable control over both the cabinet and the parliament. Though the degree of Prime Ministerial authority will vary from incumbent to incumbent depending on the personality, the endeavour of the Prime Minister is to carry with him most, if not all, of his senior colleagues in the Cabinet, particularly when it comes to major policy decisions. He is, after all, only primus interpares, first among equals. Team spirit and work culture is what a good Prime Minister should aim at.

A situation can arise, in the aftermath of a general election, when the party that holds the most seats in the House of Commons, still holds fewer seats than the opposition parties combined. In such a scenario, a party leader is selected by the Governor General to lead the government in what would constitute a minority government. However, in the interest of stability, the person chosen to form such a government must command the support of at least one other party. This precaution stems from the realisation that a minority government by its very nature would be prone to weakness and instability.

To ensure "clean" politics, Canada witnessed, in 2005, certain reforms to the party funding pattern. The new rules stipulated that a party had to receive at least two per cent of the vote nationwide to qualify for the general federal funding (disbursed quarterly) for political parties. Each vote garnered a certain amount, approximately \$1.75 for the purpose of such funding in the future. For the initial disbursements, approximations were made based on previous elections. The main reason behind this party funding reform was to ensure greater reliance on personal contributions as opposed to funding by unions or business houses. The aim was to limit their influence and impact on federal election funding, since these were not contributions from individual

The Political Scene

citizens and, therefore, not evenly spread out between parties. Unions and business houses are still allowed to contribute to election funds, but only in a minor way. Personal donations to federal parties and campaigns enjoy tax benefit, the quantum of relief naturally depends on the amount donated. Also, only those paying income tax are entitled to benefit under this scheme. Though these Party funding reforms have generally improved things, some critics do point out a snag in the funding pattern that could cumulatively exceed the legal limit by more than $60,000, by way of recurrent anonymous donations of $200 to every riding or constituency of a Party, from business houses or unions or both. But then, as experience would show, there is no such thing as, at least not as yet, 100 per cent perfection in any political system. Those determined to find some way out of various restrictions, invariably, will succeed in discovering some loopholes in the system.

The Judiciary

Going back to legalistic terminology, under the Canadian system, it is the responsibility of the Sovereign (presently-2013-the Queen) to render justice to all her subjects and is traditionally viewed as the FOUNT OF JUSTICE. However, the Sovereign does not personally rule in judicial cases, instead the judicial functions of the Royal Prerogative are performed in trust and in the name of the Queen (the Sovereign) by officers of Her Majesty's courts.

The country's highest court, the court of last resort, the Supreme Court of Canada, has nine judges appointed by the Governor General and headed by the Chief Justice of Canada. The mandatory age of retirement is 75 years. The Supreme Court Act restricts eligibility for appointment to persons, who have been judges of a superior court or members of the bar for ten or more years. Members of the bar or superior judges of Quebec, by law, must hold three of the nine positions on the Supreme Court of Canada. This representation is intended to ensure that at least three judges have sufficient experience of the civil law system to handle cases involving Quebec laws. Here, a quick word on the legal system in Canada would be called for. While it is the English common law for all matters within federal jurisdiction and in all provinces and territories, as for Quebec, it is the Civil Law based on the Custom of Paris in pre-revolutionary France as set out in the Civil Code of Quebec. The Supreme Court hears appeals from decisions rendered by the various appellate courts from the provinces and territories. Below the Supreme Court comes the Federal Court, which hears cases arising under certain areas of federal law. It works in conjunction with the Federal Court of Appeal and Tax Court of Canada.

Federal-Provincial Relations:

Legalistically speaking, the provinces in Canada are co-sovereign, with their sovereignty passed on, not by the Governor General or the Canadian Parliament, but through the Crown itself. Flowing from this concept, the Crown is "divided" into eleven legal jurisdictions, into eleven "Crowns" – one federal and ten provincial. However, normal to any federation legislative powers of the federal and provincial governments are limited and divided by the Constitution. The provincial legislatures can pass laws only on subjects set aside or allotted to them under the Constitution. These include education, provincial officers, municipal government, charitable institutions and "matters of a merely local or private nature". Any matter not under the exclusive jurisdiction of the provincial legislatures falls within the purview and jurisdiction of the federal Parliament. Thus, the federal Parliament in Ottawa alone can legislate on subjects, such as the postal service, the Census, the military, criminal law, navigation and shipping, fishing, currency, banking, weights and measures, bankruptcy, copyrights, patents, First Nations and naturalization. There can be and indeed are areas where this division of legislative authority between the federal and provincial governments is either vague or can overlap. Thus while the federal government regulates marriage and divorce in general, the actual solemnization of marriage is regulated by provincial legislatures only. Similarly, both the federal and provincial legislatures can legislate on matters like imposition of taxes, borrowing of money, punishing crimes and regulating agriculture. This pattern allows an overall national perspective without diluting local or provincial differences or variations.

Like in most other federations, federal-provincial relations remain an active ingredient, if not a controversial aspect of the Canadian political scene. The Western provinces constantly strive for greater control over their abundant natural resources, energy reserves in particular. The highly industrialised Central Canada is ever conscious of its high manufacturing capacity and wants a greater say in the national voice. The Atlantic provinces, being less affluent, invariably demand a greater share of the national pie so as to economically keep abreast of the rest of the country. And, Quebec, historically speaking has been a thorn in the side of Canada. Its constant endeavour to preserve and strengthen its distinctive nature often rankles and irritates the rest of Canada. Quebec indeed keeps stressing how it is different from the rest of the country. It is proud of its linguistic difference, French, as against English which is the language elsewhere in Canada. It likes to project itself as a different entity even to the outside world. It has a separate department of international relations. When newly arrived foreign envoys pay their first protocol visit to Quebec City, the capital of Quebec province, the local authorities ensure that the formal schedule of courtesy calls and meetings starts with a meeting with what they call the Minister of International Relations. The diplomatic corps based in the federal capital, Ottawa, is deemed by Quebec as automatically accredited to it, but not when it comes to certain diplomatic privileges, such as exemption from local taxes. Elsewhere in Canada, you simply produce your diplomatic identity card issued by the Foreign Ministry in Ottawa and the taxes are knocked off on the spot on the purchases made by you as a diplomat. Not so in Quebec. There they insist that you apply separately along with the vouchers in original to their "foreign ministry" and then get your refund. This tedious pattern very often discourages diplomats from shopping in the Quebec province, but, apparently, the local authorities are not bothered, at least not much. For them, the assertion of a principle, so very dear to them, is more important.

These oddities, if one may call them so, about Quebec are at best tolerated by many in the rest of Canada, if not often resented. The view is often expressed that Quebec is pampered too much and allowed to get away with too much. It is because of Quebec that officially Canada is a bilingual country, English and French, even though one hardly comes across any traces of French outside the borders of Quebec. Monarchs, governor-generals, prime ministers are now expected to be at least functional, if not fluent, in both English and French. In selecting leaders, political parties tend to give preference to Canadians, who are fluently bilingual. Three of the nine judges of the federal Supreme Court in Ottawa must under law be from Quebec. Quebec province in Canada is the only one to still follow the French civil law as distinct from the rest of the country, including the Territories, who follow the English common law for all matters within federal jurisdiction. Except for three short lived transitional or minority governments, prime ministers from Quebec have led Canada continuously from 1968 to early 2006. Quebecois led both Liberal and Progressive Conservative governments in Ottawa during this long period. Stephen Harper, the current (2013) Prime Minister, being from Alberta, has been a major shift in this long established tradition or practice. And yet, Quebec does not feel happy or satisfied is the widespread complaint widely voiced across Canada.

The background to this separatist or secessionist sentiment in Quebec has already been dealt with in an earlier chapter. National unity has been a major issue in Canada since the forced union of Upper and Lower Canada in 1840. But obviously, the passage of time and all the concessions to Quebec have not entirely succeeded in healing this rift between English speaking and French speaking Canada. Since the "Quiet Revolution", sovereignist sentiments in Quebec have been variably stoked by the passage of the Canadian constitution in 1982 (without Quebec's consent) and by the failed attempts at Constitutional reform by way of special political status for Quebec, notably in recent times through the Meech Lake Accord (1987) and the Charlottetown Accord (1992), the latter being rejected in a national referendum. Two referendums in Quebec so far have rejected proposals for sovereignty for Quebec. The first one in 1980 did so by 60 per cent. But the second one in 1995 almost made it since it got rejected by a very slim margin of 50.6 per cent only. In fact, in 1995, the separatists in Quebec were so confident of making it that on the eve of the referendum, the Quebec authorities did two things, which normally elsewhere would qualify as acts of sedition and open defiance. They issued an appeal to all those from Quebec in uniform, the armed forces and the police, that once Quebec declared its independence, they should declare their allegiance to it and, in return, they were promised continuance in service in the same rank and with the same pay and perks. The second act in this context was a long formal letter, in French with an official English translation, sent by the Quebec government to all foreign envoys based in Ottawa giving details as to how an independent Quebec would be viable in economic and all other respects. This was then followed, in the same formal communication, with the request for early recognition of Quebec, as an independent country, by various foreign governments. The federalist victory in the 1995 referendum by nothing short of a wafer thin majority (50.6%) served almost as a wake-up call for all those committed to preserving the unity of Canada. In 1998, the government of the then Prime Minister of Canada, Jean Chretien, himself from Quebec, made a reference to the Supreme Court of Canada regarding the legality of unilateral provincial secession. The Supreme Court's verdict was that a unilateral declaration of secession by a province would be unconstitutional. This paved the way for the passage of the Clarity Act in 2000. It also sent a clear message to the separatists in Quebec that their trying to break away from the rest of Canada would be riddled with legal and other impediments.

The Canadian political scene has indeed evolved gradually. An evolutionary process as opposed to a revolutionary one, as in the case of their neighbour to the South, the USA. It is the British Parliament, through the British North America Act (now known as the Constitution Act, 1867) that Canada's governmental structure was originally established. But the evolving of the federal model and the division of powers between the Centre and the provinces was to be the gradual handiwork of Canada's own political leaders. In a way, World War I was a turning point for Canada. Its participation and impressive performance in it gave the Canadians a new sense of identity, national pride and confidence. Seeing the emerging mood and the writing on the wall, Britain started reacting accordingly. In the Balfour Declaration of 1926, the British Government made clear its intention to grant full autonomy to its Dominions. This was followed in 1931 by the British Parliament passing the Statute of Westminster, which put the stamp of legal recognition to the autonomy of Canada and other Dominions. However, Canadian politicians were slow in reaching consensus on a process for amending the Constitution. This was finally accomplished only in 1982, when Pierre Elliot Trudeau was the Prime Minister. Otherwise, till that date, any amendment to Canada's Constitution continued to require the approval of the British Parliament. Similarly, the Judicial Committee of the Privy Council in Britain continued to make the final decision on criminal appeals from Canada until 1933 and on civil appeals until 1949.

Political Parties

By all reckoning, Canada is a stable democracy with a parliamentary form of government. For years, the two main parties on the federal scene have been the Progressive Conservatives and the Liberals, with the two interchanging control of the federal government from time to time. The other two players deserving mention are the National Democratic Party and the Bloc Quebecois (BQ), a sovereignist party fielding candidates only in the Quebec province and formed by a group of MPs, who left the Progressive Conservative Party along with several disaffected Liberal MPs. The BQ first fielded candidates in 1993 in the federal elections. Over the years, the feeling of alienation amongst the Western provinces has been giving rise to some political parties from time to time. These include the United Farmers of Alberta, who first won seats in 1917, the Progressives (1921), the Social Credit Party (1935), the Cooperative Commonwealth Federation (1935), the Reconstruction Party (1935), New Democracy (1940) and, most recently, the Reform Party in 1989. The Reform Party's catchy slogan "The West Wants In" changed into reality as "The West Is In" with Stephen Harper from Alberta becoming the Prime Minister of Canada in 2006.

However, since the 1990s the Canadian political scene has witnessed some dramatic shifts and changes. The 1993 general election virtually decimated the Progressive Conservatives (PCs) under Kim Campbell (reduced to just two seats in the House of Commons) and the Liberals under Jean Chretien formed the government. Under Jean Chretien, the Liberals remained in clear control for the next ten years. In fact, at the start of the 21st century, in 2000, Jean Chretien became the first Prime Minister to lead three consecutive majority governments since 1945. But, with Jean Chretien's departure from the centre stage of Canadian politics in December 2003, the run of luck of the Liberals also ran out. Under his successor, Paul Martin, the Liberals in the June 2004 general election won a minority victory only, having lost seats in the House Of Commons, going down from 172 of the 301 total Parliamentary seats to 135 of the total of 308. They also suffered loss of the popular vote, down from 40.9 per cent to 36.7 per cent. A regional party, the Canadian Alliance, which had done well in Western Canada in the 2000 election, failed to make any significant impact in the East. Political expediency and realism prompted them to merge with the Progressive Conservative Party (PC) to form the Conservative Party of Canada in late 2003. In the meanwhile, the minority Liberal government under Paul Martin did not last long and the country was in for another general election in 2006. The Conservative Party kept gradually improving its position. The Alliance-PC combine, after its formation in 2003, did moderately well in the 2004 elections increasing its tally of seats from 78 in 2000 to 99 in 2004, though the share of the popular vote of the new Conservatives fell from 37.7 per cent to 29.6 per cent. But hereafter, there was a distinct swing in favour of the Conservatives. In the 2006 elections, led by Stephen Harper from Alberta province, the Conservatives managed to dislodge the Liberals, but with only 124 seats, they were able to form a minority government only. Significantly also, the Conservative share of the popular vote increased from 29.6 per cent in 2004 to 36.3 per cent. In another development worthy of note, the Conservatives made major breakthroughs in Quebec, winning as many as ten seats as against none in 2004. The general elections of 2011 further confirmed this changing political landscape in Canada. With 167 seats, the Conservatives under Stephen Harper were able to form a comfortable majority government in Ottawa. The declining fortunes of the Liberals were further highlighted when they got dislodged as the official opposition by the National Democratic Party (NDP). The NDP had won 102 seats, while the Liberals were down to an abysmal 34. Some other interesting outcomes of the 2011 elections were that the Green Party won a seat (Elizabeth May) for the first time and the Bloc Quebecois (BQ) just four and, thus, losing its official party status. Whether this marked the beginning of the decline at least, if not end, of the sovereignist sentiment in Quebec, only time will tell.

The raising of the curtain on the 21st century has, thus, seen some significant changes in the Canadian political scene. As of now (2013), the once powerful Liberals have been virtually decimated. The NDP has emerged as a new force as the Official Opposition and that too with almost one third of the total seats in the House of Commons, 102. The Bloc Quebecois have lost their official party status. The Conservatives, under Stephen Harper as the Prime Minister, appear to be well entrenched. Even the political centre of gravity has shifted somewhat with Stephen Harper being neither from Quebec nor from the influential Ontario, but from Alberta. Stephen Harper, by successfully challenging the long term dominance of the Liberals, has achieved what Brian Mulroney failed to do during his years in office. So far at least, Stephen Harper has proved to be more determined, systematic and successful. How it shapes up in the future only time will tell. In politics, fortunes can swing once again. After all, in 1993, the Conservatives had been reduced to a mere two seats in the House of Commons. In less than two decades, they have made nothing short of a remarkable recovery and comeback.

Before winding up this Chapter on the Canadian Political Scene, it would not be out of place to conveniently list together some basic data and information on Canada.

NAME: Canada (for conventional and legal use; "Dominion of Canada" remains legal, but rarely used.

CAPITAL: Ottawa (Ontario)

ADMINISTRATIVE UNITS: Ten provinces and three territories. Alberta, British Columbia, Manitoba, New Brunswick, Newfoundland and Labrador, Nova Scotia, Ontario, Prince Edward Island, Quebec and Saskatchewan. The three territories being: North West Territories, Yukon and Nunavut.

NATIONAL HOLIDAY: Canada Day, July 01 (known until 1982 as Dominion Day).

CONSTITUTION: Westminster system, based on unwritten conventions and written legislation—the British North America Act of 1867 and the Constitution Act of 1982.

LEGAL SYSTEM: English Common Law for all matters within federal jurisdiction and in all provinces and territories except Quebec, which is based on the Civil Law based on the Custom of Paris in pre-revolutionary France as set out in the Civil Code of Quebec.

NATIONAL FLAG: A red maple leaf centred on a Canadian pale: three vertical bands of red (hoist side) white (white double width, square) and red with a length twice that of its height. Adopted on February 15, 1965.

NATIONAL ANTHEM: "O Canada" Adopted in 1980

GOVERNOR GENERAL (2013) David Lloyd Johnston (since October 01, 2010)

PRIME MINISTER: Justin Trudeau (since October, 2015)

Chapter Six – International Relations

Canada's foray into international relations has followed the same path as the country growing to be a modern, independent State – gradual and evolutionary.

Till the late 1840s, the British colonies in North America, what now constitutes Canada, had no or little say in the conduct of their foreign affairs. Be it wars or negotiations or treaties, the centre of activity and the final decisions rested in London, with the Canadians, at best, consulted. Whether it was disputes over fishing rights or the settlement of boundaries or the promotion of trade, it was the British government that conducted all such matters. Some significant examples from this colonial phase in Canada's history being, the Nootka Convention, the war of 1812, the Rush-Bagot Treaty, the Treaty of 1818, the Webster-Ashburton Treaty and the Oregon Treaty, the last one broadly laying down the boundary with the USA along the 49th parallel. Signs of change were visible only post 1848, when Canada won the right to self or responsible government and the setting up of an administration for the Province of Canada. Till then, the focus and emphasis of British diplomacy remained on British-American relations and specific Canadian interests were treated as a secondary consideration. The first major shift in this pattern was brought out in the Canadian-American Reciprocity Treaty of 1854. By this treaty, Canada was allowed to impose tariff duties more favourable to a foreign country (read USA) than to Britain. This treaty not only marked a significant change in relations between Britain and its North American colonies, but also ushered in a pattern of different tariffs in 1859, 1879 and 1887, despite vigorous demands for their being disallowed by London on the part of British industrialists since this changing tariff regime eroded the advantage appropriated by the British trading community in what was till then viewed as a captive colonial market.

In the wake of the British North America Act of 1867 and the ushering in of the Confederation of Canada, Canada felt encouraged towards more steps in the arena of international relations. The country's first Prime

Minister, Sir John A. Macdonald, appointed Sir John Rose as his lobbyist in London. Under the Prime Ministership of Alexander Mackenzie, Canada deputed its own representative, George Brown, to represent it at the British-American trade talks in Washington. With the Conservatives back in power in 1878, Canada appointed, Alexander Galt, as its representative to Britain as well as to France and Spain. Though eyebrows were raised in London over this nascent Canadian diplomacy, Britain finally relented and accepting the signs of changing times gave, in 1880, Alexander Galt the formal title of High Commissioner. In 1893, Charles Tupper, the then Canadian High Commissioner to Britain assisted in negotiating an agreement with France, but, at London's insistence, it was countersigned by the British Ambassador as the Queen's official representative to France. In 1894, Canada appointed John Short Larke as the Trade Commissioner to Australia. This was a follow up to a successful trade delegation to Australia led by Canada's first Minister of Trade and Commerce, Mackenzie Bowell. Larke, thus, became Canada's first trade commissioner abroad. With all this going on, Quebec was not to be left behind and it had already, as early as in 1882, ventured into the arena of international relations by appointing Hector Fabre as its representative in Paris.

But essentially, Canada still remained quite passive and inactive in international relations. Its reaction to various international events remained limited, even guarded. Thus, at the time of tensions between Britain and Russia in 1878, beyond constructing a few limited defences, Canada did little else. During the British campaign in Sudan in 1884-85, London expected Canada to contribute troops. But sensing Ottawa's reluctance to get involved, the Governor-General privately raised 386 voyagers, at Britain's expense, to help British forces on the Nile. By 1885, some Canadians, perhaps more out of a spirit of adventure than any commitment, volunteered for a potential Canadian contingent for Sudan, but Ottawa declined to act. In sharp contrast, Australia stepped in to help Britain with its troops and also paid for them.

Till the beginning of the twentieth century, Canada's relations with the USA were still largely handled by the British Embassy in Washington. But increasingly, this was proving to be an unsatisfactory arrangement. The British Embassy in Washington frequently complained that too much of its time was being taken up by Canada-US matters. Whereas there was a growing feeling in Ottawa that its relations with Washington were not receiving the attention they deserved or merited. What possibly added to this feeling or impression in Ottawa was the Alaska boundary dispute between Canada and the USA. This dispute was finally resolved by a Commission in 1903. The Canadians were not happy with the outcome. In fact, the Canadian judges on the Commission refused to sign the award that was issued on October 20, 1903. But what upset the Canadians even more was that the British delegate to this Boundary Commission had sided with the Americans. This not only caused the eruption of anti- British feelings in Canada, but also strengthened the growing feeling that for London, the interests of the Empire were above those of Canada. Quite obviously, things were slowly moving in the direction of the Canadians taking charge of their destiny and handling of their foreign relations.

An important development in this context was when in 1909, the then Canadian Prime Minister, Sir Wilfrid Laurier, established a Department of External Affairs and also created the posts of Secretary and Under Secretary of State for External Affairs. When the World War I started in 1914, Canada responded to the British call for participation without questioning it. But the exposure to the world outside that this war gave to Canada, not to speak of the heroism with which its troops fought and won laurels, gave Canada not only a new sense of identity, but also confidence as a nation. It was no longer willing to be treated as a side-kick of Britain. Canada's important contribution to the British war effort during 1914-18 could no longer be overlooked or denied by London. Not surprisingly, the Canadian Prime Minister at that time, Sir Robert Borden, insisted upon Canada being treated as a separate signatory to the Treaty of Versailles at the end of the War and it, subsequently, joined the League of Nations as a separate entity.

The ball had, thus, been set rolling in the direction of Canada pursuing a foreign policy of its own keeping in mind the preservation and promotion of its own perceived self-interests. Further evidence and examples of this new found independence in foreign affairs by Canada were to be provided during the 1920s. Between 1918 and 1921, Ottawa operated a Canadian War Mission in Washington DC, the US Capital. When William Lyon Mackenzie King took over as the Canadian Prime Minister in 1921, he took several further steps to assert Canada's pursuit of an independent foreign policy. In 1923, at Mackenzie King's insistence, Canada independently signed the Halibut Treaty with the USA.

By way of further steps in this direction, in 1925, Canada appointed a permanent representative of its own to Geneva to deal with the League of

Nations and the International Labour Organization (ILO), both headquartered at Geneva. In the aftermath of the Balfour Declaration of 1926 in which the British Government made clear its intention to grant full autonomy to its Dominions, Prime Minister Mackenzie King was quick to appoint Vincent Massey as Canada's first Minister Plenipotentiary in Washington in 1926. In 1928, Mackenzie King raised the Canadian office in Paris to legation status under Philippe Roy and the year following (1929), Canada opened a legation in Tokyo with Herbert Marler as envoy. Quite clearly, Canada's foot print on the world stage was expanding and increasing fast.

Following the enactment of the Statute of Westminster in 1931, Canada achieved legislative independence. However, in the realm of international relations, British diplomatic missions continued to represent Canada in most countries throughout the 1930s. But the outbreak of World War II changed things for Canada considerably. Unlike in 1914, when in 1939 Britain declared war on Germany, Canada was not automatically a participant on the side of Britain. The matter was first discussed at length in the Canadian Parliament and it was a full week after Britain's entry into the war that Canada joined in on its side and that too after pledges against conscription and many reservations. This not only contrasted sharply with the attitude of the other leading white Dominions like Australia and New Zealand, but also demonstrated Canada's growing determination to carve out an independent role for itself in the conduct of foreign affairs. In pursuit of this goal, Canada rapidly expanded its diplomatic missions abroad. Its widely acknowledged significant role in World War II, both in terms of heroism and economic contribution, provided a major boost to its confidence. In fact, in the post-World War II scenario, Canada emerged as a leading Western nation on the world stage, alongside the USA and Britain. Germany, Japan and Italy were vanquished nations. France was a traumatised country. Even Britain, though victorious, was an exhausted power with the beginning of the end of the once mighty British Empire very much in sight and just a matter of time. Whereas for Canada, it was, in more ways than one, an hour of glory. It had truly arrived on the international stage. It was an important founder member of the United Nations Organization (UNO) with its diplomats, known for their professional skills, serving on several international bodies and committees. It's dynamic Foreign Minister, Lester B. Pearson, later Prime Minister too, was a respected figure internationally. The Suez crisis of 1956 was a testing time for Canadian diplomacy. Britain, along with France, had made a blatant attempt by invading Egypt, to regain its status as a "Great Power." It expected the senior "white" dominions to support its Suez adventure. But while Australia and New Zealand backed Britain, Canada backed the United Nations. A resolution drafted by Canada's Foreign Minister, Lester B. Pearson, brought UN forces to intervene in the threatened area, frustrated the British-French power bid and ended the crisis that had otherwise threatened Western unity and the nascent UN itself. Canada's positive and constructive role was internationally applauded. A year later, in 1957, its Foreign Minister, Lester B. Pearson, was awarded the Nobel Peace Prize. Canada had clearly not only established its independence in the conduct of its international relations, but had also shown Britain that it was very much on its own now.

The two broad aspects of international relations and diplomacy are bilateral relations and multilateral diplomacy. Ever since reaching of age, so to say, in the conduct of its foreign relations, notably in the post-World War II period, Canada has been an active and influential player on the world scene in respect of both these aspects. It has managed successfully to project itself as a "middle power". Wisely realising that diplomacy and trade go hand in hand, in 1982, responsibility for trade was added with the creation of the Department of External Affairs and International Trade. In 1995, the name was changed to the Department of Foreign Affairs and International Trade, which is run by the Minister of Foreign Affairs, currently (2013) John Baird. As is common with most systems, the Prime Minister (the Head of Government) is very much involved when it comes to major policy decisions in the realms of foreign affairs and trade.

As regards bilateral relations, Canada's relations with its big and powerful neighbour to the South, the USA, easily occupy a position of prime importance. This has been historically so, dictated both by history and economic reality. In fact, the economies of the two countries are interdependent and inter-meshed in innumerable ways. In the realm of trade alone, nearly 75 per cent of Canada's trade is with the USA and, in reverse, Canada is the largest trading partner of the USA. In international relations, it is often said that while a country can choose its friends, it cannot choose its neighbours. Canada has been singularly fortunate in this respect. Except for the sad but brief chapter of 1812, relations between these two neighbours have been, by and large, happy with very close cooperation in virtually all areas. While there have been, from time to time, occasional boundary, maritime and fishing rights disputes, the overwhelming trend has been their amicable settlement through bilateral negotiations. Consequently, the two countries today famously share the "world's longest undefended border." Canada and the United States were close allies in both World Wars, though in both cases, Canadian involvement and participation preceded that of the US by a few years. Even in the post-World War II international scene, the two fought as allies in the Korean War and were hand in glove throughout the Cold War era. Canada is an original member of NATO and the air defences of the two countries are closely fused together in NORAD.

But it will be a big mistake for anyone to presume that because of this proximity and close cooperation, Canada's foreign policy is a carbon copy of the US foreign policy. Far from it, Canada makes it a point to emphasize that in foreign affairs, its policy decisions are very much taken in Ottawa and not in Washington. In fact, at times, Canada perhaps even feels a little uncomfortable with it's over dependence on the US, notably in the economic and commercial arenas. Over the past two decades or so, it has even been making conscious efforts to spread out more and develop close partnerships with countries and regions around the world and with a marked degree of success. A look at some examples of Canada not always toeing the US line, even differing with it, would be relevant in this context. Canada established diplomatic relations with Communist China (13th October 1970) years before the US did so (1st, January, 1979). Despite pressure from the US, it continued to maintain commercial and diplomatic relations with Cuba and also Iran. In fact, Cuba has been a favourite holiday destination for Canadian tourists trying to get away from the sub-zero temperatures of their own in winters. Canada has been reluctant to participate in military operations abroad that are not sanctioned by the UN, relevant examples being the Vietnam War and the 2003 invasion of Iraq. But where international military operations bear the stamp of UN sanction, Canada does participate. Some examples from recent times being, the First Gulf War, Afghanistan and Libya. It also willingly participated, along with its NATO and OAS allies, in the Kosovo conflict and also in Haiti. Ever since the positive role played by it in the 1956 Suez crisis, Canada has been playing a leading role in UN peace keeping efforts. In all these respects, Canada is a very different actor on the world stage compared to the USA.

As regards bilateral relations with the world at large and different regions, Canada has been active over the years and, particularly so, over the last couple of decades. It has today a good presence in Latin America with considerable focus on trade and economic ties. It has had diplomatic relations with Venezuela since January, 1953, principally because of mutual commercial interests, especially in technology, oil and gas. It is the same story in other regions, like Africa, the Middle East and Asia. Through a clever and judicious use of its high technology in certain fields and development assistance, it has made its presence felt. Canada's foreign economic aid is handled by the Canadian International Development Agency (CIDA). Canada's foreign aid policy reflects an emphasis on the Millennium Development goals and also providing assistance in response to foreign humanitarian crises. In the latter context, Afghanistan and Iraq have been large recipients of Canada's official development assistance. As a major and fast growing region of the world, Asia has been in Canada's special focus. In 1985, the Canadian Parliament passed a law to create the Asia Pacific Foundation of Canada, a think tank focussing on Canada-Asia relations. The focus very much extends to the Pacific Rim countries and economies with Canada's membership of the Asia-Pacific Economic Cooperation (APEC) forum serving as an important tool to serve and promote this goal. In Asia, China has emerged as a major partner of Canada. In fact, China now is Canada's second largest trading partner surpassing, since 2003, both Britain and Japan. Between 1998 and 2007, Canada's exports to China grew by 272 per cent and imports by almost 400 per cent. The overall two way trade is now well over $50 billion annually. Leading commodities accounting for this burgeoning bilateral trade include chemicals, metals, industrial and agricultural machinery and equipment, wood and fish products. Hong Kong and Macau being designated as Special Administrative Regions of China, the Canadian Consulate General in Hong Kong, which also covers Macau, reports directly to the Department of Foreign Affairs and International Trade in Ottawa. But Canada's other offices in China in places like Guangzhou, Shanghai and Chongqing come directly under the Canadian Embassy in Beijing and report to it.

With Europe, both West and East, including the European Union, Canada has maintained long standing and extensive relations, notably with Britain and France for historical reasons. With Eastern Europe, even during the Cold War days, Canada maintained a significant presence, particularly in Moscow. These links continue, in one form or the other, even in the aftermath of the demise of the USSR. Closer home, Canada has close relations with the Caribbean Community, which views Canada as a valued partner. Canadian banks in particular have played an important role in the development of former British West Indies colonies. Finally, Canada remains an important and active member of the Commonwealth of Nations and with those countries that still have a Dominion Status (fifteen), it even shares a monarch as its Constitutional Head of State. With India, Canada has long standing and multifarious ties, besides several commonalities, but much more on this in Part Two of this special study on Canada, devoted exclusively to India-Canada relations.

As with bilateral relations, Canada is equally active in the multilateral arena. An indication of its strong support for multilateralism is provided by the fact that it is an active member of close to eighty international and regional organizations. This includes the ADB (non- regional member), APEC, The Arctic Council, ASEAN (dialogue partner), the Commonwealth of Nations, FAO, G-20, G-7, G-8, G-10, IAEA, IBRD (World Bank), ICAO, ILO, Interpol, IPU, NAFTA, NATO, OAS, OECD, UNESCO, WHO, WTO and, of course, the UNO, to mention a few only. Two international organizations have their headquarters in Canada, namely, the International Air Transport Association (IATA) and the International Civil Aviation Organization (ICAO). In recent times, two major international treaties have been signed in Canada, namely, the Ottawa Treaty or Mine Ban Treaty (1987) and the Montreal Protocol on Substances That Deplete the Ozone Layer (1987). Though not involved in any major plan for the reform of the UN Security Council, accepting the need to adapt to changing times, it does support UN reform.

One of the unique features of the conduct of international relations by Canada is the freedom that its constituent provinces enjoy to operate internationally. The federal government has, over the years, considerably strengthened its hold over the conduct of Canada's international relations ever since they were relinquished by Britain. But the provinces, at least some of them, have always had pretensions of their own in this area. Quebec set this trend and continues to nurse it as part of its separatist mind set. As early as 1886, it appointed its first representative to France, Hector Fabre. By 1984 Quebec had its own offices in ten countries including eight in the United States and three in other Canadian provinces. British Columbia opened an office in London in the 1920s and Alberta set up an Alberta House in London in 1948. Ontario maintains thirteen delegations in seven countries. Both Quebec and New Brunswick are members of La Francophonie (separately from the federal delegation). Alberta has a semi-diplomatic office in Washington since 2005. In 2007, the then Quebec Premier, Jean Charest, even proposed a free trade agreement with the European Union. However, the saving grace is that none of the provinces can negotiate or enter into treaties with foreign countries. Also, these efforts by some of the provinces are essentially confined to matters peculiar to their needs, for instance Alberta seeking to reopen the border with the USA to the Import of Canadian beef. While the federal government constantly endeavours to involve the provinces in international matters by, for example, often including their Premiers in Canada's by now well known "Team Canada" visits abroad, none of these postures on the part of provinces, with the possible exception of Quebec, are allowed to undermine the ability of the federal government to conduct foreign affairs.

One area of Canada's international relations with potential for serious controversy, even disputes, is the Arctic region. In fact, controversies, at times quite serious, have already been erupting from time to time. The Arctic region consists of eight States, namely, Canada, Denmark (Greenland), Finland, Iceland, Norway, Russia, Sweden and the United States. The Arctic Council, a high level inter-governmental forum comprising the Arctic littoral States along with the Arctic indigenous communities and other Arctic inhabitants, was set up in 1996 to address common issues of sustainable development and environmental protection in the Arctic.

The potential areas of conflict are the conflicting territorial claims by littoral States, the use of the North Sea Route or the North Sea Passage and the exploitation of what is believed to be vast, as yet untapped, oil and gas and mineral deposits.

As regards territorial claims, the five States involved are the coastal States along the Arctic, namely, the United States, Canada, Russia, Norway and Denmark through its jurisdiction over Greenland. Russia has already staked its claim to the 1250 mile underwater Lomonosov Ridge in the UN Commission on Limitation of Continental Shelf (UN-CLCS). Russia, in support of this claim, has advanced the argument that the ridge is an extension of the Siberian landmass with the UNCLOS III providing that States can extend their jurisdiction to 350 nautical miles by submitting geological evidence to the CLCS within ten years of ratifying UNCLOS. In order to symbolically strengthen this claim, Russia startled the world in 2007 by planting its national flag on the sea bed at the North Pole and announcing that the region was connected to its continental shelf and claiming 1.2 million square kilometre area. Denmark has staked claim to the North Pole itself maintaining that the Lomonosov Ridge is an extension of the Greenland landmass. While Canada has the geographical advantage of large claims to the Arctic continental shelf, its argument that the Lomonosov Ridge is an underwater extension of its Ellesmere Island directly conflicts with the territorial claims being advanced by Russia and Denmark. Canada is also making claims to the Arctic Archipelago coast of Greenland. In the meanwhile, Denmark has already occupied Hans Island, a small piece of contested land between Canada's Ellesmere Island and the north-western coast of Greenland. In 2007, when Russia planted its flag (with the help of a submarine in use with one of its scientific expeditions) on the sea bed of the North Pole, reacting sharply to this development, the Canadian Prime Minister Stephen Harper, announced plans to enhance his country's military presence in the Arctic region in order to assert its sovereignty over the Northwest Passage. Adding to these controversies and conflicting territorial claims, Norway has advanced claims that conflict with those of Russia over their mutual border in the Barents Sea, believed to be home to an estimated 11 billion barrels of oil. In the context of the Arctic diplomacy, what further complicates the matter is that four of the five Arctic Coastal States (Canada, the USA, Norway and Denmark) are members of NATO, whose Article 5 defines the Arctic Circle as an area of its operations. This naturally results in Russia, the only non-NATO Arctic coastal State, from being concerned about any NATO initiative for the Arctic and has even cautioned that any NATO presence in the region could jeopardise regional (Arctic) security.

The second area of friction, if not conflict, is the passage of shipping through the Arctic Ocean or the Northern Route. The scene has changed considerably since the days of the Norwegian explorer Roald Amundsen, who was the first to traverse the North-West Passage (1903-1906), the North-East Passage (1918-1920), now called the Northern Route, as also to lead the first expedition to reach the North Pole (1926). However, a century later, a different scene has emerged. Due to global warming and the melting of the Arctic ice, a deep water sea route has opened up in the North – the North-West Passage or the Northern Shipping Route (NSR), mainly along Canada's Arctic coast, linking East Asia with North America, while the North-East Passage along Russia's Arctic shoreline provides an alternative sea route between Asia and North America and Europe. This Northern Shipping Route is now navigable in summer for several weeks almost until the end of November. The North-West Passage between Yokohama and Rotterdam is about 4000 kilometres shorter than the existing route through the Suez. Similarly, the Arctic route between Rotterdam and San Francisco is twelve days shorter than the one passing through the Panama Canal. Since the Arctic passage traverses very deep waters, it facilitates the passage of large container ships and even super tankers, without the constraints of size and volume restrictions imposed in much narrower and shallower passageways, like the Suez and Panama Canals. Additionally, it saves shipping freight due to much lower fuel consumption. In 2012, as many as 46 vessels sailed through the NSR (25 East-bound and 21-West bound) compared with 34 in 2011 and just four in 2010. Nearly 1.30 million tonnes of cargo was shipped through the NSR in 2012 as against 800,000 tonnes in 2011. As many as 26 tankers (18 West-East and 8 East-West) carried nearly 900,000 tonnes of oil and gas and other petroleum products. An LNG tanker sailing from Hammerfest in Norway to Tobata in Japan covered more than 6000 miles through the NSR, saving nearly twenty days. It is expected that by 2015, the Arctic will be ice free in summer, allowing more ships to sail through. Large shipping companies are already gearing up to further exploit this emerging opportunity. The route is still somewhat underdeveloped due to the lack of charts, navigation aids and lack of port infrastructure for repairs. Search and rescue resources are also still to be developed. But, these negatives being gradually overcome should be a matter of time only.

With the North-West Passage passing between the islands of Canada's Arctic archipelago, Canada is inclined to treat the Passage as passing through its internal waters. But this stance of Canada is opposed by both the USA and Russia. Things have not yet reached the flash point and, very likely, coordination and cooperation rather than conflict will be the preferred way out. The lure of the Northern route has driven the US to press for the NWP to be classified as international waters. The Canadians were upset when, in 1969, the refurbished US oil tanker Manhattan sailed through the NWP without seeking Canada's permission. In 1985, the US ice breaker Polar Sea did the same, this time despite the Canadians having enacted in 1970 the Arctic Waters Pollution Prevention Act, which asserts Canadian regulatory control over pollution within a 100 nautical mile (190 kilometres) zone of their Arctic coastline. Even then, in 1970 itself, the US had asserted that "we cannot accept this assertion of a Canadian claim that the Arctic waters are internal waters of Canada. Such acceptance would jeopardize the freedom of navigation essential for the United States naval activities worldwide." A compromise was reached in 1988 through an agreement on Arctic Cooperation, which pledges that voyages of American icebreakers "will be undertaken with the consent of the government of Canada." But even this accord failed to alter either country's basic stand. The US continued to maintain that their agreeing to ask for Canadian consent did not imply that they were obliged to do so. As recently as 2006, David Wilkins, the US Ambassador to Canada said that his government opposes the Canadian Prime Minister Stephen Harper's proposed plan to deploy military icebreakers in the Arctic to detect interlopers and assert Canadian sovereignty over those waters. In practice, as of now, for example, in the North West Passage, Canada conveniently ignores the passage of US submarines, which, otherwise, may have to notify, surface and show the flag, were Canada to insist on its claim as internal waters. Arctic diplomacy certainly lies ahead for Canada in the days to come with even more pressure than as of now.

The third aspect of the Arctic is the natural resources. It is believed that the Arctic holds the largest remaining untapped gas reserves and some of the largest undeveloped oil reserves, making it the final frontier for the development and exploitation of energy sources. The Arctic's energy and mineral resources are geographically exploitable, even if they lie mostly offshore, in the Arctic's shallow shelf. The 2008 US Geological Survey report states that over 70 per cent of the undiscovered Arctic oil resources are in five areas – Alaska, Amerasia Basin, East Greenland Rift Basins, East Barents Basins and West Greenland-East Canada. More than 70 per cent of the undiscovered natural gas is in the West Siberian Basin, the East Barents Basins and the Arctic Alaska. Nearly 84 per cent of the undiscovered oil and gas occurs offshore. This totals up to nearly 90 billion barrels of oil, 1669 trillion cubic feet of natural gas and 44 billion barrels of natural gas liquids. How far these reported enormous deposits are commercially feasible to exploit, besides the challenge posed to technology, will be the questions frequently coming up in the future. The potential for things heating up in the near future could be the discussion and possible arguments over who shall extract the oil and gas, when the ice thins and possibly disappears; how will the new marine delimitation lines be drawn; who will control the new sea passage; and, may be, at some stage, there would be a bigger question on who owns the Arctic. The clash between a "commons" position, that is, no nation has sovereignty over the Arctic (already being articulated by some) and the resources there are for all to exploit and use and the position of the five Arctic littoral States—Norway, the USA, Canada, Denmark and Russia (the A-5), which quite clearly oppose the "commons" view. Canada as one of the major littoral Arctic States will certainly be playing an important role in all such respects, more so with Canada taking over from Sweden as Chairman of the Arctic Council from May, 2013 and with the establishment of an Arctic Council Secretariat in Tromso with a budget of its own.

Chapter Seven – Culture and Art

If culture and art follow nationhood, then the Canadian scene would be relatively of recent origin. But like so many other aspects of the huge land mass today known as Canada, the people inhabiting it have evolved in this respect too over many centuries.

The beginning of that long journey or the history of Aboriginal Art in Canada would take us back to the ice age, somewhere between 12,000 to 80,000 years ago. However, the oldest surviving art works date back to about 5,000 years ago only. This is in the form of decorative and depictive carvings found in the Lower Fraser region of British Columbia, while other such pieces have been found in several parts of Canada. The prehistoric indigenous art in Canada is, at best, known in a sketchy manner only and its end date varies from region to region. In the Arctic region, the Inuit people, given their total isolation and nomadic life style had few possessions, strictly need based and their limited cultural and artistic pursuits remained restricted to items made from walrus ivory, bone, antler and occasionally stone. While some carvings were made for use, others had a spiritual significance, while yet another category like pendants, combs and tiny human figures were obviously made for pleasure. The Eastern sub-Arctic region, that is, the Eastern Canadian Shield extending from northern Quebec to Labrador and down to the Hudson Bay and James Bay provided art forms that are probably the oldest in Canada. These Algonquian speaking people—the Ojibwa, Cree, Algonquin, Ottawa, Innu, Mi'kmaq and Maliseet—were noted for their moose hair embroidery and porcupine quill work on birch bark and basketry. The Athapaskan speaking people of the Western sub-arctic region indulged in the decoration of personal gear and clothing as their major form of artistic expression. The region of the Southern Great Lakes and the valley of the St. Lawrence River extending south along the Atlantic sea board and west to the Missouri River, were the source of the prehistoric Eastern Woodlands Indian Art. The Central American Mayan civilization had touched the art forms of these people through ancient trade routes with the making of pottery as the most significant impact. As for the culture and art of the Prairie region, the vast grasslands of Saskatchewan, Manitoba, Alberta and parts of British Columbia, the Aboriginal culture and art forms, as they emerged much later by the 19th century, were a synthesis of Indigenous and White cultures. Personal art attracted aesthetic attention in the form of items, like deer hide moccasins, jackets, dresses that were adorned with porcupine quill work and beads. Yet another region in this context is the Central Plateau of British Columbia, the area between the coastal mountains and the Rocky Mountains. These plateau people were possibly the only First Nations group in Canada to have used textiles since they wove blankets from mountain goat hair. But little or nothing is known of their clothing or religious beliefs. Finally, the Northwest coast region from Vancouver to Alaska where the various tribes used oval shaped forms in their art. Their imagery was inspired by nature to include bears, ravens, eagles and humans or legendary creatures, such as thunderbirds. But speaking of the West coast art, special mention must be made of the Haida art, which shows a high level of craftsmanship. They even imported the raw materials that they lacked and turned them into refined products that were sold to other tribes on Vancouver Island and the mainland. Examples of such items included copper shields, silver and copper jewelry as well as horn bowls, spoons and goat's wool blankets. The Haida excelled in making and engraving copper shields. The Raven played an important part in the Haida mythology with many stories describing the Raven's encounters with supernatural beings and how it acquired other useful things from them for humans, things like fresh water and salmon. The Haida have almost seventy crest figures, the Killer whale being possibly the most popular crest. The Haida are also credited with the introduction of the totem pole, easily the most visible symbol today of the West coast Aboriginal Art. The world's tallest totem pole is on Victoria Island in British Columbia.

The arrival, first of European explorers and then of settlers, was to substantially change the Canadian art scene. Early sketches of the North American territory were made by French explorers like Samuel de Champlain. But more significantly, it was the Roman Catholic Church in and around Quebec City that provided patronage to art. Historically, Abbe Hughes Pommier is reckoned to be the first painter in New France. Leaving France in 1664, he initially worked as a priest in various communities till he took up painting seriously and extensively. Painters like Pommier and Claude Francois were inspired by the Renaissance art as reflected in their works, which featured religious depictions with classical clothing and settings. Call it out of modesty or whatever, few artists of this period signed their works, thus, rendering attributions difficult today.

By the end of the 17th century, while the population of New France was increasing, its link with the mother country, France, was on the decline. Consequently, few, if any, artists arrived from Europe. That is when the Roman Catholic Church stepped in and set up two art schools so that the number of artists in New France kept increasing. Pierre Le Ber from Montreal ranks as one of the most recognized artists of this period. Self-taught, he never left New France. According to the Canadian art historian, Dennis Reid, Le Ber's depiction of Saint Marguerite Bourgeoys ranks as "the single most moving image to survive from the French period".

The next stage in the development of Canadian art bore the influence of English settlers. Nova Scotia and Newfoundland were the first to experience some growth of art. However, being Protestants, these early English settlers believed in simple church décor, thus, hardly providing any scope for the encouragement of artists or sculptors. This attitude of the Protestant Church sharply contrasted with that of the Roman Catholic Church in New France, which gradually emerged as an important patron of art. But in the case of the English settlements, itinerant artists stepped in to somewhat fill this gap. They frequented these areas and visited different communities of settlers to sell their works. One such itinerant artist, the Dutch born Gerard Edema is believed to have painted the first Newfoundland landscape in the early 18th century.

In the aftermath of the battle for Quebec, September 12, 1759, that sealed the fate of New France with the entire territory coming under the control of the English, small garrisons of English troops were stationed at different strategic locations in the territory. As a pastime, and those with a talent for drawing, some of these English soldiers sketched and painted the Canadian landscape and people. Some of these works even found a market in Europe longing to get a vicarious glimpse of the exotic new lands or colonies. Even for keeping land records, with photography not yet available, drawings and sketches were the only means available to these soldiers by way of building up records. This period in Canadian art did throw up a few names, such as Thomas Davies, who recorded the capture of Louisburg and Montreal among other scenes. Scottish born George Heriot was amongst the first artist-soldiers to settle in Canada. His prints were to appear later as "Travels through the Canadas" in 1807. Forshaw Day, who worked as a draftsman in Her Majesty's Naval Yard in Halifax, Nova Scotia, from 1862 to 1879, later moved to Kingston in Ontario and taught drawing at the famous Royal Military College of Canada from 1879 to 1897.

Late 18th century witnessed art prospering in Lower Canada (Quebec). With the construction of new churches gaining momentum, more and more professional artists were commissioned to decorate the churches. New public buildings also provided another outlet for this talent. Portrait painting, in particular, was popular during this period with Francois Baillairge being one of the leading names. After studying art and sculpture in London and Paris, he returned to Montreal. The light and carefree Rococo style also influenced the artists during this period. Due to the French Revolution and the Napoleonic wars, Quebec's links with France got considerably weak, which, in a way, helped the independent growth of local art. William Berczy, who migrated to Canada from Saxony, though not living in Lower Canada, did portraits of several leading people in Quebec. The Woolsey family painted by him in Quebec City in 1808 is his best known work. In a complex arrangement of figures, the work features full-length portraits of all members of the Woolsey family besides decorative floor panels against the backdrop of a view of the landscape as seen through an open window. J. Russell Harper, an art historian, considers this period of Canadian art as the first to develop a truly Canadian character.

This flourishing artistic growth and trend continued into the 19th century. Around the 1820s, a second generation of artists emerged, a leading name of this period being Joseph Legare known for his local landscapes. Antoine Plamondon, a student of Legare, went to France to study art and, on his return, became a highly successful artist of this period executing several religious and portrait commissions. The early Canadian artists were much influenced by European trends. Cornelius Krieghoff, a Dutch born artist in Quebec painted scenes from the life of French-Canadian farmers. Another Canadian artist around this time, Paul Kane, specialized in painting scenes from the lives of indigenous people around the Great Lakes in Western Canada and the Oregon Territories.

The birth of the Canadian Confederation in 1867 and with Canada acquiring Dominion status also provided boost to the Canadian art. A group of Canadian artists led by John Bell-Smith formed in 1870 the Canadian Society of Artists, thus becoming the first organization to reflect the new emerging political reality and the spirit of national identity. This Society embraced artists with diverse backgrounds, many new Canadians and those of French heritage spread across Ontario and Quebec.

Early 20ᵗʰ century witnessed yet another significant development in this context. A group of landscape painters, called the Group of Seven, set before itself the aim of developing the first distinctly Canadian style of painting – brilliantly coloured scenes of the Canadian wilderness is what this Group of Seven specialized in. The seven being: Franklin Carmichael, Lawren Harris, A.Y. Jackson, Frank Johnston, Arthur Lismer, J.E.H. MacDonald and Fredric Varley. Without ever being formal members, Tom Thomson and Emily Carr were also closely associated with the Group of Seven. In the 1930s, this Group decided to enlarge itself to form the Canadian Group of Painters, made up of 28 artists from across the country.

Simultaneously, with the trend towards landscape painting, the main forte of the Group of Seven, there was the beginning of the movement in favour of abstract art. Kathleen Munn and Bertram Brooker, in the 1920s, on their own, experimented with abstract or non-objective art in Canada. Inspired by their personal spirituality, they experimented with symbolism and mysticism. A little later, Lawren Harris of the Group of Seven departed from the Group's focus on landscapes to switch to abstract forms and conceptual themes. These individual trends in art were to develop further in the post-World War II period and inspire several young and budding artists, thereby changing the definition of art in Canada.

The Eastern Group of Painters, founded in Montreal in 1938, had as its common interest and objective art for art's sake rather than the espousal of a nationalist view as was true of the Group of Seven or even of the enlarged Canadian Group of Painters. The Eastern Group of Painters included artists like Alexander Bercovitch, Goodridge Roberts, Eric Goldberg, Jack Weldon Humphrey, John Goodwin Lyman and Jori Smith. This group also spearheaded the growing resentment amongst several Canadian artists against the quasi-national institution that the Group of Seven had become. The view frequently expressed, including in art form, was that a group of artists based largely in Ontario could not monopolise the national vision or view of art. Artists notably based in Quebec were the most vociferous in expressing this feeling, born partly due to a sense of being ignored by the largely Ontario based Group of Seven. Since the 1930s, some Canadian painters have developed a highly individual style. Emily Carr earned repute for her paintings of totem poles, native villages and the forests of British Columbia.

David Milne's landscapes and William Kurelek's prairies also deserve mention in this context.

But taking a broader view of culture and art, for years and still to an extent, Canada has been a country striving for an identity of its own in this field. It was this realization that prompted the federal government in 1949 to set up a Royal Commission under the Chairmanship of Vincent Massey, later Governor General, with a mandate to find out how Canadians could be spurred to greater "national feeling" about their history, culture, art and traditions. The Massey Commission turned its attention to what it perceived as the country's cultural shortcomings. Its recommendations had a significant impact on Canada's cultural life. With Massey subsequently becoming Governor-General only helped further push its recommendations. One major outcome was increased support for State financed institutions, like the Canadian Broadcasting Corporation (CBC), the National Film Board, the National Art Gallery and the National Museum. The Massey Commission was emphatically of the view that such national identity that Canada possessed was largely the result of the role played by these national institutions, which, therefore, deserved increased State support and financial assistance. But the Massey Commission's most radical proposal was the creation of a body to be known as "The Canada Council for the Encouragement of the Arts, Letters, Humanities and Social Sciences". This was implemented in 1957 with the setting up of the Canada Council, thereby accepting the principle of State subsidy of the arts. Though some critics described this as Canada's experiment with culture by fiat, given the country's circumstances, the decision was widely endorsed and welcomed.

Spurring Canada's search and quest for a national identity in culture and art was the patronizing and condescending attitude towards Canada of the three countries whose culture has deeply influenced it. For the French, the first Europeans to arrive on the Canadian scene, the tendency was to view French Canada as merely a province of French Culture. As for the British, they were loathe to even grant the English Canadians the privilege of assimilation by the mother country. They refused to consider Canada as a place where art was possible with the Manchester Guardian patronizingly dismissing Canada as a "cultural backwater". England's Samuel Butler, the author of "The Way of All Flesh" and "Erewhon", after a visit to Canada, wrote an angry poem berating the Victorian philistinism of Montreal's middle class merchants with the memorable tag line "O, God! O, Montreal!" What had particularly upset

Butler was that a Greek statue had been banished to a Montreal attic, because being trouser-less, it was considered "indecent". As for the Americans, though their influence on Canadian culture and art is relatively of recent origin, though most immediate and encompassing, they are somewhat slow and reluctant to accept that Canada is different. The tendency often is to list short stories by Canadian writers as American in collections of American short stories or to show the works of some Canadian painters like Kenneth Lochhead, Jean Paul Mousseau, Harold Town or Jean MacEwen under the label, the New York School.

In the fields of literature and poetry too, Canada has been evolving gradually over the last couple of centuries or so. The earliest works were mostly unadorned narratives of travel and exploration, including mapping of people and places, heroic journeys to the vast unknown West and North and encounters with the Inuit or the First Nation people. Thus, the explorer Samuel Hearne wrote, "A Journey from Prince of Wales Fort in Hudson's Bay to the Northern Ocean (1795)." Sir Alexander Mackenzie, an explorer and fur trader described his travels in "Voyages from Montreal through the continent of North America, to the Frozen and Pacific Oceans (1801)". Simon Fraser recorded details of his 1808 trip west to Fraser Canyon (named after him). Captain John Franklin published an account of a British naval expedition to the Arctic. In 1838, Anna Jameson published "Winter Studies and Summer Rambles in Canada", an account of her travels in the New World. Frances Brooke, the wife of a visiting British military chaplain in the conquered French garrison of Quebec, wrote the first published novel with a Canadian setting. Her "History of Emily Montague" (1769) portrays the sparkling winter scenery of Quebec and the life and manners of its people.

Halifax in Nova Scotia and Fredericton in New Brunswick witnessed some early literary activity in Canada. The first literary journal, the "Nova Scotia Magazine", was published in Halifax in 1789. The literary activity of this region received something of a boost with the influx of Loyalists during the American Revolution and the efforts of Joseph Howe, a journalist, a poet and the first Premier of Nova Scotia. But as viewed by the outside world, these were at best infant first steps taken by Canada in the direction of attaining a literary standing.

The French Canadians were faring no better. Indigenous literary talent took its own time to evolve. What is possibly the most celebrated novel of French Canada, an account of rural Quebec life entitled "Maria Chapdelaine" is by Henry Wadsworth Longfellow, an American. Paris still exercises considerable influence on French Canadian writers. Books by new American writers are rarely translated into French or read in Quebec. The same is true of the works of English Canadian writers. On the other hand, it is equally rare to see a French Canadian book translated into English. Perhaps, the only French Canadian writer to attain international repute is Gabrielle Roy, whose novel on Montreal poverty (published in the US as "The Tin Flute") won France's celebrated Prix Femina in 1947.

The English Canadians too, for a long time, lived under the shadow of the literary circles of Britain, the mother country, or were just not considered worthy of serious note. J.B. Priestley, the British novelist, told English audiences on his return from a Canadian lecture tour that Canadians are "frustrated" and urged that if there is not sufficient talent in Canada, then talent should be imported. He later wrote a play for, in his opinion, the "culture starved" Canadians. This was presumably his way of conveying the kind of literary talent Canada needed to import. The play written by him closed after thirty seven performances in Toronto.

But like in the political and economic fields and also in the realm of international relations, the twentieth century was to witness Canada, surely though slowly, coming into its own in the field, notably of English literature. Writers like Alice Munro, Carol Shields, Margaret Atwood and Rudy Wiebe contributed considerably to putting Canada on the global literary map. And, now, in October, 2013, with Canada's Alice Munro winning the Nobel Prize for Literature, present day Canada has very much arrived on the international literary scene. Alice Munro also becomes Canada's first ever Nobel Laureate. The stiff upper lip British attitude of describing Canada as a "cultural backwater" would certainly not hold good any more.

Even in other fields of art, Canada has been surging ahead. Thanks to the efforts of Tom Patterson, who pushed ahead with the idea of making Stratford, Ontario, a Shakespearean center, Stratford, Ontario, became a leading Shakespearean theater in North America. Ever since the creation of the Canada Council in 1957, it has supported professional theater groups in Vancouver, Winnipeg, Toronto and Montreal. The Council gives grants to many of Canada's twenty or so symphony orchestra associations. It also subsidizes the two national ballet companies, the National Ballet Company of Canada and the Royal Winnipeg Ballet, as also a third group, Le Grand Ballet Canadien of Montreal. Additionally, the Council provides scholarships to thousands of artists, writers and students. It also helped in the setting up of a National Theater School in Montreal.

To wind up this survey of culture and art in Canada, a few words on the film industry would be appropriate. The year 1897 saw the first films shot in Canada, all at the picturesque Niagara Falls. These included: Lumiere, Edison and Biograph. A Manitoba farmer, James Freer, is widely accepted and recognized as the first Canadian film maker with the documentaries made by him shown as early as 1897. From documentaries, Canada soon graduated to making feature films with Hiawatha, The Messiah of the Ojibway, the first fiction films made in 1903 by Joe Rosenthal. The first Canadian feature film, Evangeline, was a production of the Canadian Bioscope Company in 1913. It was shot in Nova Scotia. The Ontario province set up in 1917 the Ontario Motion Picture Bureau, with the Canadian Government Motion Picture Bureau following in 1918. In 1938, the Canadian Government invited the British film maker and critic, John Grierson, to advise it on the government's film making and the outcome was the National Film Act of 1939 and the establishment of the National Film Board of Canada (NFB) as an agency of the government. The National Film Act of 1950 defined the mandate of the NFB as "to interpret Canada to Canadians and to other nations". Through the 1950s and 1960s, the federal government took several measures to encourage the development of a feature film industry in Canada and in 1968, the Canadian Films Development Corporation (CFDC) was set up with $ 10 million invested by the government in this venture. British born, Michael Spencer, who immigrated to Canada at the age of twenty, was to become the first and the longest to serve as the Executive Director of the CFDC, known today as Telefilm Canada, nick named "Hollywood North". For his outstanding contribution to the growth and development of the film industry in Canada, Michael Spencer was deservedly awarded the Order of Canada in 1989.

Since 1911, almost one thousand Anglophone-Canadian and six hundred Francophone-Canadian feature films have been produced in Canada at several film studio centers, mostly located in its three largest metropolitan centers, Toronto, Montreal and Vancouver. In 2011, Toronto ranked third in total film industry production in North America, behind only Los Angeles and New York City. Notable film makers from English Canada include David Cronenberg, Guy Maddin, Atom Egoyan, Allan King and Michael Snow. Prominent French Canadian film makers include Claude Jutra, Gilles Carle,

Denys Arcand, Jean Beaudin, Robert Lepage, Dennis Villeneuve and Michael Brault.

Despite there being a distinctly Canadian cinematic tradition, the cinema of English speaking Canada is closely linked to the cinema of the neighbouring USA. Canadian-American co-productions filmed in Canada include: "My Big Fat Greek Wedding" and the "Saw" series. American films shot in Canada include the "Night at the Museum" and "Final Destination" besides hundreds of others. Besides, there are several American films with Canadian directors and/or actors. Those in the former category (Canadian directors) include Norman Jewison, Jason Reitman, Paul Haggis and James Cameron. It is worth mentioning in this context that James Cameron, the Canadian director, wrote and directed the highest and second highest grossing films ever to come out of Hollywood, namely, "Avatar" and "Titanic". Likewise, quite a few Canadian actors have achieved notable success in Hollywood including names like Mary Pickford, Norma Shearer, Donald Sutherland, Jim Carrey and Ryan Gosling and many others, too numerous to enumerate. There is yet another category of Canadian directors or actors, who, despite starting their early career in Canada, later preferred to move to Hollywood to further pursue their careers because of better prospects, wider exposure and the much bigger reach of Hollywood, both nationally and internationally. Well known in this category would be David Cronenberg, John Candy, Lorne Michaels, Dan Aykroyd, Michael J. Fox, Mike Myers, Ivan Reitman, Derek Harvie, Seth Rogen, Eugene Levy, Tom Green, Scott Mosier and Paul Hagus.

However, from the point of view of the film industry in Canada, particularly the English Canadian sector, there is a negative fall-out of these close links with Hollywood. The US film industry is not only much bigger and with an international reach and appeal, it also substantially controls the market, including the film distribution network. This has a somewhat strangulating effect on English language productions in Canada. Interestingly, the French Canadian film industry has escaped this negative fall-out on account of the overriding influence of Hollywood. The protective barrier of language has helped the Quebec film industry and French-Canadian films, being in the French language, continue to do better, at least in Quebec, than their English-Canadian counterparts.

But all said and done, films and the related thriving industry, roughly estimated at about $ four billion a year in Canada today, have a future in

Canada. Given the country's talented actors and directors, high technological skills, excellent infrastructure and facilities, the stunningly beautiful landscapes and outdoor locales, Canada has carved out for itself an impressive niche in the film world internationally, including when it comes to shooting films. Even Bollywood has not entirely escaped the lure of Canada in this respect. Simultaneously, other film related activities help considerably to put and keep Canada on the world map of the film industry. The Toronto International Film Festival, today ranks as one of the most important events in North American films, showcasing not only Hollywood films, but cinema from around the world, including Canadian films.

Chapter Eight – Canada: 'A Bird's Eye View'

This concluding chapter of Part I of this work on Canada is not meant to be a travel guide in the traditional sense of the word. That purpose stands much better served by numerous books in the market providing detailed guidelines on travelling in Canada. If one has the time, the resources and the urge to discover and observe first hand, then Canada is a traveler's delight. The infrastructure is excellent, the variety and choice of landscapes and places are endless and fascinating with stunningly beautiful scenery. And, on top of it, the people are friendly and helpful. If you speak English, then language is no barrier, not even so much in Quebec, though some knowledge of the French language would be an asset there. This chapter seeks to provide a racy overview of Canada, a vast country stretching from the Atlantic Ocean in the East to the Pacific Ocean in the West and from the Arctic in the North to the USA in the South, mostly along the 49th parallel. This bird's eye view of the world's second largest country, in geographic size, seeks to capture essentially what may be termed as the general flavor of Canada based on the author's personal experience of traveling all over Canada, quite literally. Besides the well inhabited and developed parts of Canada, the coverage will include what is commonly referred to as Canada North. This huge chunk of the country, lying beyond the Arctic Circle, hardly ever even finds mention in the general run of travel guides on Canada. Very few people, in fact, go to this part of the country. It is not easy to access, the infrastructure is poor, the distances vast, the population extremely small and travel facilities not just very sketchy, but very expensive, if at all available. Thanks to the unique circumstances of the author's five year stay in Canada, as his country's High Commissioner (Ambassador), he was extremely fortunate to see this relatively unknown part of Canada and visit places, whose names were not even known to most Canadians. This rare experience would be covered in some detail.

Starting from the Atlantic Ocean in the East, Canada starts with the province of Newfoundland. It was the last territory to join Canada, as recently as 1949, and thus become its tenth province, completing the map of

Canada as it is today. Its Capital, St. John, owes its name to Giovanni Caboto from Venice (also known as John Cabot), who sailed into the enclosed and natural harbor on St. John's Day in 1497, claiming the land for England, whose then monarch, Henry VII, had commissioned Cabot's voyage and paid him Pounds ten for his effort. The Capital St. John must not be confused with Saint John in New Brunswick. Though the latter was also named after the same Saint, it was founded much later in 1630. To avoid confusion, the former (the Capital of Newfoundland) is always spelt as St., while the latter spells the word Saint in full, John being the common denominator in both.

Newfoundland juts out the maximum into the Atlantic Ocean of all the land points on the entire American continent, North and South. At this extremity, there is a sign according to which, from there you are closer to London (UK) than to Toronto. It was this that apparently prompted Guglielmo Marconi to be in Newfoundland in 1901 to receive the first wireless transatlantic message. Fishing is the main stay of the local economy, cod being the most plentiful, though there are enough commercial stocks of sole, flounder, redfish and turbot. For those fond of sea food, Newfoundland would be the place to be in. The most popular drink of Newfoundland is SCREECH, more interesting than refined and is often chased down with beer to reduce the kick.

Tourism apart, mining and forestry are the other industries. The offshore discovery of gas and oil deposits in recent times has provided further boost to the local economy. The Trans-Canada highway starts in Newfoundland going all the way, nearly 10,000 kilometers, to the Pacific coast. It serves as a major transport artery of the province. The province also boasts of some National Parks like the mountainous Gros Morne National Park with its fjords and wild life like whales, seals, caribou and moose. There is then the Terra Nova National Park on the east coast, the Cape Spear National Park, the province's most easterly point and the Signal Hill Park, which boasts of having witnessed several events of historical importance. Newfoundland is also known for its humour with "Newfy" jokes popular all over Canada. Where else would a cemetery get described as an underground condominium?

One of the four Atlantic Provinces, Prince Edward Island (PEI), Capital Charlottetown, is the smallest of Canadian provinces. It is often called "the cradle of the Confederation" since the 1864 meeting, which led to the formation of the Dominion of Canada three years later, was held in Province House, the first public building of the province. Potato is grown in abundance, indeed is the principal crop leading some to describe PEI as two beaches divided by potato fields. The province has a cute charm of its own with several wooden structures and the lovely spires of St. John the Baptist church. A major tourist attraction of the island is the Green Gables House that attracts visitors from far and wide, who come to see the settings described by L.M. Montgomery in his famous book "Anne of Green Gables". In the 1990s, a thirteen kilometer long bridge, a feat of engineering indeed, was commissioned, thus providing a road link between the island and the mainland.

New Brunswick, Capital Fredericton, often gets described as the gateway to the Maritime region. Its magnificent forests cover over eighty per cent of the land, thus resulting in a substantial paper and pulp industry. The Saint John River is the lifeblood of New Brunswick. The city of Saint John is located along the Bay of Fundy at the mouth of the Saint John River. For a panoramic view of the city and its waterfront, there is the Fort Howe and the Carleton Martello Tower. The mouth of the Saint John River provides the sight of a unique phenomenon. Twice each day, the tides of the Bay of Fundy reach such heights that they force the Saint John River to flow upstream. This natural and unique spectacle has been named by the locals as the Reversing Fall Rapids. The Christ Church Cathedral in the Capital Fredericton, completed in 1853, is considered to be one of North America's finest examples of decorated Gothic architecture.

The fourth of the Atlantic provinces, Nova Scotia, Capital Halifax, as its very name suggests, has been home to Scottish highlanders only to be preceded by the Micmacs, the French, the English and Loyalists from the American colonies. Today, over seventy per cent of Nova Scotians are of British descent and about ten percent of French. Nova Scotia also has the largest indigenous black population in Canada.

The first and second largest cities of Nova Scotia, Halifax (founded in 1749) and Dartmouth are located on opposite sides of one of the world's great harbours connected by two suspension bridges. The Halifax harbour, the second largest natural one in the world, is free of ice the year round. As the Capital of the province and as a major commercial and educational center, Halifax understandably dominates over its twin city of Dartmouth. Halifax boasts of several tourist attractions including museums, historical buildings like the Province House, Canada's oldest standing legislative building described by Charles Dickens as "a gem of Georgian architecture" and St. Paul's Church (1750), the oldest Protestant Church in Canada. Cape Breton Island is a very popular tourist attraction in Nova Scotia, particularly its Cabot Trail, named after John Cabot, the explorer, who sighted land here in 1497. The Trail is a 300 kilometer loop that roller coasts around the northern part of Cape Breton, offering some stunningly beautiful scenery and richly deserving the label of one of the most spectacular drives in North America. There is then also the industrial part of Cape Breton with its coal mines and steel mills, including the famous rail track making plant in Sydney, the only one in North America specializing in the longer lasting rail tracks made of extra hardened steel.

Moving further west, one comes to the heartland of Canada, the Ontario province with Toronto as its Capital. It is densely populated, in parts at least, with a large immigrant component. It is, in many ways, the gateway to Canada with the Toronto airport being a major hub. The province is a major commercial and manufacturing center with several of Canada's big industries located in and around Toronto and also in cities like London, Windsor, Hamilton and Sudbury, which has a huge aluminium plant. It is also a major center of education and learning, boasting of quite a few world class universities and institutions. For a visitor, the province has several attractions including Toronto's CN Tower, one of the tallest in the world, the next door unique stadium, which, with the press of a button, gets converted into an indoor one giving protection against rain or snow. The roof takes about twenty minutes to close. Ontario also is home to the world famous Niagara Falls where Lake Erie overflows into Lake Ontario at the rate of 35,000 cubic liters per second. Ontario also has some wineries and produces the unique ice wine made from frozen grapes. It tastes more like sweet liquor, is quite potent and expensive too. With its lakes and rivers and beautiful forests, Ontario has a lovely countryside including its Muskoka lake district with sprawling luxury lakeside villas. Ontario, particularly Toronto, with its large immigrant population, offers cuisines from around the world making it a food lovers' delight. And, not to forget, Ontario is also home to the nation's Capital Ottawa, by itself a beautiful city of little over a million with the Ottawa River flowing past. The bend in the river provides an impressive view of the Parliament building and the Chateau Laurier hotel, both in beautiful Gothic style. It is really a tale of two cities with Hull in Quebec on the other bank of the Ottawa River connected to Ottawa by several modern bridges enabling one to hop over from Ottawa (Ontario) to Hull (Quebec) within minutes. It is this location, a political statement indeed, that finally swung things in favour of Ottawa being declared the national Capital by Queen Victoria, something for which Kingston, a beautiful and historical city in Ontario as a strong contender for this status, will perhaps never forgive Queen Victoria. Ottawa also has a few impressive museums and art galleries including the Museum of Civilization in Hull just on the other side of the Ottawa River. The building of this museum is by itself a fine example of modern architecture. On the outskirts of Ottawa, there is another museum that is quite unique, the Museum of Aircraft that has on display an impressive collection of military and civil aircraft from days gone by. The largest one in its collection, a World War II vintage Liberator bomber, is a gift to the museum from the Indian Air Force.

Adjoining the Ontario province is the province of Quebec or French Canada, thus making Canada a bilingual country. Quebec has a history and personality of its own, already covered in detail in the chapters on history and the political scene. The present day Quebec is a developed and prosperous part of Canada with a good concentration of industry and manufacturing. It remains proud of its French culture and background. Montreal, its largest city, is a major hub of industrial and commercial activity, an important banking center, boasts of several centers of art and culture, including the famous Musee des Beaux Arts, besides several educational institutions, including the famous McGill University. The city has several tourist attractions including some lovely parks with one boasting of the largest collections of bonsai trees, almost three hundred with some over a century old. The city received a major spurt in its growth and development when it was chosen as the host to Expo 1967 to mark the centenary of the birth of the Canadian Confederation. The silver dome of Montreal's Expo, 67 still dominates the city's skyline.

Quebec City, the Capital of the province of Quebec, is a delight to visit. It differs considerably in character and looks very different from almost all other major cities in Canada, one could perhaps even say, the entire North America. Standing sentinel over the St. Lawrence River, it is the only walled city on the Continent north of Mexico. Called by some as the Gibraltar of North America, its giddy heights, its citadel suspended, as it were, in the air, its massive and famous cliffs with the famous hotel, Chateau Frontenac, and its turrets dominating the city's skyline, picturesque narrow cobbled streets and gateways and splendid views make it a photographer's delight and a joy for a visitor. It is a city, particularly the old part, where the best is to walk around and leisurely take in the various sights and the overall ambience. On a bright sunny day in the balmy summer months, its roadside and pavement artists are reminiscent of Montmartre in Paris. The other attractions of Quebec City include its horse drawn carriages, fine French cooking behind charming facades, the Dufferin Terrace, the Petit Champlain, lined with crafts shops and tiny galleries, Notre-Dame-des-Victoires Church, the city's principal church, Basilique Notre-Dame-de-Quebec, the Universite de Laval and some museums. The seminary's museum is possibly the city's finest general museum and has an impressive collection of Baroque and Renaissance art and some good examples of 19th century Canadian art. This museum also has on display, in a sealed glass case, a rare sight, an unwrapped mummy from the time of Tutankhamen. Even outside Quebec City and Montreal, the Quebec province offers several attractions, it's beautiful countryside, small little villages and hamlets, the Laurentian mountains, geologically one of the oldest in the world, the Gatineau Hills with their lovely drives and, not to forget, Quebec is famous for one of Canada's national delicacies, the maple syrup, the sap of the national tree, the maple, with several large farms producing and marketing it. In March-April Quebec's temperatures are ideal for this product.

Moving further West beyond the provinces of Ontario and Quebec, one finally touches Canada's famed prairies and the vast flat lands, no longer bound by a corridor of ragged trees and rolling on and on to a distant horizon. The first of these provinces is Manitoba with Winnipeg as its Capital. No other province is so dominated by one city with at least half the population of Manitoba living in Winnipeg, with the Canadian-Ukrainians being particularly prominent in Winnipeg. Other than the down town area with its curved avenues skirting around the ASSINIBOINE and Red Rivers, thus avoiding the usual straight lines of most modern cities, not to miss is the junction of Portage and Main, considered to be the widest, windiest and coldest street corner in Canada.

The next province in the westward direction is Saskatchewan with Regina as its Capital. The province was formed in 1905. Recalling Canada's first Prime Minister John A. Macdonald's telling comment that: "If you had a little more wood, and a little more water I think the prospect would be improved", the city leaders of Regina accepted the challenge, dammed the muddy WASCANA Creek and created a small lake. With water thus available, tree planting and the laying out of gardens with fountains followed, including one from London's Trafalgar Square. The city's imposing legislative building, the Wascana Center with its woods and water bodies and the nearby Willow Island are today some of the popular sights of Regina. The University of Regina's art center and the Museum of Natural History, one of the finest in Canada, are some of the other attractions of Regina. One of the training centers of Canada's elite police force, the RCMP, is also located in Regina.

The other major city of the Saskatchewan province is Saskatoon, founded in 1884, with the South Saskatchewan River flowing through it with its wooded banks. The University of Saskatoon gives the city its cultural and academic profile along with its theater groups and orchestra.

Moving further West is the province of Alberta with Edmonton as its Capital, Canada's most northerly metropolis. It ranks as a world class city with its famous Edmonton Mall, the largest in North America, the Citadel Theater, Canada's largest, the Space Sciences Center with Canada's biggest planetarium and the Western World's largest Zeiss-Jenastar projector. The city is famous for its beautifully laid out gardens, walks and jogging tracks, opera and classical ballet companies, a symphony orchestra and several professional theater groups. It is also home to the famous University of Alberta. The city's industrial muscle is best demonstrated by Refinery Row, which produces almost ten per cent of Canada's petrochemical products. For, after all, one of the major sources of Alberta's prosperity is its oil bearing rich and extensive sand deposits. Add to this, its fertile farm lands, coal and gas deposits and the incomparable beauty of the Canadian Rocky Mountains and the famous Calgary stampede or the Rodeo that are a big draw for tourists from far and wide. The province is home to two world famous National Parks, Banff and Jasper and given its excellent connectivity and infrastructure, they are highly popular tourist destinations not just from Canada and the neighbouring USA, but from countries far and beyond. In fact, the entire Canadian Rockies are a delight to float around with their numerous streams and rivers, placid lakes, big and small, thick forests and snow clad peaks as the backdrop. A convenient and highly enjoyable way to relish the Canadian Rockies is to take the Rocky Mountain Express from Calgary to Vancouver. This special train is an ideal way to enjoy this extremely pretty and picturesque part of Canada. You leave Calgary in the morning travelling in first class comfort with meals and drinks served at your seat. A nice commentary keeps giving all the highlights on the way. Wherever the scenery is particularly spectacular, the train slows down to a virtual crawl for you to take pictures and for the night halt, the train stops at Kamloops, a decent sized town, where stay in a comfortable hotel is included in the train ticket. Next morning, you resume your train journey reaching Vancouver by late afternoon. Thus, by not travelling after dark, this train journey ensures that no sights are missed.

Besides the Capital Edmonton, Calgary is the other big city of Alberta. It is considered to be Canada's longest city and also known for its over-walks that ensure safe walking around for pedestrians without their having to cross the roads. The city is a major hub of activity, a gateway to the famous Banff National Park, just about an hour's drive away and also a good entry point to the Alberta Badlands, once part of a sub-tropical swamp that was home to a vast array of prehistoric life. Preserved along the Red Deer River is the Dinosaur Provincial Park, one of UNESCO's world heritage sites. The William Tyrrell Museum of Paleontology has one of the best collections of dinosaur fossils in the world.

Finally, one comes to Canada's western-most province of British Columbia, facing the Pacific Ocean. Though Vancouver is easily its best known and largest city, it is not the Capital of British Columbia. That honour goes to Victoria on the not too far Vancouver Island. Apart from its impressive array of government buildings, museums, art galleries and the famous gardens, perhaps the best known landmark of Victoria is its Empress Hotel on the ocean front. A cup of tea with a pastry or a plate of cucumber sandwiches, in the true English style, at this hotel is supposed to be the done thing, while on a visit to Victoria. Regular ferry services connect Vancouver to the Vancouver Island.

But the main action is in Vancouver, a large and a beautiful city facing the Pacific Ocean with a backdrop of mountains and thick forest. The city is a major center of commerce, Canada's premier port and the most important one on the North American West Coast. It is a major academic center and a hub of art and culture. It has a very sizeable population of immigrants, notably from India and China. Its China-town is not only famous but is the second largest in North America, next only to the one in San Francisco. And, its Punjabi Market, where even the road signs are in English and the Gurmukhi script, is a veritable Punjab transplanted on Canadian soil.

Having thus traversed across Canada from the Atlantic to the Pacific with this racy coverage, or a bird's eye view, it is now time to look at what is commonly referred to as Canada North. This would include the Yukon, the North-West Territory and Nunavut. These are the vast, the least inhabited underdeveloped parts of Canada that even most Canadians are quite unfamiliar with, except that they see them on the map as a vast expanse stretching all the way towards the North Pole and the Arctic Sea. While Capital cities like Whitehorse (Yukon), Yellowknife (NWT) and Iqaluit (Nunavut) are better known and relatively easy to access, served as they are by regular commercial flights and have a reasonably good infrastructure, the rest is mostly empty wilderness dotted with tiny little communities living under truly tough, even harsh, conditions.

Normally, as an Ambassador posted to Canada, you would have neither the urge nor even, in most cases, the possibility to see these parts of Canada. It was precisely this realization that prompted Jean Chretien, later a successful Prime Minister, to decide when he was Minister for Northern Affairs several years ago to initiate an officially sponsored trip, in the mid- summer of every year, to Canada North for Heads of Mission based in Ottawa. The thinking, rightly so, was that while foreign Ambassadors to Canada could and did indeed travel on their own to the developed and easy to access parts of Canada, including all major and even small urban centers, Canada North remained a total blank in their perception of Canada. To rectify this, the annual practice of a trip to Canada North for a group of Heads of Mission in Ottawa was started. The selection of the group each year was determined strictly in order of seniority going by the date of the presentation of credentials by you. When your turn came, you got a formal letter of invitation from the Foreign Minister that covered complete hospitality including travel by a well-equipped and comfortable transport aircraft of the Canadian Air Force, flown by an experienced cockpit crew and a polite well trained cabin crew. Accompanying our group of twenty Ambassadors (in June 1994) was also the Chief of Protocol and two senior officials from the Northern Affairs Department to keep explaining various features of Canada North to us with the help of detailed maps. Spouses could not be included on this trip because of the very limited, almost primitive, infrastructure at some of the places on our itinerary. I was fortunate to get my turn for this trip in June, 1994, that is, a year and a half from the time of presentation of credentials by me in early December, 1992. Confirming the impression of those, who had already done it, the trip indeed turned out to be an experience of a life time.

Taking off from Ottawa on the early morning of June 16, 1994 we headed north towards Iqaluit. After a couple of hours of being in the air, we were already beyond the tree line. Dotting the landscape were numerous lakes, big and small, with many of them, as we were told, not even bearing any name since nobody lived in those areas. One was already seeing the vast emptiness of Canada. Iqaluit was a quiet little place, but the airport had a smooth and an exceptionally long runway. This was understandable since during the peak of the Cold War, the huge B-52 bombers of the US Strategic Air Command were based there and a few of them were all the time, in turns, airborne and equipped with nuclear weapons.

At Iqaluit, we were split into two smaller groups and shifted to smaller aircraft capable of landing on the short landing strip on Baffin Island, where Pangnirtung was to be our first night halt point. Only the Davis Strait separated us from Greenland. Pangnirtung turned out to be a small little community of under a thousand inhabitants, tiny little wooden structures along a short dust road and with a modest sized community center. When we left Ottawa, it was a balmy +33 degrees Celsius. Due to some snow flurries, Pangnirtung was about -3 degrees Celsius and the single dust road, or rather a track, muddy and slushy. We were all put up in a small hotel, the only structure, besides the community center, built of concrete, two Ambassadors in a room. We were served an early simple dinner after which we were welcomed by some seniors of the local community. With the help of a big wall map of the world, each one of us was requested to point out on the map the country we came from and very briefly introduce it to the assembled local gathering. Our entire interaction with the locals had to be through an interpreter, as they spoke no or very little English. We were also apprised of the problems faced by this small community. Unemployment ranked high with the virtual end of hunting and fur trade, the traditional occupations. Alcoholism was a common problem and suicides high. All this was quite an eye opener and the realization dawned as to why this region was called the "Third World" of Canada.

After the night halt and an early morning breakfast, we were back in our two small aircrafts to take off for Iqaluit where we once again boarded our much bigger and comfortable aircraft. Thus, we were on to our next destination, the Lupin gold mine. For me it was the first to be visiting a gold mine and it was an interesting and educative experience. We were treated to a simple lunch at the mine's cafeteria before boarding our plane for our next night halt point, a small little community again of about a thousand inhabitants, called Resolute. We were already at 85 degrees North Latitude, way beyond the Arctic Circle that starts from 60 degrees North Latitude.

Soon after landing there and a brief refreshment, we were again shifted to two much smaller aircrafts that took us to Polaris, the highest mine (copper and zinc) in the world at 87 degrees North. We were given a conducted tour of the mine and also shown the living quarters of the small work force. Interestingly, despite the extremely tough living and working conditions, no wives no children allowed, the jobs at the mine were in great demand because of the exceptionally attractive remunerations and other perks and facilities that the Polaris mine offered. Back in Resolute for the night halt, we took a walk about this small one street place. Resolute had a major radar and weather forecasting station. It also served as possibly the last inhabited place for those undertaking expeditions to the Arctic. The hotel accommodation here, after Pangnirtung, was a distinct improvement since we had a separate room each. At one time, Resolute was home to a person of Indian origin (from Tamil Nadu) by the name of Bezal Jesudasan. In Resolute, he married a local and ran a business organizing tours to the Arctic. National Geographic honoured him with an hour long film describing him as the "King of the Arctic" and an outstanding adventurer. Sadly, he died of heart attack on August 9, 1995. He last visited Chennai in 1993. His wife, Terry, continued to live in Resolute after his death and run the business started by him. Unfortunately, I could not meet Jesudasan, as he was on a visit to Montreal when I was in Resolute. But I did meet his wife and it was a pleasant encounter, as she was particularly happy to meet someone from her husband's far off land of origin.

Taking off from Resolute, we first flew further north till we were over the magnetic North Pole. Till then, I did not know that the magnetic North Pole is different from the North Pole and that it keeps shifting and overlaps with the North Pole only once every few years. Flying over the magnetic North Pole is not easy since the compass of the aircraft does not work. But our experienced flying crew was used to this problem and managed very well. After an aerial view of the island of Tuktoyaktuk, in the extreme North-West of Canada, we landed at the small town of Inuvik, not far from Canada's border with Alaska (USA). Our visit to Inuvik coincided with a local festival "The Midnight Madness". Being the third week of June and virtually 24 hours of day light at that latitude, the whole town was in the throes of fun and frolic and our group happily joined in all these celebrations.

After a night halt at Inuvik, our next halt, the following day, was a brief one at Old Crow on the Porcupine River, a tiny little community of around three hundred aboriginals. Proceeding further, we flew on to Dawson City in the Yukon for our night halt. With a population of about three thousand, Dawson City owes its origin to the days of the gold rush in the late 19th century. Most of the houses are low wooden structures, roads not metalled, but the side-walks covered with wooden planks so that you do not have to walk through mud and slush in rainy season or when the snow melts. In the summer season, the town attracts tourists, including from Alaska by steamers down the Alaska River that flows past Dawson City. Due to this tourist rush in summers, the population of the town swells temporarily by a few thousand. The town, besides offering plenty of the old world charm, including gold panning, to the visitors, it also prides itself over having the first and, therefore, the oldest and still functioning casino in Canada, Diamond Tooth Gerties.

From Dawson City, we were driven in a luxury coach along the Alaska highway for our next night halt at a place called Burwash Landing, essentially a camping site along the Alaska highway. The following day, we flew into Whitehorse after reboarding our plane at Burwash Landing. Whitehorse, the Capital of Yukon had, in 1994, the time of our visit, a population of 18,000 only and, I am quite sure, this figure could not have changed much since then. A huge painting on display in the local museum explains the origin of the name Whitehorse. In earlier days, when the river flowing through the town had not been tamed, its rapids looked like the manes of white horses, hence the town getting its name Whitehorse.

After a night halt at Whitehorse, we flew on to Yellowknife, the Capital of the North West Territory. But after taking off from Whitehorse, our aircraft first flew low over some glaciers in the area and also circled over Mt. Logan (16,000 feet), the highest mountain peak in Canada. A city of just about 20,000 inhabitants situated next to the Great Slave Lake, Yellowknife, after what we had been experiencing over the last few days, looked quite modern with proper roads and shops and its Explorer Hotel, where we were put up, had most of the basic modern amenities. The town also boasted of its impressive Legislative Assembly building, besides the Prince of Wales Museum. Our group was given a conducted tour of both with the local Premier personally welcoming us at the Legislative Assembly premises along with the other local dignitaries. Earlier, in April 1993, my wife and I had visited Yellowknife on our own. The night temperature at that time of the year was still -17 degrees Celsius and we even drove on the Great Slave Lake that was still frozen solid. We had also experienced a dog sleigh ride over a stretch of a few kilometers with a team of about twenty huskies pulling the snow sleigh at a fairly good speed.

From Yellowknife, it was a long haul back to Ottawa with a refueling halt at Churchill on the Hudson Bay. By the time we landed at Ottawa, a week after departure from there, we had been in the air for a little over 32 hours, clocking nearly 14,000 kilometers. This Canada North trip was indeed an experience of a life time. As mentioned earlier, visiting most of these remote corners of the great Canadian expanse and wilderness on your own would be nearly impossible and prohibitively expensive. Thanks to this annual gesture of the Canadian government towards foreign envoys to Canada, one had seen and visited those parts of the country that would otherwise be only tiny dots on the map, perhaps not even figuring in any travel guide book. One came back with a true understanding and appreciation of the famed vastness and emptiness of Canada. Even the names of some of the places visited, derived obviously from their history and background, were fascinating. Where else would one come across names of places like Resolute, Old Crow, Porcupine River, Whitehorse, Yellowknife! Add to this list, indicative only, names like Moose jaw, Rose Town, Red Deer River and you get a different flavor of Canada. But, what was impressive was that no matter where we went and however small, all places had basic amenities like electricity, potable water and communications like telephone and even fax. No matter where we were, one never felt out of touch with the rest of the world. True, in many ways the Third World of Canada, and yet not so in all respects.

PART – II

RELATIONS WITH INDIA

Chapter Nine – An Overview

"Friendship to be real, must ever sustain the weight of honest differences."

Interestingly, this quotation from Mahatma Gandhi was used in his reply speech in New Delhi in January, 1996 by the then Prime Minister of Canada, Jean Chretien, at the welcome State Banquet in his honour hosted by the then Prime Minister of India, Narasimha Rao. Chretien was on a State visit to India, the first by a Canadian Prime Minister in nearly a quarter century.

Jean Chretien always chose his words carefully and his quoting Mahatma Gandhi was intended not merely to flatter his Indian hosts. He very much meant it having fully realized what ups and downs India-Canada relations had been through over the last half century.

In a Chapter entitled India and Canada that I had contributed to the special voluminous issue on "Indian Foreign Policy: Challenges and Opportunities." Brought out by the Foreign Service Institute, New Delhi, in 2007, this is what I had to say on India-Canada relations.

"Over the last nearly sixty years, since India's independence in 1947, India-Canada relations have been something of a roller coaster ride. Starting with a phase of "special relationship" to the emergence of certain irritants, to harsh language and accusations of "betrayal" following India's Pokhran-I in 1974, to a near freeze bordering on indifference, to the injections of mutual suspicion in the 1980s when India was rocked by militancy, to the re-discovery of India by the mid-nineties, to a renewed setback in 1998 in the aftermath of India's Pokhran-II, to hopefully the final realization that if put and kept on a mature course, these relations can and should realize their full potential. This has been, in brief, the story of India-Canada relations in the last six decades."

The story started off on a very happy note indeed. Due to its active participation in and significant contribution towards the allied war effort, Canada was on a high in the post- World War II period. With the collapse of France and the occupation of most of Western Europe in 1940 and the entry of the United States into the war in 1941, Canada was the third most important country in the western alliance and it remained so until the mid-fifties. By then, France, Italy and Germany had regained much of their normal influence that they had lost due to defeat or occupation. It was during this period that Canada, as a member of the inner group of the three western nations, alongside the USA and Britain, was very much involved in the drawing up of the agreements that set up international organizations like the Food and Agriculture Organization (FAO), the United Nations Relief and Rehabilitation Agency (UNRRA), the International Monetary Fund (IMF), the World Bank, the International Civil Aviation Organization (ICAO), and the North Atlantic Treaty Organization (NATO). Canada took to this role of pursuing an active foreign policy quite naturally and enthusiastically, thereby earning the label of the golden age of Canadian diplomacy for Canadian foreign policy during this period lasted for over a decade.

Coinciding with this Canadian role on the world scene was the emergence of India post-independence (1947) as an active actor on the world stage. Nehru with his world vision and international standing was the logical spokesman of the Afro-Asian world with most of this region still struggling to throw off the yoke of colonialism and imperialism. China was still in the throes of internal strife and even after the Communist takeover by 1949, it was occupied with internal problems and consolidation. Canadian enthusiasm in foreign affairs found a perfect match in Asia in the form of Nehru's independent India.

The foundation of the special relationship between India and Canada was laid during this period and under these circumstances. The Canadian leadership, at the time Louis St Laurent as Prime Minister and Lester B. Pearson, who almost simultaneously became Canada's Foreign Minister, took to Nehru very positively and shared several commonalities with him, including in terms of attitude and style.

The Commonwealth bond between Canada and India was to play an exceptionally important role. At this point of time, the British Commonwealth was still a very small grouping and all white – Britain, Canada, Australia, New Zealand and South Africa. It was the entry of India, Pakistan, and Ceylon (Sri Lanka) that earned this group the appellation, "the new Commonwealth". It was no longer an all-white club. In December 1946, just three months after the formation of the interim government in India, India formally suggested to the Canadian government to persuade the government of its province of British Columbia "to confer the franchise on the small Indian community in that province and, thus, rectify the present anomalous position, which is a source of humiliation to Indians." Indicative of the prevailing Canadian attitude towards India, by April 1947, this was accomplished; the franchise conferred and Nehru sent a telegram to Ottawa thanking it for the prompt action. To complete this part of the story, four years later, Canada removed a second "source of humiliation to Indians" by ending its immigration rule that barred Indians (as indeed the other "Asiatics") from entering Canada as immigrants unless they were wives or unmarried children under eighteen of Canadian citizens legally resident in Canada. Following a formal agreement with India, Canada threw open immigration to Indians going beyond "close relatives" to cover a hundred and fifty Indians annually. It should be mentioned in this context that the size of this general quota was less important and more relevant was the symbolic gesture on Canada's part of removing a legal discrimination. Significantly, this agreement was signed on India's Republic Day, January 26, 1951. Nehru, in a message to his Canadian counterpart, Prime Minister Louis St Laurent, described this agreement as "another step in the developing friendship between our two countries".

Realizing fully the importance of India as a member of the "new Commonwealth", many Canadians were unhappy with India's decision in 1949 to become a Republic. But true to its newly acquired high profile diplomatic role, including in Asia, Canada was determined to find a way out. It, thus, played a leading role in working out a formula that sought to reconcile India's desire to remain in the Commonwealth with its decision to become a republic. The formula being that India accepted the King (or the Queen as the case may be) as the symbol of the free association of the independent nations of the Commonwealth and as such the head of the Commonwealth. Also, at India's instance the term "British" before the appellation Commonwealth was dropped since it was suggestive of British hegemony, something India could not agree to. This development, in which Canada had played an important role, truly made independent India the keystone of the arch of the new Commonwealth. This formula was, in subsequent years, really to ensure that the Commonwealth did not face total extinction. If today, this voluntary organization of independent nations across Asia, Africa and the Caribbean consists mostly of Republics and only a handful of Dominions, the credit goes to this significant development of the late 1940s.

The next step in this context was the realization that the new Commonwealth had to be made relevant to the emerging needs, particularly of some of its new members in Asia. Ever since the end of the Second World War, Canada had been giving economic aid in various forms to Britain and West European countries. At the Commonwealth Foreign Ministers' meeting at Colombo in January 1950, the plan to address the pressing economic growth needs of the newly independent nations of South and South East Asia was addressed. Indicative of the new and growing Canadian interest in forging ties with Asia, within the ambit of the new Commonwealth, was Canada's decision to participate in the Colombo Plan for Cooperative Economic Development in South and South East Asia. Since this involved a Canadian annual contribution of $ 25 million towards the Colombo Plan fund, the idea was a bit of a hard sell back home for Canadian diplomacy. In fact, initially, it was rejected by the Canadian Cabinet. Canada, the feeling was already somewhat overstretched in its various economic assistance programmes and commitments to Britain and countries of Western Europe. What ultimately worked in favour of Canada joining the Colombo Plan was the irresistibly attractive notion that the Colombo Plan was a Commonwealth concept that must be encouraged and pursued. It is this that enabled Foreign Minister Lester B. Pearson to sell the proposal to Prime Minister Louis St Laurent and for the latter to finally push it through his Cabinet.

It was in the midst of such positive atmospherics that Prime Minister Nehru of India visited Canada in October, 1949. Nehru was coming straight to Canada after a visit to the United States. By all accounts, Nehru's visit to the US had not gone off well. He perhaps found the Americans a little too overbearing. He was exposed to too much lecturing by the US leadership. With Dean Acheson, the US Secretary of State, in particular Nehru could rarely come on the same wavelength. In short, there was nothing much to write home about, as they say, about the visit. By contrast, Ottawa presented a different scene. Nehru had already met and interacted with Prime Minister, Louis St Laurent at the Commonwealth conferences. Both St Laurent and Pearson were gracious in their references to India and to Nehru and to his role in the struggle for independence. At the same time, they were modest in their references to Canada and its achievements. Nehru, altogether, felt a lot more comfortable in Canada than in the USA and this visit marked an important step in the evolving special relationship between India and Canada. Nehru was even extended the courtesy and honour of addressing a joint session of the Canadian Parliament on October 24, 1949.The second time an Indian Prime did so was Indira Gandhi on June 19, 1973.

For Canada, with its newly found vigour for foreign affairs since the end of World War II, Asia seemed to be the flavor of the month. That is where the action was. The wave of independence from colonial rule was sweeping across. The Indonesian struggle against Dutch rule that began in 1945 was to culminate successfully in 1950 with Soekarno dominating the scene. Malaya (now Malaysia) and Burma (now Myanmar) were in turmoil on account of Communist insurrection. With a military presence of close to two hundred thousand troops, the French were fighting the Vietnamese led by Ho Chi Minh. China was settling down after a bitter civil war at the end of which Chiang Kai-shek was forced to flee the mainland and seek shelter in Formosa (Taiwan). The Korean War had broken out in the summer of 1950 marking possibly the beginning of the bi-polar era and the subsequent Cold War. The US occupation of Japan was still there and was to last till 1952. The US as the leader of the Western Alliance, already forged in the form of NATO in 1949, was increasingly getting determined to contain Communism. US Senator Joseph McCarthy's witch hunt in the name of fighting and opposing Communism combined with General Douglas MacArthur's bellicosity were already beginning to strain US relations with some of its NATO allies, Canada included, who had a different perspective of the post War world. Canada's more restrained and cautious approach increasingly contrasted with the much more strident US style of conducting its foreign policy, particularly during this period. In fact, Canada's style of conducting its foreign affairs was closer to that of the newly independent India than of its powerful neighbour to the south, the USA. Canada was favourably inclined towards the Indian view that a better and more enduring way of stemming the spread of Communism was to support the nationalist sentiment and forces in the newly independent countries and to address positively their legitimate aspiration for rapid economic growth.

Recalling this positive ambience that marked India-Canada relations during this period is vital to understand the flowering of this special relationship in the early stages. Nuclear cooperation was to constitute an important element of this growing relationship. The first step was when in the autumn of 1947, the Government of Canada agreed to supply a ton of crude uranium oxide for the Bose Institute in Calcutta for fundamental research in nuclear physics and the possible use of atomic energy for industrial purposes.

Even at that stage, India had clarified to Canada that the ultimate objective of this research was the use of uranium extracted from Indian rocks and minerals for the construction of an atomic reactor. Canada's interest, it is believed, in securing thorium from India was at least a contributory factor in Canada agreeing to this Indian request for the supply of uranium oxide. It was against this background that as a further step in cooperation in this field, Canada agreed to supply to India in 1954 CIRUS (Canadian-Indian Reactor, US), a research reactor at the Bhabha Atomic Research Center (BARC) in Trombay near Bombay (now Mumbai). CIRUS used heavy water (deuterium oxide) that was supplied by the US and was to be the second nuclear reactor to be built in India. It is important to clarify here that this reactor was not under IAEA safeguards, since they did not exist when the reactor was sold to India. The grey area emerged since Canada stipulated and the US supply contract for the heavy water explicitly specified that it only be used for peaceful purposes. However, at a capacity factor of 50-80 per cent CIRUS could produce six to ten kilograms of plutonium a year. CIRUS, therefore, not only produced some of India's initial weapon grade plutonium stockpile, but also presumably supplied the plutonium for India's Pokhran-I in May, 1974, understandably described by India as a PNE, Peaceful Nuclear Explosion. Having lived its life span, despite mid-term refurbishment in 1997, CIRUS was finally shut down on December 31, 2010.

It was in this positive atmosphere that India-Canada witnessed close cooperation in the early 1950s. Be it over the Korean crisis or the turmoil in Indochina, Indian and Canadian foreign policy postures converged a lot more than perhaps the worldview taken by Canada and the USA. As Canada's then High Commissioner to India, Escott Reid (1952- 57) observed in one of his dispatches to Ottawa, a few months after taking up his post in India: "My impression is that there is perhaps no western democratic country, whose foreign policy is closer to that of India than Canada." Interestingly, while this period roughly coincided with the special relationship phase of India-Canada relations, it also witnessed a progressive decline in India-US relations. India with its independent and non-aligned foreign policy was increasingly viewed by Washington as bothersome and an irritant. Military alliances and bases is what the USA was constantly working for while India steadfastly stayed away from any such tie-ups. This alienated India from the USA. Washington with its vigorous pursuit of its policy of containing Communism saw things only in black or white. Either you were with the USA or against it. The then US Secretary of State John Foster Dulles even dubbed the policy of non-alignment as something unethical and immoral. Reportedly, Canada was neither happy nor comfortable with such extreme rhetoric but, even if it tried, it could not restrain the USA.

A major irritant in India-US relations was when in 1954 Washington, decided to start giving military aid to Pakistan, despite India's strong opposition to this, convinced as it was, and rightly so, that Pakistan happily joining the US policy of containment of Communism was merely a ruse to build up its military capacity against India. India's cautioning the USA was of no use and its protestations fell on deaf ears in Washington. Once again, Canada was reportedly uneasy with these developments, but could do nothing or not much in the matter. The India-Canada special relationship possibly touched its highest point by 1956 when Canada played an active and very positive role in resolving the Suez Crisis of 1956 that had provoked a very strong reaction from India (Nehru describing the Anglo-French invasion of Egypt as "naked aggression"). Egypt's then leader, Abdul Gamal Nasser was a prominent member of the then trio, the other two being Nehru of India and Tito of Yugoslavia, leading the Non-aligned Movement. Canada's Foreign Minister, Lester B. Pearson, earned laurels for himself and his country and praise from India. The active role played by Pearson in resolving the Suez Crisis even earned him the Nobel Prize for Peace in 1957. Ottawa apparently managed to persuade Washington not to endorse the Anglo-French action, something that considerably helped the Canadian efforts.

In the meanwhile, the clouds of the Cold War were gathering fast. The Hungarian Crisis of 1956 and India's stand on it further disillusioned the West, Canada included. The Kashmir question at the UN and the West's blatantly obvious soft spot for Pakistan was progressively making India view the Soviet Union as a dependable friend. Indo-Soviet relations were on an upward swing in the aftermath of the Khrushchev-Bulganin visit to India in November, 1955. The divide between India and the West was only widening. This was beginning to strain the India-Canada special relationship as well. In the meanwhile, a new constant irritant was slowly emerging in India-Canada relations. Following the Geneva Accords of 1954 on Indochina that had set up the International Control Commissions for Vietnam, Laos and Cambodia, India was the Chairman of all three Commissions with Poland and Canada as members. Justified or not, Canada as a member increasingly felt unhappy with India's role as Chairman, which it perceived as invariably favouring the Communist side. In the eighteen years (1954- 1972) that these three Commissions functioned, it is roughly estimated that as many as nearly two hundred Canadian diplomats served on these three international bodies because of the policy of a quick turn over. Indochina assignments were viewed in Ottawa as hardship postings and, therefore, short. Most of these Canadian diplomats went back with somewhat unsavoury feelings about India and the role it was playing as the Chairman. Thus, gradually, a sizeable number of Canadian diplomats, mostly young and with years of service still left were to constitute a lobby at the Foreign Ministry in Ottawa that did not quite help India-Canada relations, to put it mildly. This factor was to play a negative and an important role as these "disillusioned" with India Canadian diplomats were to keep moving up in seniority over the years.

As one stepped into the 1970s further complications were to emerge. The year 1971 was particularly crucial. The East Pakistan crisis resulting very much from the wrong doings of West Pakistan, the resultant huge influx of refugees into India rightly viewed by it as another form of aggression and the unfriendly attitude of the West, the USA in particular. Between President Richard Nixon and his Secretary of State Henry Kissinger, there was no doubt left as to where their sympathy and support lay. The tilt was clearly in favour of Pakistan. The break-through in US-China relations following Kissinger's visit to China in the summer of 1971 had further altered the equations in the South Asia region with Pakistan feeling further emboldened in its nefarious designs against India, aided and abetted by the USA and also China. India was almost getting encircled by hostile intentions. It was under these circumstances that the Indo-Soviet Treaty of Peace, Friendship and Cooperation was signed in August, 1971. The brief India-Pakistan War of December, 1971 followed against this immediate backdrop of events. Pakistan was dismembered and humiliated. What was East Pakistan emerged as the new and independent nation of Bangladesh. Ninety five thousand Pakistani troops had laid down arms and surrendered to India, the largest number of POWs ever taken in history. The USA in particular and its Western allies in general (Canada included) were furious with India. So was China. Moscow was happy, while India was on top of the world. The Cold War divide was becoming even more prominent. With this new stature and confidence, India carried out its Peaceful Nuclear Explosion in May 1974 that infuriated the West and even more so Canada with its then Prime Minister, Pierre Trudeau, describing it as an act of "betrayal" by India. The special relationship between India and Canada had been laid to rest. But the overall context in which this happened and as explained above is most important and relevant. The way things were moving for several years, at least since the mid-50s, this was coming. India's nuclear test of May, 1974 may have only provided the final push down this road to what in the late 40s and early 50s was indeed a very special relationship.

For the next two decades, India-Canada relations were to get relegated to a very routine nature. Gone were the special warmth, cordiality and proximity. If anything, further complications were to hit this relationship from the 1980s and well into the 90s. Militancy and terrorism by the supporters of the so called "Khalistan" movement had their principal support in countries like Canada, the USA and West Europe, notably the UK and West Germany. Canada was a major point and the source for funding and, above all, providing a safe haven for the perpetrators of such acts of terrorism against India. The blowing up in mid- air of the Air India flight from Montreal resulting in the loss of over three hundred innocent lives, the "Kanishka" tragedy of 1985, caused further strains in India-Canada relations. India, for valid reasons, was not convinced that Canada was doing enough to check such elements openly hostile to India and operating from its soil. Canadian contentions of their liberal laws and, consequently, their pleas of helplessness did not cut much ice with India. The fact was that with the growing influence of the Sikh community in Canada, in certain constituencies at least, it was vote bank politics that Canada was indulging in. The continuing low in India-Canada relations did not generate enough pressure on the Canadian authorities to curb effectively the activities of such extremist elements operating from its soil with near impunity, however small their number. They were the small, but vociferous minority, while the large majority felt too vulnerable to raise their voice against them.

This was, over all, the scene as India-Canada relations entered the 1990s. But the 1990s witnessed some significant developments that were to have a positive effect on India-Canada relations. Asia was fast emerging as the Continent of the future providing a huge market and immense investment possibilities. Canada was beginning to feel and realize the need to spread out more into other markets, notably Asia and, thus, progressively reduce what was clearly its over dependence on the next door US market. The political scene too underwent a major change in the aftermath of the 1993 general election. The Conservatives were voted out of office and the Liberals under the leadership of Jean Chretien came to power. All this coincided, more or less, with major changes underway in India. The 1991 general election brought back the Congress Party to power, but this time under the leadership of P.V. Narasimha Rao. The Indian economy was in a bad shape indeed. Rao introduced the bold economic reforms that were to unleash India's economic capacity and potential. The world was quick to take note and almost overnight India acquired a major economic sex appeal. The Foreign Ministry in Ottawa was asked to work on a special report on India appropriately called "Focus India". The report's message was loud and clear. Canada must focus on India in a big way if it were not to miss out on the attractive opportunities offered by this huge market of over a billion people, a fast expanding middle class and a substantial number of highly educated and technically trained and qualified people. Come January 1996 and the Canadian "Team Canada" led by Prime Minister Jean Chretien and two plane loads full of top politicians and business executives descended upon India. As the Canadian Prime Minister declared in his very first address to a select large group of top Indian business executives, "Canada is back in India and we are here to stay". By all accounts, the visit was a success with substantial business deals concluded. Canada's post 1974 boycott of India, if one may put it that way, was over. If not yet a special relationship, the old warmth, cordiality and cooperation certainly promised a come-back after nearly a quarter century.

But, unfortunately, a major glitch was to develop again. India had consistently refused to sign the Non-Proliferation Treaty (NPT) and also the Comprehensive Test Ban Treaty (CTBT). In India's considered view, both these treaties were unequal in content and spirit and only sought to prolong the nuclear weapons monopoly of the five declared nuclear weapons States— the USA, Russia, the UK, France and China. India was for a total ban on and elimination of nuclear weapons, including by the above five. Finally, in May, 1998 by carrying out a series of nuclear tests, and formally declaring itself to be a nuclear weapons State, India showed to the world that it meant business. Not unexpectedly, India's action was denounced by the West, as also by China. Canada joined the Western bandwagon, condemned India and its then Foreign Minister, Lloyd Axworthy, even spoke of "punishing" India. Many Western countries imposed sanctions against India, Canada included. Invitations already extended by Ottawa, including to some senior Indian Ministers, were unceremoniously withdrawn, all high level interaction was stopped and all the hype and good work done in the very recent past in the context of India-Canada relations was virtually undone. It was a sad spectacle indeed.

Fortunately, this time, the near freeze in India-Canada relations was short lived only. The realization that India was too big and important a country to be shunned and ignored for long, dawned fast. Gradually, all the sanctions imposed were lifted, including by Canada. Normal exchanges and visits slowly resumed till things were back to normal. India was accepted as a responsible nuclear weapons State. Also, this time, there was to be no going back to what India-Canada relations were in the early days when Canadian economic aid to India was a crucial component of this relationship. It was to be no longer a donor-receiver equation. Instead, it was to be an active and growing partnership. Bi-lateral trade picked up momentum and Indian investments in Canada and vice-versa were to be the pattern of the future now. High level visits were resumed and increased in frequency. The Governor- General of Canada visited India twice, in 1998 (pre India's nuclear tests) and again in February, 2014. The Canadian Prime Minister, Stephen Harper, too has been to India twice, 2006 and 2012, both being highly productive visits. There have been numerous bi-lateral agreements covering a wide range of subjects. Even the supply of uranium by Canada to India is now very much on the anvil. Finally, the realization seems to have dawned that honest differences notwithstanding, this bi-lateral India-Canada relationship is much too important in mutual interest to be exposed or allowed to be effected by honest policy differences. The focus, instead, should be on areas of cooperation and partnership where the scope is enormous and the potential considerable. In other words, this relationship now appears to have entered the phase of maturity and balanced approach on both sides. The true meaning and significance of the quotation from Mahatma Gandhi: "Friendship to be real, must ever sustain the weight of honest differences" seems to have finally been grasped. Hopefully, this will be the trend of the future in the management of India-Canada relations. No longer they need to resemble a roller coaster ride. Instead, the trajectory should continue upwards only.

In this context, a highly significant development was the Indian Prime Minister Narendra Modi's official visit to Canada in mid-April, 2015. It was after a gap of forty two years that an Indian Prime Minister was paying a bi-lateral visit to Canada. That it was overdue would be obvious from the fact that since 1996, there had been as many as three Prime Minister level visits from Canada to India – Jean Chretien in January, 1996 and two by Stephen Harper, 2006 and 2012. Two Governor Generals of Canada also visited India in early 1998 and again in February 2014. This perceptible imbalance needed to be rectified and the Indian Prime Minister's visit in April, 2015 did exactly that. The fact that this visit took place during Mr. Narendra Modi's first year in office only added to its importance and significance.

Symbolic importance apart, the visit yielded a lot in substantial terms. A number of agreements and MoUs were signed covering diverse fields, such as education, research, technical cooperation, defense and cyber security, economic and trade relations, energy, infrastructure, manufacturing and skills, smart cities and agro-industry. But the deal that attracted maximum attention was the one under which the Canadian producer CAMECO agreed under a commercial agreement signed during the visit to sell more than three thousand metric tons of uranium to India over the next five years, beginning from 2015 itself, at an estimated cost of $ 254 million, for its nuclear reactors. This made Canada the first Western country to do so as regards India. So far, only Russia and Kazakhstan were supplying uranium to India. Canada had banned the export of uranium to India in the 1970s following India's PNE (Peaceful Nuclear Explosion) of May, 1974. The signing in 2013 of the Canada-India Nuclear Cooperation Agreement had marked the turning of a new page in India-Canada relations. But the commercial details and other modalities had yet to be worked out. To facilitate the commercial agreement, Canada's Prime Minister Stephen Harper took the important step of waiving Canada's initial demand for tracking of the nuclear fuel by its own authorities and agreeing instead to IAEA inspections, a position acceptable to India. Hopefully, this breakthrough decision by Canada will serve as an example for similar arrangements for the supply to India of uranium by the US and Australia, among others. Underlining the significance of the nuclear deal, Prime Minister Modi rightly stressed that: "It is not just commodities that we are dealing with when talking about uranium, it is the show of faith and trust between the two countries and it is really a building block for the future." Prime Minister Stephen Harper of Canada was expressing similar sentiments when he observed: "There have been unnecessary frosty relations for too long (between the two countries) and it is time to move ahead." And, Prime Minister Modi clearly pointed out the path ahead when he said that: "Few countries in the world can match Canada's potential to be a partner in India's economic transformation."

Chapter Ten – Political

It is quite common, while discussing India-Canada relations, to talk of the commonalities between the two countries. And, indeed, there are many. Both have vigorous parliamentary forms of government. Both have a federal structure. Both are successfully functioning democracies. Both have an independent judiciary. Both have a vibrant media. Both are multi-cultural societies and are proud of it. Both relish their unity in diversity. Both have a legal system inspired largely by the Anglo-Saxon system. Both are essentially English speaking countries. Both are members of the Commonwealth of Nations, India as a Republic and Canada with Dominion status. Further scrutiny might very well bring out more commonalities.

While all such commonalities do help in fostering close and cooperative relations, as past experience of India-Canada ties shows, they alone are no guarantee of good relations. In fact, this would be generally true of other countries as well. Commonalities do help and even facilitate meaningful interaction, but their role needs not be overemphasized or over-rated. India itself provides a good example of this dictum. It continues to have problems with most of its neighbours, with some serious, despite sharing so many commonalities with them, including history, culture, religion and geography. Coming back to India and Canada, even the presence of a huge Indian Diaspora in Canada does not necessarily help or promote friendly ties. While this element can and does play an important role in building bridges of friendship and cooperation, the significance of this role remains limited. Though the label, of Indian origin, is common to all, quite a few migrated to Canada from elsewhere, Africa and the Caribbean included. Even this label keeps fading away with each generation. Besides, for many, the main focus remains on areas of immediate interest rather than building and strengthening the nebulous entity called India-Canada relations. Some, even if a very small minority, might even work against it as it fits in better into their own nefarious agenda, more on this later in the separate chapter on the Indian Diaspora.

The geographic location of a country plays a crucial role in determining its political stance and attitude, indeed of so many other policy aspects. Canada's geographic location and, therefore, its circumstances vastly differ from those of India. Canada has only one land neighbour to contend with, the USA to its south, and with that neighbour, for nearly two centuries now, it has had tension free, friendly and increasingly cooperative relations. The Canada-USA border is easily one of the longest unguarded one in the world. The economies of the two countries are heavily entwined and the two-way trade is a highly important aspect of their relationship. The same holds good for cultural flow and the movement of people. In many ways, it is a unique relationship and the two pose no security threat to each other. Indeed, they are close partners in this important area, including as founder members of the North Atlantic Treaty Organization (NATO).

As compared to all this, India is very differently placed. It is a sad fact that India has a troublesome, unsettled, and to an extent at least, a hostile neighbourhood with no choice, but to deal with it. As is often said, a country, like an individual, can choose its friends, but not its neighbours. From the very beginning since independence, India has had to contend with this unfortunate reality and situation, something that has quite naturally played a crucial role in the formulation of its policies, both domestic and even more so foreign. It is, therefore, essential, or at least desirable, that any country working on its relations with India, keeps this factor in mind and, better still, shows sufficient understanding of it and sensitivity towards it. India's policy of non-alignment has been very much a product of this consideration of its circumstances as also its extra proximity to certain countries in the conduct of its foreign relations.

Since the mid-1950s till the demise of the USSR in 1991 and even after that with Russia as the successor State, India's close ties with cooperation in several crucial fields, provides a good example to illustrate this point. During the early years of "special relationship" between India and Canada, the latter, it seems in hindsight, had a different understanding of it. Canada's focus on Asia, the happening Continent, gelled well with the role that India was actively playing under Nehru's leadership. Unlike with Washington, India's role in world affairs as an acknowledged leader of the emerging group of non-aligned nations, was viewed differently and positively by Ottawa. Indeed, the two countries cooperated closely and the respective leadership of the two sides got along very well. But as the Cold War atmospherics spread, national postures also underwent change with consequent complications. A stage came, mid-1950s onwards, when the West, Canada included, increasingly viewed with suspicion, even disapproval, India's growing proximity to Moscow. But what the West conveniently chose to ignore or overlook was that its own handling of India was, to a considerable extent, responsible for gradually almost pushing India towards the Soviet Union. Over the Kashmir question before the UN, the West tried hard to put India in the dock, so to say, by solidly backing the aggressor Pakistan just because it willingly became a party to the West's containment of Communism policy and happily offered its territory to US military bases. On numerous occasions, it was the Soviet veto that bailed India out of the anti-Indian resolutions sponsored and pushed by the West in the UN Security Council. When it came to economic growth and development, India, with its emphasis on the role of the State or public sector, again the West was either lukewarm or downright unwilling to offer the hand of assistance and cooperation. Post 1962, when India was made to realise the importance of defence preparedness, again the West was unwilling to help in any meaningful long term manner. Even with regard to the supply of vital military equipment, it either refused or quoted terms, both financial and political, that were clearly beyond India's reach and, therefore, unacceptable. Compared to all this, it was Moscow that offered the hand of friendship and cooperation on terms that were attractive enough for India to accept. This included the supply of hardware, including military, transfer of technology and all under the convenient Rupee-Rouble agreement that did not put additional strain on India's desperate hard currency situation. Friendly and soft, long term loans further padded up the Soviet offers. It is to be regretted that the US led and influenced the West, who refused to take any of this into account and instead kept creating situations simply not acceptable to India. This was because of the focus on Pakistan, who was more than willing to be an active partner in all the Western designs. It is a different matter that all this pampering of Pakistan including generous aid, both military and economic, did not do much good to Pakistan either. Today, including the same West, it is widely viewed as a failed or failing State, torn by internal divisions and virtually a safe haven for terrorists and extremists, whose main target is the West, notably the USA. On the economic side, Pakistan has proved to be a basket case and a bottom less pit. The West seems to have realised all this, but one wonders if it is willing to acknowledge and accept its faulty policies of the past. Either willingly or reluctantly, to give it the benefit of doubt, Canada went along with all this, thus letting its view of

India get increasingly prejudiced. A sad chapter indeed when one recalls the days of "special friendship" between India and Canada.

Even India going nuclear was the result of geo-political circumstances that the West was unwilling or unable to accept and comprehend. India's nuclear programme, much maligned and misunderstood by its critics, was so because they refused to take note of India's genuine security concerns. Following the brief border war with China in 1962 that had totally exposed India's military unpreparedness', China was going ahead full steam to become a nuclear weapons State. It achieved this target by 1964 and, thereafter, it was essentially a question of building up its nuclear arsenal along with a matching delivery system. True, the West, notably the USA was its principal target, but its fast growing nuclear muscle also posed a serious threat to India with which it had and still continues to have an unsettled and a long border. Either India could totally cave in by rendering itself totally vulnerable to this new threat posed by China or do something about it. It reluctantly chose the latter path in the process, if anything, wasting away precious time and letting the threat only grow, as the critics would rightly say. Simultaneously, through its "all weather friend" Pakistan, China actively helped it to develop nuclear weapons. China was, thus, in its own scheme of things, encircling India and increasing the pressure on it. It is hard to believe that the West was unaware of all this. It simply chose to look the other way, while Pakistan was, with Chinese assistance and also that of North Korea (for the delivery system by way of missiles), by all accounts, virtually sitting on a "basement bomb", but the West again chose to remain a silent spectator. How else can one explain Pakistan carrying out its own nuclear tests literally within days of India doing so in May, 1998?

While Canada took all this as almost a personal offence since it had been the first country way back in the 1950s to extend the hand of nuclear cooperation to India, the West and its close friends indeed took a very harsh view of India going nuclear. Instead, if only this group of countries had taken a more realistic view and shown better understanding for India's genuine security concerns, things need not have turned ugly the way they did. Canada tries to follow an independent foreign policy, but as a member of the Western alliance, it generally has to go with the thinking and posturing of its allies, notably the USA. Its ability to influence the USA is there and possibly it even tries to do so from time to time, but its capacity in this respect should not be overrated or over-estimated. It has its own geopolitical and other limitations.

Both Canada and India will have to accept and reconcile themselves with this reality, while dealing with each other, namely, a balanced understanding of each other's circumstances and, consequently, the policy curves, even when there are honest differences. Hopefully, this realization has finally dawned upon both sides now.

While a sound political relationship is essential to any bi-lateral relations, to make them truly enduring and meaningful, economic and commercial padding is not just desirable, but very necessary. It was this that brought Canada back to India in the mid-1990s, it was this that kept its period of annoyance with India post May, 1998 short and it this that is now pushing ahead Canada-India relations in the right direction. If since the turn of the century, India- Canada relations have been maintaining an upward trend, including by way of high level visits and exchange of other important delegations, it is because of the factor of mutual benefit accruing from an active and growing economic and commercial relationship. Two-way trade is growing fast and on the economic side, both countries are being increasingly drawn towards each other by investments. The recent (March, 2014) purchase by the Indian Oil Corporation of ten per cent in Canadian shale and LNG business worth $ 900 million and the Canadian Pension Plan Investment Board (CPPIB) deciding to enter the Indian market are just some of the latest indicators (as of March, 2014) to show that things seem to be moving in the right direction between the two countries. This trend, if maintained, should prove to be a much better guarantee of an enduring and a mature political relationship.

Summing up, the partnership dimension that India-Canada relations have now acquired is to be welcomed. The potential for growth is considerable. The two countries do not pose any serious or major threat to each other's vital interests, be it political, security, economic or commercial. And yet, the scope for further growth and expansion in all such and more areas is appreciable. After the ups and downs in this relationship, over the last six decades or so, both sides appear to have realised that as long as they respect and understand each other's sensitivities and areas of vital interest, no further road blocks need be encountered. One hopes that this realization will get firmly ingrained in the conduct and management of this vital and mutually beneficial relationship.

Chapter Eleven – Economic and Commercial Ties

The pattern of Canada-US relations has benefitted both sides considerably and continues to do so. More specifically, on the economic and commercial side, the two countries are heavily dependent on each other. Canada with its rich natural resources satisfies substantially the ever growing demands of a huge economy like the US. The big neighbour to the South, the US, also absorbs a major segment of Canadian manufactured products and whatever else is covered by its exports. For years, this arrangement has been working smoothly and to the benefit of both sides. Not only Canada's abundant natural resources, but also its high quality and wide range of manufactured goods find easy entry into the next door US market. However, there is a down side to all this, a realisation that has gradually dawned upon Canada and its economic and commercial community. This over-dependence on one market is like being in a tight and warm hug, comforting and convenient may be, but also, at times at least, somewhat disconcerting. In a way, it even makes you feel somewhat vulnerable. If the other side acts tough at times and even tries to pressurise, your options suddenly emerge as limited. In any case, it gives only a limited exposure to your strengths and attractions to the wider world that lies beyond North America because you have seldom made a serious and determined effort to venture into markets and opportunities that are available elsewhere. The slow realisation of all this, spurred by the emergence of huge new markets and opportunities in Asia, Africa and Latin America, has been a major factor favouring a change in the Canadian economic and commercial mind-set. This process has been particularly active and visible since the 1990s and has been picking up momentum over the last two decades now. The results are already beginning to show. From a little over eighty per cent of its foreign trade being absorbed by one market, the US, the figure has progressively come down to the early seventies and the trend continues. The same goes for Canada's economic forays abroad, distant markets and destinations included. In short, Canada is now marketing itself a lot more vigorously and its economic and commercial footprint is gradually getting noticed. With this has also come the realisation that it has a lot to offer to the emerging and developing markets of the world and to get a lot from them too. The growing India-Canada economic and commercial ties should be seen in this context.

Without indulging too much in the blame game, it may be said that matching the Canadian smugness was perhaps the Indian indifference. For much too long, North America for many in India meant essentially the USA. Much bigger in territory compared to the USA, Canada living in the shadow of its neighbour to the South seemed to be quite happy with its lot and others treated it with matching neglect. Few bothered to look at the enormous opportunities offered by Canada or the attractions of actively dealing with it. But while talking of India and Canada, there were blissfully some redeeming features.

Even before India attained independence in 1947, a few major segments of corporate Canada, multinationals like Bata and Alcan had entered the promising Indian market way back in the 1930s. By all indications, both have and continue to perform in India harmoniously and successfully with Bata, because of the nature of its products (footwear) almost becoming a household name, even in the remotest village or hamlet with, interestingly, few being aware of its Canadian origin. Howe India could be given as another example. It uses its Canadian engineering and managerial experience in successful cooperation with its highly professional staff in India. Thanks to the low profile and modest approach of Corporate Canada, many of Canadian manufactured and sophisticated products have been widely in use in India over the years without an average Indian realising that they are of Canadian origin and manufacture. Products of the De Havilland Aircraft Company of Canada, notably the Beaver, the Otter, the Twin Otter, the Dash Seven and the Dash Eight are all well-known names to the Indian aircraft industry. The same can be said of Bombardier of Canada that is currently supplying coaches to the fast growing urban metro rail service in India, including the Capital, Delhi. Even in a highly crucial and important sector like nuclear energy, it was Canada that supplied India its first nuclear reactor, the CIRUS, way back in the 1950s. A few other major examples of direct Canadian Corporate presence in India would include Agra International Ltd, Bank of Nova Scotia, Balcorp (India) Ltd, Bell Canada International (Tata Services), Lucas Aerospace Ltd, Northern Telecom, Seagrams India Private Ltd, SNC

Lavalin Inc and Raytheon Canada. These are only a few illustrative examples to show that Canada's highly sophisticated manufacturing capacity has not been unknown to India. But for a variety of reasons, it has not made the same splash in India as say manufactured products from sources like the USA, the UK, Germany, France or Japan. Perhaps, the Canadian marketing has not been vigorous enough. As already explained, for much too long Canada was happy with a huge next door outlet like the USA and did not pursue things beyond. May be the Indian side remained too US centric while dealing with North America. But, happily, the scene is changing; indeed it has already changed considerably. Both India and Canada appear to be fast discovering each other with happy results already there to see.

Starting from the 1990s, this process of mutual awareness between India and Canada has been on the increase and since the turn of the century, the momentum has picked up encouragingly. Besides growing high level interaction between the business communities of both the countries, including corporate leadership, the two sides are increasingly in touch with each other by way of visits, etc. On the economic side, the fundamentals of this relationship have also undergone a sea change. Though appreciative of the generous economic aid that India received from Canada in its early years after independence, with Canada being among the very first countries to undertake a major development assistance programme in India under the Colombo Plan, the trend now is for both sides to view it as a partnership, equally benefitting both sides rather than as giver and receiver of generous aid. Canada's CIDA (Canadian International Development Agency) played a significant role till the transformation of this growing relationship into what it is now, a partnership. The focus now is more on mutual investments. Recent examples like the buying by the Indian Oil Corporation of ten per cent in Canadian shale and LNG business worth $ 900 million and the Canadian Pension Plan Investment Board's (CPPIB) decision to enter the Indian market are significant pointers of the likely future trends by way of economic cooperation between the two countries. According to Statistics Canada, the two way foreign direct investment (FDI) between Canada and India reached record levels in 2009 at $ 3.6 billion. Of this, Indian investment in Canada totalled nearly $ 3 billion, while Canadian FDI in India in 2009 totalled $ 601 million.

That the opportunities are enormous is now well recognized by both sides. The areas of interest are many and clearly identified. From India's point of view, Canadian expertise in several vital areas should be of particular interest. These would include hydroelectric projects and technologies (the first Canadian built hydroelectric project in India was completed in the State of West Bengal in 1953), telecommunication equipment and technologies, equipment and technologies for the oil and gas sector, computers and communication systems for informatics, development and use of forest wealth including waste management, equipment and technology for the exploitation of oceanic resources including tidal power, mining and metallurgical development equipment and technology, long term contracts for the purchase of primary products like sulphur, zinc, potash, (uranium hopefully to be added soon to this list), newsprint and paper, transportation equipment and technologies for railways (including electric locomotives of 5000 horse power and above and special long lasting rail tracks of hardened steel), equipment for ports (specially self-unloaders), smaller aircraft for regional air couriers, equipment for airports including miniature remote vehicles for use in airport security systems and avionics, mass urban transport systems and defence including some highly specialised electronic devices for naval ships, high-tech electronic and electrical equipment and technology including remote sensing equipment, food processing equipment and grain handling equipment and technology. The list, though already quite exhaustive, could get expanded as interaction between India and Canada increases. This is what some experts would call matching Canada's technological capabilities with India's growing requirements.

Of particular interest and significance is that, notably in the last decade, India-Canada economic cooperation has acquired an omni-directional character. Many sectors of the Canadian economy are now developing or executing India related strategies. The two visits to India by the Canadian Prime Minister, Stephen Harper, in the space of three years (2009-2012) and at least fifteen ministerial visits to India since 2006 resulted in path breaking agreements on civil nuclear cooperation, the launch of research partnerships between major Canadian research-intensive universities and their Indian counterparts, the ongoing negotiations on CEPA and FIPPA as well as the opening of a new Consulate in Bengaluru. Earlier Canada had opened trade offices in Hyderabad, Kolkata and Ahmadabad in 2009. The total number of Canadian missions in India now stands at eight, one of Canada's largest networks abroad. All these recent developments have moved India-Canada relations to a new transformative stage. Prime Minister Manmohan Singh visited Canada in 2010 for the G-20 Summit combining it with a bilateral visit.

Nothing speaks more or better than hard facts. The fast growing and wide ranging economic cooperation between India and Canada is perhaps best brought out through statistics and related details. Notably, in the last decade, Canada has welcomed large scale Foreign Direct Investment (FDI) by India in different sectors of the Canadian economy. From a measly figure of C$ 29 million in 2001, the figure had jumped to C$ 4.4 billion by 2011, thus, placing India in the 13th rank in terms of FDI into Canada. Though considerably lagging behind, Canadian FDIs into India during the same period, however, kept increasing at an assuring pace to move up from C$ 145 million in 2001 to C$ 587 million in 2011 putting Canada 40th in terms of Canadian FDIs abroad. Recent trends, mentioned earlier, indicate a promising future for this important aspect of India-Canada economic cooperation. Further confirming this encouraging trend is the fact that two major Indian Banks, the State Bank of India and the ICICI Bank have already six branches each in Canada. Two other major Indian Banks, the Punjab National Bank and the Bank of Baroda are expected to make an entry into the Canadian market soon. The Royal Bank of Canada and Scotia Bank already have branches in India. Since good Banks know where and when to enter the market, these trends do augur well for India-Canada economic co-operation. Till the end of the last century, only the State Bank of India, with two branches, operated in Canada and only Scotia Bank the other way round in India.

As the above figures clearly show, Indian investments in Canada have been moving up quite impressively in the last few years, especially in the information technology and software sectors. Indian companies with substantial operations in Canada include VSNL (TATA), Aditya Birla Group, Hindalco, Essar, Tata Consultancy Services, BFL Software, Patni Computer Systems, Satyam Computer Services, WIPRO and Infosys Technology. Other areas of significant Indian investment in Canada are financial services and pharmaceuticals. For more details, see Annexure I to this Chapter.

Considering that at one stage India was possibly the largest recipient of Canadian overseas development assistance, this list (and still growing) of Indian FDIs in Canada along with Canadian FDIs in India clearly bring out how the fundamentals of this bilateral relationship have changed from the earlier donor recipient nature to a healthy, growing and mutually beneficial partnership.

Keeping pace with this welcome trend towards mutual investments, trade relations between India and Canada have been showing an equally promising upward swing. Compared to the 1990s when even touching or crossing the C$ one billion mark in the two-way trade was virtually a cause for celebration, the bilateral trade during the period 2006-2011 increased from $ 3.1 billion to $ 5.2 billion. The global economic recession, however, did not spare India-Canada trade, which in 2009 fell by $698 million or 16 per cent in US dollar terms. India's overall exports to Canada showed a 15 per cent decline in 2009 as compared to the 2008 figure. Likewise, Canada's exports to India fell by 17 per cent for the same period. Encouragingly, bilateral trade picked up in 2010 with India's exports increasing by 17.8 per cent with imports from Canada increasing by 5.9 per cent with the total bilateral trade thus showing an increase of 11.6 per cent over the previous year (2009). This positive trend continued in 2011 when bilateral trade crossed, for the first time, the $5 billion mark, that is an increase of 28.35 per cent over 2010. India's exports to Canada registered a handsome growth of 25 per cent while imports from Canada were up by 31.7 per cent.

Items figuring prominently on Indian exports to Canada include: Medicines, garments, diamonds, chemicals, gems and jewellery, petroleum oils, sea food, engineering goods, marble and granite, knitted garments, rice, electric equipment and plastic products, etc. Major items of Canada's exports to India being : Pulses, fertilizers, newsprint, aircraft and aviation equipment, diamonds, copper ores and concentrates, bituminous coal, wood pulp, unwrought aluminium, asbestos, photographic equipment, lumber and ferrous waste, etc.

Accepting the growing importance of India-Canada commercial ties, a multi-product Brand India Expo was organized in March 2012 at Ottawa's prestigious and centrally located Convention Centre. The obvious aim of this effort was to expose Canadian business, consumers and decision makers to the range, quality and richness of products from India. Taking part in this Expo were nearly fifty business houses from India. Items on display included carpets, textiles and apparels, jute, decoration items, fashion jewellery and accessories, tea, spices, coffee, sea food, wines, rice and processed food. The India Tourism Office and the State Bank of India also participated in this Expo. The Canadian Department of Foreign Affairs and International Trade (DFAIT), the Trade Facilitation Office (TFO Canada), the India-Canada Ottawa Business Council (ICOBC), the India-Canada Chamber of Commerce (ICCC), the Canada-India Business Council (CIBC) and the State Bank of India were Knowledge Partners in organizing this Expo that was inaugurated jointly by Canada's Minister of Foreign Trade, the Indian High Commissioner to Canada and the Chief Minister of the Indian State of Arunachal Pradesh on a visit to Canada. Present on this occasion were several Canadian dignitaries, members of the diplomatic corps in Ottawa, leaders of Canada's commerce and industry and of the Indo-Canadian community besides the media. The effort was a success by all accounts.

Very much indicative of the fast growing cooperation between India and Canada, both in terms of quality and quantity, the two countries have established various mechanisms to interact on an annual basis in areas of mutual interest. For a detailed picture of this aspect see Annexure II to this Chapter.

To further bolster bilateral cooperation in economic, commercial and other related fields, the two countries have established a number of mechanisms with the objective of further expanding cooperation. These include Trade Policy Consultations, Annual Trade Ministerial Dialogue, Science and Technology Committee, Joint Industrial R and D projects in the areas of Nano Sciences/Nano Technology, Information and Communication Technology, Biotechnology, Health Research and Medical Devices, Alternate Energy and Sustainable Environmental Technologies, Earth Sciences and Disaster Management, Environment Forum, Agriculture Cooperation, Post-Harvest and Processing Technology, Food Safety, Quality, Packaging and Agricultural Marketing, etc. The list is essentially indicative of the growing multi-dimensional cooperation between India and Canada. There is also an Energy Forum, Cooperation in the field of Mining, a Health Steering Committee with areas identified for cooperation in Life Style Diseases, Public Health and Disease Surveillance.

This increasing cooperation naturally entails more frequent interaction and visits. Air services between India and Canada have been the beneficiaries from this. India and Canada signed an Air Services Agreement on July 20, 1982. Entering into force on August 31, 1982, this agreement underwent subsequent amendments in 1987, 1991 and 1998. Following a successful round of negotiations on Civil Aviation in 2005, the two sides agreed to substantially increase flights both ways and Air India restarted a direct service between New Delhi and Toronto. From September, 2007, Jet Airways, a private Indian airline also began its flight on the sector New Delhi-Brussels-Toronto as agreed by the two countries.

During the first official visit to India of the Canadian Prime Minister, Mr. Stephen Harper, in November, 2009 the Prime Ministers of the two countries jointly announced the celebration of the Year of India 2011 in various locations in Canada. The inaugural event was followed by a variety of cultural programmes in Ottawa and fourteen other cities in Canada. The year 2011 also witnessed the launching of the Canada-India Centre for Excellence in Science, Technology, Trade and Policy. In this context, the year 2011 also saw a Canada-India Innovation Summit, a Festival of Indian Writing, a CAPEXIL trade show in Canada, an Indian Film Festival, the 150th Birth Anniversary celebrations of Rabindranath Tagore, to mention a few highlights only. The Brand India Expo in March, 2012 was a logical follow-up to all these developments and events in 2011. India was, thus, very much on the map of Canada.

While considerable satisfaction can legitimately be derived by both sides because of this unfolding scene marking a new high in India-Canada relations, there should be no room for complacency. It has taken considerable effort by both sides to bring these bilateral relations to this level. This should only encourage them to keep building up further on this super structure. The potential is there for anyone to perceive. The process must go on, if anything with increased momentum.

Chapter Twelve – The Indian Diaspora

The Indian Diaspora in Canada today numbers a little over a million (nearly a quarter from Punjab) in a country with a total population of thirty five million. In other words, one out of every thirty five Canadians presently is of Indian origin, an impressive ratio indeed. And, it is not just the numbers, those of Indian origin in Canada are doing well for themselves in virtually all walks of life and occupations. Even in the political field, they have established their presence well and constitute today an important constituency. They are to be found as elected members of Provincial legislatures and also of the Federal Parliament. This was first accomplished following the general election of 1993, when as many as three members of the House of Commons in Ottawa were of Indian origin, including, for the first time in the history of the Canadian Parliament, a turbaned Sikh, Gurbax Singh Malhi, from Toronto. Subsequently, political leaders of Indian origin were to occupy posts of Federal and Provincial Ministers. In the late nineteen nineties, the province of British Columbia was to even have an Indian origin Premier, Ujwal Singh Dosanj. In short, in the last one hundred years, the Indian Diaspora in Canada has indeed come a long way, in numbers, prominence, influence and stature. But this journey over a century has not at all been an easy one. It is, if anything, a saga of hardship and struggle, under extremely difficult conditions that included blatant discrimination, at times even insults and humiliation. This struggle required considerable grit, determination, patience and resolve to survive till things started changing for the better and today's reality was firmly established. For all this, the Indian Diaspora in Canada deserves to be saluted. But the almost painful and heart rending beginnings of this saga cannot and must not be forgotten.

In all probability, the first Indians to set their eyes on Canada were the Punjabi soldiers from the Hong Kong regiments travelling through Canada after participation in Queen Victoria's Diamond Jubilee celebrations in London, England, in 1897. What they saw of Canada impressed them, lots of good land, thick forests, scenic landscape and good weather. Even cold weather did not quite deter them because they were used to it, given the harsh winters of the land of their origin, notably Punjab and the other North-Western parts of India. Altogether, Canada looked like a land of opportunity, which when matched with their capacity for hard work, promised good rewards. Word of all this travelled fast to India and the adventurous types, and there were plenty of them, soon started making travel plans to make it to this far off land, but otherwise full of opportunity. The first wave of immigrants from India, mostly Sikhs from Punjab, was to reach Canada between 1904-1908. Nearly five thousand East Indians, as they were locally labelled, but mostly young male Sikhs from the Punjab province of India, came to British Columbia looking for jobs on railway construction, in the lumbering mills and in forestry. Though mostly unskilled and uneducated, they nevertheless found favour with their employers as they were hard working, dependable, willing to work for long hours and the white employers favoured them since they could pay them less than white men for the same work. This was to gradually even result in some resentment amongst the white work force.

It can be surmised that these early immigrants from India did not even have long term plans of staying on or settling down in Canada. Initially, the lure that brought them to Canada was to make money and return to India. They had come to a cold and visibly hostile environment. The handicaps they suffered from were many – language problem, poor education, lack of proper housing and health care and above all the culture shock. And all this combined with open racial discrimination and segregation. There was more than an undercurrent of anti - Asian feeling amongst the whites that these early Indian immigrants encountered. Fellow Asians like the Chinese and the Japanese came across the same unwelcoming attitude, often bordering on hostility. The Chinese head tax had been raised to $500 per person in 1903 and all Asians were lumped together when it came to this discriminatory treatment. The local media painted all Asians with the same brush often portraying them as dirty, diseased, uncivilized beings, who were incapable of adapting to Canadian ways. Photographs of that period show that the Indian immigrants even took to dressing like Westerners and how even their women, at least in public, took to wearing long skirts, stockings and shoes, so that they could merge with the local scene and be acceptable. What must have been a very hard decision from the point of view of their religion, many Sikh immigrants even shaved off their beards and cut short their hair. Even this almost cruel decision posed problems. White barbers would not oblige them with their services leaving them with no choice but to turn to Japanese or Chinese barbers. As if all this was not enough, the working and living conditions of the early Indian immigrants were abysmal, to put it mildly. Far away from home, no family life or comfort, long working hours, low wages, poor or no medical facilities and almost shocking living conditions with dozens of single men packed into communal bunk houses. Between 1904 and 1920, there were only nine women immigrants from India. Life for these early immigrants was indeed cruel, lonely and harsh. To cap it all was the open discrimination and segregation they were constantly exposed to. Even reaching Canada was not easy; first by train to Calcutta and then by steamer to Hong Kong. All immigrants seeking entry had to come to Canada by continuous journey and with through tickets from the country of their birth or nationality. There being no direct passage those days from India to Canada, via Hong Kong was the only choice available. An immigrant from India was also required to possess at least $200, while immigrants from Europe needed only $25. They were obliged to undergo medical and sanitary examination upon arrival in Canada and their being accepted in Canada was subject to favourable labour conditions prevailing at the time. Thus, it was hardship of the long journey made worse by the element of uncertainty at the end of it. Racism and injustice were a fact of life for all Asians in Canada. For those from India, who were technically British subjects, it was made worse by open political and racial discrimination. As British subjects, they had the right to vote in all elections. But this was blatantly denied to them and in 1907, the government of British Columbia passed a bill into law to disenfranchise all natives of India not born of Anglo-Saxon parents. Thus, all immigrants from India were automatically denied the right to participate in municipal or provincial or indeed any elections. The implications of this were to be far reaching and till Indian independence in 1947, all Indian immigrants remained excluded from the political process in British Columbia and were denied the right to become Canadian citizens. As if all this was not enough, fed by strong anti-Asian feelings among trade unionists, politicians and the media, the Canadian government adopted a new policy and issued an order-in-council on January 08, 1908 with the intention of drastically curtailing, if not completely stopping, immigrants from India. No wonder, from 1908 to 1920, only 118 immigrants from India entered Canada. In fact, in 1908, there was even an effort or at least a proposal made to deport all those, who remained in Canada to British Honduras so as to effectively rid the country of "Hindoos" (a term loosely used to denote all those from India) in order to "keep Canada white". H.H. Stevens, the leader of the Asiatic Exclusion

League and a City of Vancouver alderman, went on record to state in 1907: "We contend that the destiny of Canada is best left in the hands of the Anglo-Saxon race, and are unalterably and irrevocably opposed to any move which threatens in the slightest degree this position--- As far as Canada is concerned, it shall remain white, and our doors shall be closed to Hindoos as well as to other Orientals." Faced with today's reality, Stevens surely must be turning in his grave now, but it has been a long and tough journey for Indian immigrants to Canada. The infamous "Komagata Maru" incident of 1914 has to be seen in the context of such openly hostile and racist atmosphere then prevailing in Canada.

Since immigrants were required to come to Canada only via continuous passage and there being no direct passage available from India to Canada, an enterprising Indian businessman, Gurdit Singh, thought of a way out. He chartered a Japanese freighter, "Komagata Maru" to challenge the Canadian immigration laws. Picking up passengers along the way in Hong Kong, Shanghai and Yokohama, besides a cargo of coal in Japan destined for Canada, "Komagata Maru", with Gurdit Singh himself on board along with 376 Indian immigrants (mostly Sikhs from Punjab) arrived in Vancouver on May 23, 1914. The ship was forced to anchor in the harbor as the Canadian immigration authorities refused permission for the ship to dock. The Khalsa Diwan Society of Vancouver, founded in 1907 to look after the affairs of the Vancouver Gurdwara, tried their utmost to persuade the Canadian authorities to let the passengers on board "Komagata Maru" land. They even offered to pay the mandatory $200 per person. But all appeals to the Canadian government's sense of justice fell on deaf ears. Only twenty two of the three hundred and seventy six passengers on board were allowed to land, since they fell into the category of former residents of Canada.

This legal wrangling went on for two months in what was the peak summer season on the West coast. The shore committee formed to face this crisis took care of the hapless passengers on board the "Komagata Maru" by way of food, essential supplies, charter costs and all other expenses during their internment aboard ship. An estimated $70,000 were spent on all this, all raised voluntarily within the small Indian community. The summer heat and the increasingly intolerable conditions generated considerable tension. An attempt by the local police to board the ship failed as they were pelted with coal. Finally, the Canadian authorities ordered their navy cruiser "Rainbow" to blow up the ship if it did not leave Canadian waters. Faced with this impossible and hopeless situation and the firm resolve of the Canadian authorities not to relent, "Komagata Maru" left Vancouver on July 23, 1914, exactly two months from the date of its arrival. It was escorted out of the Canadian waters by the cruiser "Rainbow" and left for India with its passengers feeling utterly despondent, frustrated and humiliated. While "Komagata Maru" was on the high seas, Canada became involved with World War I, which had just broken out. Months later, when "Komagata Maru" reached Calcutta all aboard were charged with attempting to overthrow the British government. Troops opened fire on unarmed men, killing over fifty. The rest were imprisoned and tortured, with many even hanged.

This entire extremely sad episode caused serious repercussions. The Indians in Canada felt devastated, their morale touched a new low, they lost faith in Canadian institutions and their sense of justice and fair play. A corrupt immigration official, William Hopkinson, was shot to death and an Indian named Mewa Singh was hanged for his murder. A sense of gloom generally prevailed across the small Indian community. Many went back to India having lost all hope and faith. Some migrated to the next door United States in search of better social and economic conditions. Not surprisingly, by 1918, the number of Indians in British Columbia had dropped to a low of about seven hundred. In the year 1914 not even one Indian immigrated to Canada. The following year, 1915, saw only one and the figure remained stuck at zero in 1916, 1917, 1918 and 1919. It very slowly picked up pace in subsequent years, never touching the figure of even one hundred, the highest being in 1930 at eighty. The only somewhat positive development during this entire phase was that in 1919, the immigration restrictions on bringing over wives and children under eighteen were lifted. But family reunification was not instant. It was not until 1920 that women and children started coming out from India. But the number of immigrants from India again dipped to a low of three in 1941 and none at all for three years running, that is, 1942, 1943, 1944 and only one in 1945. World War II apparently had its impact on this. But the scene slowly, very slowly, changed in the post-World War II period. With the Canadian economy booming and a lot more attention being paid to general reforms and improvement, fields like education and health care received special attention. There was demand for skilled hands like teachers and doctors. The 50s, 60s and 70s witnessed a fair number of university level teachers and doctors from India being not just accepted, but welcomed in Canada. From the figure of 1,154 in 1964, Indian immigrants to Canada had increased to 5,313 by 1971.

The stigma of second class residents with no voting rights was removed only in 1947. Just three months after the formation of the interim government in India, preparatory to independence, in December 1946, India formally suggested to the Canadian government to persuade the government of its province of British Columbia "to confer the franchise on the small Indian community in that province and thus rectify the present anomalous position, which is a source of humiliation to Indians." Indicative of the prevailing Canadian attitude towards India, by April 1947, this was accomplished and the franchise conferred. Four years later, Canada removed "a second source of humiliation to Indians" by ending its immigration rule that barred Indians (as indeed other Asians) from entering Canada as immigrants unless they were wives or unmarried children under eighteen of Canadian citizens legally resident in Canada. Following a formal agreement with India, Canada threw open immigration to Indians going beyond "close relatives" to cover a hundred and fifty Indians annually. It should be mentioned in this context that the size of this general quota was less important and more relevant was the symbolic gesture on Canada's part of removing legal discrimination. Significantly, this agreement was signed on January 26, 1951, India's Republic Day.

Tracing in some detail this background is essential to comprehend and appreciate as to how painfully slow and difficult this journey has been for the Indian Diaspora in Canada. The "Komagata Maru" episode happened exactly a century ago (1914). The scene today (2014) has changed beyond recognition. Nothing brings this out better than hard facts. In 2013, 33,000 Indians immigrated to Canada. Around 60 per cent were economic migrants and the rest were families. Most in the former category were technical entrepreneurs and even venture capitalists. A further sign of the changing times is that in 2013, Canada issued more than 1,30,000 visitor visas to Indians and 14,000 Indian students went to Canada for higher studies. The days of "Komagata Maru" are definitely behind us now. But it has been a tough and long journey.

The large Indian Diaspora in Canada today indeed does India proud. Canadians of Indian origin are to be found in virtually all walks of life and most of them, by all accounts, are doing well and contributing impressively to the growth and prosperity of Canada. Apart from trade and agriculture, people of Indian origin are there in various professions including science and technology, the IT sector, banking and finance, real estate, education and the medical field. Today, there would scarcely be a hospital in Canada without at least one doctor of Indian origin and the same goes for the universities and colleges across the country. And, it is not just the numbers, many of Indian origin have excelled in their respective fields of work, occupying senior positions, and are held in high regard for their professional acumen and dedication to work. The Indian Diaspora distinguishing themselves in the political field has already been mentioned at the beginning of this chapter.

The sentiment openly expressed a century ago that Canada is best left in the hands of the Anglo-Saxon race is today as irrelevant as it would sound misplaced, almost to the point of being ridiculous. Today, it is openly acknowledged that Canada is very much made up of immigrants and indeed depends on immigration to maintain the dynamism of its economy. This aspect is best brought by the fact that over 3,00,000 new immigrants come to Canada every year, with nearly ten per cent from India. In fact, Canada prides itself in being a highly diverse country – both in terms of landscape and natural resources and in terms of population. In 1971, Canada became the first country in the world to adopt a multiculturalism policy affirming the equality of all citizens. Canada's mosaic culture not just allows, but encourages (to an extent even financially) the preservation and growth of various cultures that immigrants from different parts of the world have brought along with them.

The Indian Diaspora, while merging well with the overall Canadian scene, has, as a result of this policy of multiculturalism, successfully preserved its identity and thereby only added to the richness of the Canadian cultural mosaic. Be it the dress or the performing arts, the rich Indian cuisine or religious diversity, all co-exist and thrive in Canada. The entire landscape of the country is dotted with Hindu temples, Muslim mosques, Sikh gurdwaras and places of worship of other religious denominations. Indian classical music and various dance forms are taught and performed at various places across the country. The huge number of Indian restaurants proves the growing popularity of the Indian cuisine even amongst those of non-Indian background. Indian art finds a place of pride in museums and art galleries across Canada. A walk down Toronto's Gerard Street or Vancouver's Punjabi Market would be like being anywhere in India except for the overall unique Canadian ambience, weather included, besides, of course, the general surroundings.

Though Canadians of Indian origin (the Indian Diaspora) are to be found literally in all parts of the country; in numbers and concentration, the scene varies from province to province. According to the National Household

Survey of 2011 in the ten Canadian Provinces and three Territories, the largest number to emerge was in Ontario at 6,78,065 followed by British Columbia at 2,74,065. But in proportion to the total population of the province, British Columbia was first at 6.3 per cent followed by Ontario at 5.4 per cent. The other major concentrations to emerge were Alberta at 1,25,105 or 3.5 per cent of the total population, Quebec at 48,535 or 0.6 per cent of the total population, Manitoba at 21,705 or 1.8 per cent of the total population and Saskatchewan at 10,040 or 1.0 per cent of the total population. Provinces like Nova Scotia (4,640 or 0.5%), New Brunswick (2,605 or 0.3%), Newfoundland and Labrador (1,395 or 0.3%) and Prince Edward Island (255 or 0.2%) had comparatively small numbers. Amongst the three Territories, Yukon led with 310—0.9 per cent, followed by North West Territories 165—0.4 per cent and Nunavut 80—0.3 per cent. But, to repeat, there is no part of Canada that does not have at least some people of Indian origin. Amongst the cities, Toronto leads with 5,72,250 or 10.4 per cent of the total population followed by Vancouver with 217,820 or 9.6 per cent of the total population. In other words, in Toronto and Vancouver nearly one out of every ten inhabitants of the city is of Indian origin. Other Canadian cities with substantial Indian Diaspora are Calgary (66,640-5.6%), Edmonton (49,795-4.4%), Montreal (45,640-1.2%), Ottawa (25,545-2.1%), Winnipeg (19,855-2.8%), Hamilton in Ontario (18,270-2.6%), Kitchener in Ontario (16,305-3.5%) and Victoria in British Columbia (7,260-2.2%).

A few other highlights that may be mentioned in passing are: Toronto today has the largest Indian community in Canada. Around 20 per cent of the entire Indian community in Canada resides in the Vancouver area with the highest density concentrations to be found, besides Vancouver, in Surrey, Burnaby, Richmond, Abbotsford and Delta. Though a large majority of Indo-Canadians in the Vancouver area are of Punjabi Sikh origin, there are also Indo-Canadians of other ethnic backgrounds including Gujarati, Tamil, Malayalees, Bengali, Goan Christians and Sindhi. Calgary, with five per cent of the Indo-Canadian community residing there, has one of the fastest growing Indian communities in Canada with Indians being now the second largest minority in Calgary after the Chinese.

As regards places of worship, the first Sikh gurdwara of North America was built in 1911, the Guru Sikh Temple at Abbotsford BC, though some claim that a gurdwara was built earlier in 1908, but shut down a few years later.

Some other prominent gurdwaras in Canada include the one in Mississauga or the Dixie gurdwara. Another large gurdwara is the Sri Guru Singh Sabha in the Toronto area and is connected to England's gurdwara Sri Guru Singh Sabha. The Khalsa Diwan Society is responsible for most of the gurdwaras in Canada as well as the Guru Sikh Temple.

The largest Hindu temple in Canada is the Shri Swaminarayan Mandir in Toronto covering a total of 3000 square meters. Hindu temples, big and small, are to be found in other parts of Canada as well.

Many Indian Muslims along with Muslims of other nationalities worship at one of the largest mosques in Canada, the ISNA Centre in Mississauga.

The Ismailis have the first Ismaili Jamatkhana and Centre at Burnaby in British Columbia. This high profile building is the second in the world with other locations in London, Lisbon and Dubai.

The majority of people of Indian origin from Goa in Canada are Roman Catholics. They share the same parish churches as other Roman Catholics of Canada.

The Indo-Canadians or the Indian Diaspora in Canada reflects not just the religious and cultural diversity of India, but also its linguistic diversity. Almost all of them speak English with varying levels of proficiency. Being one of the two official languages of Canada and much more widely in use compared to French, the other official language, and hailing from India where widespread use of English is still the norm, even as a link language, Indo-Canadians have no choice, but to be proficient in English, notably those in different professions and active in public life. This is widely the case and it would be rare indeed to come across an Indo-Canadian, who does not possess at least a good working level knowledge of English, with quite a few excelling in it.

But the link with their original Indian language is still very much there, notably with the older generation. The most widely spoken Indian language is Punjabi, which is in wide use in Punjab, Haryana, Himachal Pradesh and Delhi. But those in Canada originating from the Punjab province of Pakistan also speak Punjabi. Tamil is another widely spoken language not only amongst those coming from the Indian State of Tamil Nadu, but even by Sri Lankans originating from the Tamil speaking parts of Sri Lanka. Urdu is primarily spoken by Indians from certain parts of Northern India and also those from the Hyderabad region of South India besides those from Pakistan. Hindi is used by Indo-Canadians from across North India and also by some of Indian descent from Africa and the Caribbean. Gujarati is used by those from the Indian State of Gujarat and also by Indians (Ismailis) from East Africa. Though Marathi is common amongst those from the Western part of India, some Zoroastrians from the same region, though only a small percentage of the Canadian population, also speak Marathi. Bengali is in common use amongst those from the Indian State of West Bengal, but as a language they also share it with those from Bangladesh. The number of those speaking Malayalam is quite large and they hail from the Indian State of Kerala. There is a small community of English speaking Goans from East Africa, but only a few of them have retained their original language, Konkani. The Indian Diaspora in Canada is, thus, a true linguistic mosaic.

This linguistic, ethnic and religious diversity also largely determines how they are organized to pursue their cultural and related activities. Thus, one comes across bodies like the Gujarati Samaj, the Bengali Association, the Kerala Samaj, the Tamil Association, etc. and yet they generally manage to also function under an umbrella body like an Indian Association. Canada's official policy of multiculturalism renders the functioning of all such bodies easy and yet they are very conscious of their overriding identity as Indians.

Though Indo-Canadians have largely managed to preserve their original cultural norms, something called Indo-Canadian culture has also been evolving, particularly amongst the second and third generations, notably the youth. This is easy to understand since this age group was largely born and brought up in Canada surrounded by a very different ambience. Consequently, Indo-Canadian culture has today developed its own unique identity compared to people from India. It is, thus, quite common to come across variations of the traditional Indian cultural elements identifying with mainstream North American cultural norms. Fusing the two cultures often produces interesting results, including what is referred to as fusion music. To cite another example, Punjabi youth in Canada are prone to mix the traditional Punjabi folk dance, "Bhangra" with hip hop based rhythm and beats, including with rap music entertainers.

Thanks to Canada's multiculturalism, the Indo-Canadians have the choice and easy access to Indian programmes and news directly from India. Following private initiative and a deal with the Canadian Radio-Television and Telecommunications Commission (CRTC), a Company known as Asian

Television Network ensured in 1997 the establishment of Indian television networks from India on Canadian television. Under this agreement with the CRTC, Indian television networks based in India are allowed to send a direct feed to Canada. All such channels have been branded under the private company called Asian Television Network. Indo-Canadians, and indeed even those outside this category but interested, now enjoy the facility of subscribing to TV channels from India by purchasing TV channel packages from the local satellite/cable companies. In the Greater Toronto Area, there are Radio Stations (FM) regularly broadcasting Indo-Canadian programmes and content. In some major urban centers, the Indian Diaspora has even started newspapers particularly focused on areas of interest to the large Indo-Canadian community. Some major examples would be: Canindia News in Toronto and Montreal, The Asian Star and The Punjabi Star in Vancouver and The South Asian News in Edmonton and Calgary. The film industry, both in India and Canada, has also been quick to catch on with this trend. In the past few years, there have been quite a few films with Indo-Canadian subject matter. Some examples would be: Masala in 1992 in English, Taal in 1999 in Hindi, Tum Bin – Love Will Find a Way in 2001 in Hindi, Jee Aayan Nu in 2003 in Punjabi, Dus in 2005 in Hindi, Neal 'n' Nikki in 2005 in Hindi, Humko Deewana Kar Gaye in 2006 in Hindi, Sweet America in 2008 in English, Kismat Konnection in 2008 in Hindi and Cooking With Stella in 2009 in English.

An interesting and significant feature of the Indian Diaspora in Canada is that besides tracing their origin directly to India, quite a few in Canada come from other parts of the world as part of the global Indian Diaspora. Faced with political turmoil and even prejudice, many Indians residing in East African countries, like Uganda, Kenya and Tanzania and some even from Zambia and South Africa left the region for Canada and other Western countries. Possibly, the largest chunk of immigration to Canada in this category was in the 1970s, when nearly 50,000 Indian-Ugandans were forced out of Uganda by the dictator Idi Amin with a sizeable number of them finding refuge in Canada. Some Indo-Caribbeans have also moved to Canada over the years bringing along with them a unique cultural blend of Indian, Western and "Creolised Caribbean" due to a long period of isolation from India. Some from this category do associate themselves with the larger Indo-Canadian community, but most prefer to stay within the fold of the Indo-Caribbean community. There has also been migration of some Indians from the Middle-East to Canada. A few Indian businessmen and professionals in countries like the

UAE, Oman, Kuwait and Saudi-Arabia have moved to Canada essentially for the sake of better educational facilities for their children post schooling. The Malayalis constitute a sizeable number of such migrants to Canada. Fiji in the South Pacific has been another source of some Indo-Canadians. Though constituting nearly 50 per cent of the population, since Fiji's independence increased hostility between the native Fijian population and the Indo-Fijians and the resultant political confrontation has, over the years, prompted some Indo-Fijians to move to countries like New Zealand, Australia, the USA and Canada. Finally, some Indo-Canadians have moved over to Canada even from countries like the UK and the USA, essentially for economic and family re-union reasons. The Indian Diaspora with this background has not only settled well in Canada, but done well and contributed to the richness of the Canadian mosaic. Some examples would be an award winning novelist like M.G. Vassanji known for works on the plight of Indians in East Africa. Some attained prominence in television broadcasting (Suhana Meharchand, Nirmala Naidoo and Indira Naidoo-Harris), all migrants from South Africa. Two high profile Indo-Africans deserving mention would be Zain Verjee and Ali Velshi. Varjee was educated in Canada, while Velshi's father, Murad Velshi, was the first member of the Ontario legislature of Indian descent. Irshad Manji, an Indian of Ugandan origin, who settled down in Canada, became an acclaimed advocate for secularism and reform in Islam. These are just a few illustrative examples to show how some migrants to Canada of Indian descent contributed richly to the overall Canadian scene.

The growing importance of the Indian Diaspora across the world, roughly estimated to be around thirty million, is very much recognized by the mother country, that is, India. "The Pravasi Bharatiya Diwas" observed each year on January 09 and the creation of a separate Central Ministry for Overseas Indians are clearly an acknowledgement of the significance attached to the role of the Indian Diaspora. Over the years, there had been a demand on the part of the Indian Diaspora for dual citizenship. Many of them had acquired the citizenship of the countries in which they had settled down. And yet, they wanted to maintain close links with India, including the facility of being able to visit India without going through the hassle of acquiring a visa. While agreeing to dual citizenship posed certain practical problems, a convenient way out was found by India starting to issue two types of documents to those interested and otherwise qualified for them. The PIO (Person of Indian Origin) card that allows visa free entry into India up to fifteen years and the OCI (Overseas Citizen of India) that allows this facility for life. This latter category (OCI) was the closest that India could go to dual citizenship. It allowed all privileges due to an Indian citizen except for the right to vote and acquire agricultural land. These facilities that have been available for quite a few years now seem to have largely satisfied the Indian Diaspora, though the right to vote still keeps coming up from time to time, at least from certain quarters.

But without appearing to be belittling the role and importance of the Indian Diaspora, not just in Canada, but across the globe in general, one must not lose sight of certain ground realities. India's approach to its Diaspora has evolved over the years since independence. The realization has been there since the beginning that people of Indian origin, who have, for whatever reasons, adopted a foreign land as their home owe, first and foremost, loyalty and commitment to the country that has adopted them. That is where they live now, that is their true home now, that is where they have raised their families, educated and settled their children; that is where most of their worldly possessions are now, their circumstances in life are very much dependent on the overall situation in that country, in short, their destiny in life is very much interlinked with the situation prevailing at any given time in that country. This is the unavoidable reality that must never be ignored or overlooked. Nor should any attempt be made to encourage elements, such as dual loyalty or commitment. Where the scope lies is to try and ensure that they continue to view the fact of their Indian origin with pride and an urge to forge closer ties between and act as a bridge of understanding and cooperation between the country that is their home now and the country of their origin. If relations between the two countries are cordial, friendly and cooperative, the task of the Diaspora is rendered a lot easier. But, if unfortunately, these relations turn sour, for whatever reason, the Diaspora truly has to fend for itself. The mother country or the country of their origin can and will in most likelihood voice concern over their legitimate interests if they are threatened, but it is unlikely to go beyond this. Yes, if the mother country has considerable clout, military, diplomatic, economic or commercial, things may turn out to be somewhat different. But there are limitations even of power and talking specifically of India, this factor was sadly demonstrated in the case of Uganda in the 1970s and again in the case of Fiji in more recent times. There were the expected expressions of concern on India's part, there were plenty of tea and sympathy on offer, but in concrete terms, India was either unwilling or unable (more likely) to do much beyond remaining a distressed spectator to the sad unfolding events and trying to arouse the conscience of the world.

The Diaspora, on its part, cannot be expected to easily forget or forgive such harsh realities.

Emotions, family ties and memories are alright to an extent as a bonding factor, but their strength need not be stretched beyond a point. There are other factors at play too. Not all Indians living abroad necessarily left their home country under happy or pleasant circumstances. Some, however small their number may be, insist on carrying the baggage of the past with them. Some continue with a limited agenda in life that includes either actively working against the interests of the country of their origin or, at least, remain indifferent towards this factor. They have chosen a new home for themselves and, if their current interests do not so demand, India is just another country for them. Even when at play, emotions and memories tend to fade with the passage of time. This is more so with each new generation. The parents or the first generation will necessarily have different feelings that do not get automatically passed on to their children, or the next generation, and even less so in the case of subsequent generations. They may carry on with the label "of Indian origin", but for all practical purposes, they are the products of a different country, society and system. They have been born there, educated and brought up there, have adopted the local mores and practices; very likely, do not even speak any Indian language; therefore, to expect them to have any special feelings for India is, frankly speaking, stretching things a bit far and being somewhat unrealistic. At best, India for them is a far off land, an ancient country and culture, perhaps exotic in some ways, but none of this by itself is enough to stimulate and induce a strong bonding or commitment towards India, the country of origin of their forefathers.

What will then keep alive the interest, and hopefully commitment, of the Indian Diaspora in general in the country of their origin, India? First and foremost would be the general image of India overseas. If it keeps getting projected as a country ridden with problems, like poverty, disease, lack of basic amenities like even safe drinking water, poor infrastructure, political squabbling and extreme slowness of vital decision making along with widespread corruption, the attractiveness of India will be a difficult product to market abroad. Emotional and sentimental bonds alone will not suffice. Presuming that a vast majority of the Indian Diaspora would be keen and happy to maintain active links with India; to cash in that feeling, India will have to project itself as a vibrant country where things are moving and where, at least, the basics are easily available. Just to illustrate, over the years, India has been trying hard to promote itself as a major and a popular tourist destination. Tourism, as is widely recognized, can be a major industry. Several countries, with much less to offer, have already demonstrated this and remain way ahead of India in this respect. As a tourist destination, India has almost everything to offer, its diversity, cultural richness, famous historical sites, endless variety of cuisines, its colourful costumes and oriental bazaars throbbing with activity and, not to forget, its geographic attractions ranging from stunningly beautiful mountain resorts to exotic beaches along its long coastline. One could easily further expand this list. And yet, what puts off many a visitor to India, the Diaspora included, who have got used to a different life style abroad, is the filth and squalor that unfortunately remains a common sight in many places, including those otherwise popular with tourists. Add to this our touts and beggars, who insist on harassing, almost pawing foreigners or anyone, who even remotely looks like a well to do visitor out to enjoy India. Even basic amenities like clean and usable toilets still remain only a wish in many places. It is not that those in charge or in a position to remedy the situation are not aware of these problems. They even talk about them. But till all this gets translated into reality on the ground, India's enormous and acknowledged potential as a major tourist destination will continue to suffer. It is action and efficient implementation that are lacking, not the awareness of the existence of such problems and shortcomings.

But apart from the general run of the Indian Diaspora, there is another category within this much larger group; small in number, but very influential and doing exceptionally well in life. They can not only serve as an important and effective pro-India lobby abroad but, at least, some among them have the financial capacity to become active partners in India's growth efforts by way of directly investing in different vital sectors of the Indian economy. This category certainly deserves special attention and consideration. When from 1991, India went in for, in a reasonably big way, economic reforms and liberalization of the country's economy, foreign investors apart, this category of the Indian Diaspora began to show keen interest in India and was even enthusiastic about it. But as the pace of economic reforms and the opening up of the Indian economy began to slacken, this interest in India also began to waver. Quite understandably, such people are, if at all, moved by emotions and sentiments only to a very limited extent. They are essentially hard-nosed pragmatic businessmen, who have achieved high success abroad because of this approach. The lure of doing something for the mother country may be there, but hard core business considerations are what ultimately count.

And, this is where India has been faltering. Doing business with India or investing in its economy still remains something of a challenge for many. Our various rules and regulations; the numerous time consuming, often frustrating, clearances involved; corruption and influence peddling, to name a few, very often put off many, who are otherwise interested in India and in doing business with it. Unfortunately, for a quarter century, since 1989, India has suffered the curse of weak coalition governments at the center and regional forces have been gaining ground. This has often prevented either the formulation of clear cut and attractive policies or their implementation, even if somehow they were pushed through. This has considerably tarnished India's image abroad, including amongst the Diaspora. Weak, unstable, indecisive governments do not attract potential investors or partners. Annual events like the Pravasi Bharatiya Diwas (January 09) do not go far enough to change this image. Make investing in India simple, safe, speedy and efficient and things will change for the better and soon. Increase India's economic sex appeal, if one may put it that way, and people will come on their own. After all, India has several features going in its favour in this respect. It is rich in resources, both natural and human, it has a huge educated and trained work force, it is increasingly becoming a high consumption society, particularly its growing middle class, it is a huge market of over a billion people hungry for a better deal in life. As the world acknowledges, India's economic potential is enormous and the country is raring to go ahead and fast. What is needed is the right conditions and atmosphere.

Hopefully, the recent (May, 2014) dramatic change in the country's political landscape and the emergence, after twenty five years, of a stable and a strong government at the Center, will bring about the much awaited, desired and needed change and for the better. The task is not going to be easy. Several hurdles have still to be overcome and crossed. A new mind set and work culture have to be evolved. Many cobwebs have to be cleared. But, at least, there is hope now. Once India transforms itself from the present category of "an emerging great power" to actually being a great power in the economic, commercial, military and political sense, it will automatically instill a different sense of pride amongst most of the Indian Diaspora and from that will emerge a different commitment towards working for the interests of the mother country, that is, India. Annual events, like the Pravasi Bharatiya Diwas will then acquire a different meaning and significance, going beyond the symbolic importance that they represent as of now.

The outcome of the general elections of October, 2015 further confirmed the growing role, clout and importance of the Indian diaspora in Canada. In a House of 338 elected members, as many as nineteen were of Indian origin, nearly 6%. The general elections of 1993 had brought in, for the first time ever, three MPs in the Canadian House of Commons who were of Indian origin. This component kept increasing gradually over the years so as to touch nearly 6% of the total membership of the House of Commons in a span of just over two decades. It was a proud moment indeed for the Indian diaspora and a further confirmation of its growing involvement in Canadian affairs and politics.

Chapter Thirteen – The Road Ahead

When in the year 2014, Canada opted to send a Canadian of Indian origin, one Mr. Patel, as its' next High Commissioner to India, it was obviously not a routine diplomatic appointment. It was a clear further signal on Canada's part of its keen desire to strengthen and improve its relations with India even more, a process that had been clearly picking up momentum of late. In the historical context, this move on Canada's part had special significance too. This gesture coming exactly a century after the sad and tragic episode of "Komagata Maru", when in 1914, Canada refused just a few hundred hapless potential immigrants from India to even disembark on its soil. It was like finally putting the lid on this unfortunate century old episode. Canada was now not just ready, but visibly very keen to do business with India, welcome Indians on its soil and to build a strong partnership with India. The significance of the timing of this appointment was too evident to be missed, much less not to be appreciated.

It is quite common to enumerate the long list of commonalities shared by India and Canada. Both are vibrant democracies committed to a rule of law. Both have a federal structure and a parliamentary form of government. Both believe in multiculturalism. Both are examples of unity in diversity. Both are consciously pursuing the path of respect for basic human rights. Both are active members of the Commonwealth of Nations and share a common language, English. These are only a few commonalities and one could easily further expand the list.

But, however important these commonalities may be, they have not consistently ensured a cordial, friendly and cooperative relationship between the two countries. Enough has already been said in some earlier chapters of this book to bring out how turbulent this relationship has been over the last century. The beginning was particularly sad, as has been brought out in considerable detail in the chapter immediately preceding this one, the one on "The Indian Diaspora". In fact, the first half of the twentieth century was hardly a phase worth recalling. It is only after India gained independence in 1947 that things changed, in many ways almost dramatically and for the better. For a while, it was even a "special relationship". But this phase was relatively short lived. From the late fifties and through the sixties, seventies and eighties, India and Canada were cordial at best and indifferent, if not openly hostile, at worst. There were long spells when it was essentially a routine relationship. The nineties of the last century witnessed a promising upswing only to once again nose dive as the twentieth century was coming to a close. Much has already been written in this volume on this roller coaster ride of a relationship so that details and the reasons need not be repeated. A major shift occurred in the Canadian view of India as the two countries stepped into the twenty-first century and this happy trend appears to be not just continuing, but is increasingly picking up momentum. Why so, one may legitimately ask?

As regards the political and security aspects of this relationship, the two countries do share certain common objectives and have often even worked together to try and achieve them. Their commitment to peace and security, democracy, human rights, a free and vibrant media, to name a few aspects, is beyond question and is broadly accepted by both sides. But when it comes to translating these ideals into action, there can and will be honest differences of opinion. In the past, such differences, whenever they occurred, were allowed to cast a negative spell on the overall relationship. The realization seems to have dawned now that such occasional honest differences, because of the very different circumstances of the countries, have to be accepted in a mature manner and not be allowed to hit the fundamental interest of the two sides in maintaining and developing a friendly and cooperative relationship. It is this fundamental shift in how the two sides perceive each other that has possibly been the most encouraging development in recent times in India-Canada relations.

Talking of circumstances, Canada is, in many ways, very differently placed as compared to India. It shares its land border with only one country, the USA. A long border no doubt, but it is one of the most peaceful and tension free borders in the world. Since 1812, there have been no hostilities between Canada and the USA. That is two centuries now and any departure from this continuing scenario looks out of question. Canada is a close partner of the USA in virtually all fields, including security. Both are members of NATO and the two have fought side by side in several theaters from World War II onwards, including in recent times in Iraq and Afghanistan. In short, the two pose no security threat whatsoever to each other. In fact, Canada is a very fortunate country in many respects, including in terms of an important factor like national security.

In the case of India, things are not just very different, but almost the opposite. It lives in a troubled, unstable and, in many cases, an unfriendly if not openly hostile neighbourhood. It has in the North and the West nuclear armed States, China and Pakistan, and continues to have an unsettled border with both. Infiltrations, tensions, even occasional hostilities, are not uncommon. In less than seven decades since independence in 1947, India has had to fight five wars – 1947, 1962, 1965, 1971 and 1999, not to speak of continuing tensions or at least alerts, along its long land borders. No wonder the Indian armed forces, notably the army and other land security forces are possibly the most battle hardy in the world. Defense preparedness involving heavy financial burden has become a sheer necessity for India. India has no choice in the matter. Even its going nuclear in 1998 has to be seen in this context. This, no doubt, irked and upset certain countries, including Canada. But what India found unacceptable was the failure or refusal of such countries to look at things from India's perspective. If your national security is not directly threatened, you can afford to pontificate on the merits of peace and disarmament. But not if some of your neighbours are constantly posing a threat and trying to destabilize you. This cardinal difference between the circumstances faced by Canada and India, if not understood and appreciated, will keep causing setbacks to relations, even leading to misunderstandings and honest differences. Possibly, the most significant development in recent times has been the realization on Canada's part that India's circumstances are very different, its needs are different and these should at least be understood, if not appreciated. This change of mind-set, one would like to believe, has cleared a major roadblock that, in the past, kept disrupting the smooth flow of relations between the two countries. Just as India understands Canada's commitments to its Western allies, in both political and security matters, it expects reciprocal understanding from Canada, and indeed the wider West, of its circumstances that dictate certain postures and approaches. This new maturity in the bi-lateral relationship appears to have finally set in now, so that, in future, one can legitimately expect to realize the full potential of India-Canada relations, managing them to mutual advantage within the framework of honest differences that might keep cropping up from time to time.

Focusing next on the areas of agreement, economic and commercial ties will be the best guarantee of a healthy India-Canada relationship. Canada is very much a trading nation. Of all the G-7 countries, the Canadian economy is possibly the most dependent on trade. It draws a quarter of its income from international commerce. Canada's foreign policy vigorously pursues the objective of contributing to its economic prosperity and the creation of more jobs and with this in mind, it actively engages with a diverse group of trading partners around the world. Whether the country has a democratic form of government or not; whether it has respect for human rights in the traditional sense or not, Canada pursues this objective relentlessly. Its burgeoning economic and commercial ties with China would be a classic example to illustrate this point. It is pragmatism, not idealism that ultimately decides. Where its economic and commercial interests are not at stake, idealism can take the front seat with vocal emphasis on freedom, democracy and human rights. In a highly competitive world of international trade, Canada has the advantage of a sound economy that gives it the reputation of being a reliable trading partner. Its efficient economic management enabled it to weather the 2008 global economic crisis, or at least a slow-down, reasonably well, unlike its big neighbour to the South, the USA. Among the group of G-7 countries, Canada has had the strongest record of growth and job creation over the economic recovery. Canada is also the only G-7 country to have more than fully recovered the business investment that was lost during the global economic slow-down of 2008. And, Canada continues to counter challenges that emerge from the state of the world economy. Indicative of this objective on its part is its determination to get back to a balanced budget by 2015-16 through a judicious mix of spending reductions and further initiatives to stimulate the economy even more. Blessed with a lot of natural resources, including oil, gas and minerals, Canada has traditionally been a resource based economy. But the services sector has, over the years, come to play a very major role contributing today to over two-thirds of Canada's economic output.

In view of its heavy dependence on international trade, Canada is understandably focused on diversifying its economic and commercial opportunities with new and emerging economic powers, while consolidating its access to traditional markets in North America and Europe. The USA remains its largest trading partner. Canada's comprehensive relationship with Mexico continues to grow under the umbrella of NAFTA (North American Free Trade Agreement). Its trade relations with the European Union continue to be strengthened through the Comprehensive Economic and Trade Agreement. Canada is also actively deepening its engagement with Brazil and the Pacific Alliance countries.

Fully realizing that the global balance of power continues to shift with the rise of China, India, Brazil and other major regional players like South Africa, Indonesia, Japan, South Korea, Turkey, Mexico and the UAE, Canada is actively engaging with new partners in new ways—bilaterally and regionally—while continuing to capitalize on its key traditional allies and multilateral relationships. One of Canada's priorities in Asia includes promoting Canada as a reliable and stable supplier of liquefied natural gas to Asia's fastest growing energy market.

There is a clear message in all this for India and its matching keenness to further strengthen economic and trade relations with Canada. There is an obvious realization on both sides that instead of continuing to harp on the inevitable honest differences, the best guarantee of a strong mutually beneficial bi-lateral relationship is to focus on its economic and commercial content. Canada's future prosperity will increasingly be linked to the success of rising economies in the coming years. It is this factor that both India and Canada must constantly keep in mind while deliberating on the road ahead as regards India-Canada relations that are increasingly in the category now of a partnership. As brought out in detail in the Chapter on Economic and Trade Ties (Chapter 11), in recent years, India-Canada trade has been showing an impressive upward swing, and so have direct investments. More than four hundred Canadian companies currently operate in India and another eight hundred engage in regular transactions with Indian partners. Bilateral trade touched $5.2 billion in 2011, up 23 per cent from the previous year, and the two sides have been expressing a strong desire to take this figure up to $15 billion by 2015, an ambitious but not entirely an unrealistic goal. At least, the two sides are thinking big now. As for direct investments, if anything, currently at least, Indian direct investments in Canada are way ahead of Canadian investments in India. But serious efforts are afoot to rectify this imbalance and further improve things. The Economist Intelligence Unit has rated Canada as the number one place to do business in the G-7 group of countries. Present Indian investment in Canada is valued at about $3.7 billion and Canadian investment in India at around $644 million. Even if these figures are probably somewhat understated, it is realized on both sides that there certainly is room to improve. In order to encourage more Canadian investment in India, a Foreign Investment Promotion and Protection Agreement (FIPA) is being seriously negotiated by the two sides. The efforts (since November 2010) aimed at the early conclusion of a Comprehensive Economic Partnership Agreement (CEPA) between India and Canada should be viewed in the same context. With the recent (May 2014) dramatic changes on the Indian political scene and the increasingly visible signs of policy changes towards greater economic liberalization and reform, a framework as envisaged under these two proposed agreements should hopefully be materializing soon. CEPA, when concluded, will be a broad based free trade agreement. Canada's pension funds – amongst the largest in the world – are well placed to invest in India's infrastructure projects. Canada has the world's third largest oil reserves. Its natural gas resources are equally impressive. India, with its fast growing energy needs, is already focusing on Canada as a long term and reliable source of supply, including substantial direct investment in this sector of the Canadian economy. There is also considerable potential in the field of nuclear collaboration. Canada having got over its decades old reservations in this respect, with the Nuclear Cooperation Agreement now in force (since October, 2013) between the two countries, Canadian and Indian firms are now in a position to work together for the supply of materials, equipment and technology to meet India's energy security needs. There are four sectors where collaboration is already strong and where the potential for growth is particularly high, namely, food and energy security, innovation, education and infrastructure. These are the sectors where India's requirements are matched perfectly by Canada's strengths and capabilities.

As regards food security, Canada is already the largest supplier and exporter of pulses to India and a close collaborator in the fertilizers' sector. In 2012, Canada exported more than one million tons of Potash to India. All this places Canada in a position of a dependable partner in India's quest for its food security objectives. Besides, there is close ongoing cooperation between the two countries in areas, such as dairy and agricultural production, processing, distribution and monitoring.

On energy security, besides oil and natural gas where there is already close collaboration (in 2011, India imported approximately $ seventy five million worth of petroleum products from Canada), immense possibilities in respect of renewable sources like solar and wind energy are now recognized, while nuclear energy is now increasingly being viewed as a promising field in the near future.

As for education and innovation, Canada with its recognized excellence in the field of higher education is fast becoming a popular destination for Indian students. In 2013, more than 13,000 students from India chose Canada for higher studies, a four-fold increase from 2008. Besides the decades old links under the Shastri India-Canada Institute (SICI), Canadian institutions have entered into close to three hundred agreements with their Indian counterparts for student and faculty exchanges, joint programmes, curriculum development and research partnerships in areas like science, engineering, arts and humanities. Leading edge, high-tech Canadian companies are already present and operating in the Indian market. Additionally, as an acknowledged global leader in mobile applications, 3-D animation tools, gaming, wireless technologies, digital media, life sciences, aerospace and renewable energy, Canada is ideally placed to partner with India in these industries.

Infrastructure, which remains a weak link in India's growth efforts, is yet another area of close cooperation between India and Canada that has considerable potential. Canadian pension funds – amongst the largest in the world – are already well poised to invest in India's infrastructure projects. But going beyond the provision of funds, Canadian companies with their known expertise in engineering, management and construction of projects to build roads, bridges, railways, ports, airports and communication networks should make ideal partners in India's efforts towards a much more improved and efficient infrastructure so that it ceases to be a drag on the country's faster economic growth and development.

It should be clear by now that the potential for close cooperation between India and Canada is enormous. The particularly promising areas have been clearly identified, there is willingness and enthusiasm on both sides and positive trends in the growth of this relationship in recent decades and time provides the necessary push to go further and fast. The potential, in short, is enormous.

However, it will help a great deal in realizing fully this potential if people, which means the man in the street, the common man in both India and Canada feels a lot more committed and enthusiastic about making the most of this emerging partnership. This potential is generally well recognized amongst those in government and the corporate sector in both countries, besides of course a few other well informed sections of society. But this, though welcome and very helpful, is clearly not enough. What is needed is much more heightened mutual awareness. This shortcoming is there on both sides. There would be many in India for whom North America is almost synonymous with the USA. They view Toronto and Ottawa as far off places, but not New York or Washington. It is the same with many Canadians. They only have a somewhat hazy picture of India as a far off country ridden with problems. This mind-set needs to change on both sides. How many in India, for instance, know or realize that a substantial percentage of pulses that constitute an important and regular part of an average Indian's diet are imported from Canada? How many residents of Delhi know that several of the comfortable metro coaches, otherwise the pride of the national Capital, are supplied by Bombardier of Canada? Millions of commuters by India's massive rail network possibly do not know that the most powerful electric locomotives in use by the Indian railways are of Canadian manufacture and some are now being made in India with Canadian collaboration. Or that the special railway tracks, made of extra hardened steel, on certain very busy sectors or junctions come from the only plant making such tracks in the whole of North America (the USA included) situated in Sidney (not to be confused with Sydney of Australia) located in the North-Eastern part of Canada. These are just a few examples to show how wide the information gap is between the people of the two countries. An average Canadian is no better. He or she only has a somewhat hazy picture of far off India, the country of the Taj Mahal, but very little beyond that. The size of India and its population, its variety and diversity, the fact that it has high mountains, vast flat plains and a coast line of thousands of kilometers dotted with some exotic beaches and tourist resorts are amongst the little known facts about India. Even less realized is that India is the only country in the world to have an ocean bearing its name, the Indian Ocean. The focus somehow remains more on India's problems of poverty, malnutrition and other such areas of concern. What receives scant, if at all any, attention is from where India started at the time of independence in 1947 to where it has reached now. A country now of 1.2 billion (it was 360 million in 1947) being able to feed its people alone is something of a miracle. India's Green and White Revolutions have enabled the country not just to have sufficient agricultural and dairy products, build up reserve stocks, but to even export some of these products. Another area worthy of mention is the great strides made by the country in science and technology. The same goes for the health care system and the giant pharmaceutical industry. Scourges like small-pox and polio have been eradicated and the average life span of an Indian has risen from 29 years in 1947 to 68 now. When such bits of information about India are shared with an average Canadian, the reaction invariably is one of disbelief. One wonders as to how many Canadians know or realize that since independence, India has made impressive strides even in manufacturing and industry. From a country that in 1947 had to import even bicycles and sewing machines, India today has a major automobile industry. Leaving the bicycle age far behind, the country is today manufacturing its own scooters, motor cycles, automobiles, commercial vehicles like trucks and buses and all of a quality and reputation as to enable these products to be exported world-wide to several countries besides fully meeting the fast growing demand of the domestic market. Going beyond, India is now manufacturing its own military aircraft, war ships and tanks, etc. besides a range of other weapons to include sophisticated missiles of different categories. The country is now launching its own satellites as part of the communication revolution to hit the country. The number of mobile telephones alone now is close to a billion and still growing. Television transmissions via satellite are a routine and common feature serving even the remotest parts of the country. And, all this is just the tip of the iceberg as regards India's growth story.

If the two countries have to get closer and provide more flesh to this partnership, then mutual awareness must increase manifold.

Chapter Fourteen – India and Canada: A Quick Comparison of Some Basic Features

For the convenience of the reader, this Chapter seeks to compare India and Canada, very briefly indeed, in respect of some basic features.

Geographically, the two countries are located far apart, India in South Asia and Canada in North America. India with a land area of 3.29 million square kilometers is the seventh largest country in the world. Canada with a land area of 9,976,140 million square kilometers is the second largest country in the world, next only to Russia. India has a coast line of 7,516.5 kilometers whereas Canada's is 202,080 kilometers long, the longest in the world. India has the Arabian Sea to its West, the Bay of Bengal in the East and the Indian Ocean in the South. It is the only country in the world with an Ocean bearing its name. Canada has the Atlantic Ocean on its East, the Pacific on the West and the Arctic Sea to the North. India shares land borders with Afghanistan, Pakistan, China (Tibet and Sinkiang), Nepal, Bhutan, Myanmar and Bangladesh. Canada shares a land border with only one country, the USA, to its South. India is essentially a tropical country located between Latitude 8.4 degrees to Latitude 37.6 with the Tropic of Cancer almost running through its middle. But the entire Indian land mass is located above the Equator. Like Canada, therefore, it is very much in the Northern Hemisphere. India is known for its long hot summers, at least from early April till late September with temperatures, during peak summer, touching +47 degrees Centigrade at some places in the vast Indian plains. The summer season does get some respite from these scorching temperatures once the monsoon rains come, from mid-May in the South till July, August and part of September when rains, with varying intensity, cover the entire Indian sub-continent. But during the monsoon period, while the temperatures may not be too high, around mid to high thirties Centigrade, the humidity level goes up very high, at times touching 90 to 100%, thus making it very muggy and sticky. But in the mountainous regions, mostly in the North, starting from the Himalayan foothills, say from around six thousand feet, the long summer season is very pleasant, cool and agreeable. This accounts for several hill resorts, even large towns and cities, at this altitude and beyond. While in the Southern half of the country, the period from November till March is quite pleasant, the vast Northern plains experience a cold winter, with night temperatures around 3 to 4 degrees Centigrade, even hovering around zero at some places and with frequent heavy fog. During the same period, the Northern mountainous parts of the country have sub-zero temperatures as a normal feature with occasional to frequent heavy snow. Further North are the great Indian Himalayas with some peaks going up to 7000 to 8000 meters and beyond with heavy snow-fall from mid-September till late April or, at times, even early May. Some people living at altitudes much beyond 10,000 feet is not uncommon. In terms of climate and temperatures, therefore, India is a land of considerable variety. While some places can be hot, hotter and hottest through-out the year, others can be pleasant to cool to bitterly cold. In the extreme Northern part of the country, Dras in Ladakh ranks as the second coldest place in the world with the temperature dropping to -35 degrees Centigrade in winter. Though commonly viewed as a hot country, in truth, some places in the country most definitely defy this general categorization.

Like India, Canada too is in the Northern Hemisphere, but way to the North in North America, starting from 49 degrees Latitude going up virtually to the North Pole. During the short summer period, say from June till August, the lower parts of the country, from coast to coast, can have some balmy days and weather, with more in the Western parts than in the Eastern region. But a major portion of the country lies to the North, from 60 degrees Latitude and, therefore, in the Arctic zone with the usual cold to bitterly cold weather throughout the year. The Southern parts of the country, say up to a depth of 300 kilometers or so are, therefore, the places where most Canadians prefer to live. A common description is that where the coldest parts of the USA end, the warmest parts of Canada begin. Beyond 60 degrees north, it is essentially the vast openness and wilderness of Canada. If, in the popular imagination, India is a hot country, then by the same norm, Canada is a cold country. Even it's Capital, Ottawa, ranks along with Moscow (Russia) and Ulan Bator (Mongolia) as one of the coldest Capital cities in the world. Temperature dropping to 35 or 40, if not even lower, degrees below zero Centigrade is not entirely uncommon during the peak winter months and, of course, with plenty of snow.

In terms of population, India with 1.2 billion is the second most populous country in the world, next only to China. Canada's population is just about 35 million. Population density too offers a sharp contrast. As against India's 371 persons per square kilometer, the figure for Canada is just 0.3 person per square kilometer. India has not just a much larger population, but also a much younger one, the median age being 26.7 years as against Canada's 41.5 years. The average life expectancy in India is 68 years as against Canada's 81.5 years. The infant mortality rate in India is much higher at 44.6 deaths per thousand births as against Canada's 4.78 deaths per thousand births. Fertility rate is higher in India at three children per woman as compared to Canada's 1.59 children per woman. Birth rate too is higher in India at 20.2 per thousand as against Canada's 10.3 per thousand. India is also slightly ahead in sex ratio with 1.08 males per female with Canada at 0.99 males per female. In terms of literacy rate, Canada is way ahead at 99% as against India's figure of 62.8%.

Taking a quick comparative look at the economies of the two countries, India's GDP stands at $4.76 trillion as against Canada's at $1.51 trillion. But the prosperity of Canada comes out when one looks at the per capita income. Canada's per capita income is $40,500 while that of India's is just $3,900, though in PPP (Purchasing Power Parity) terms, it is about $12,000. India's growth rate has been around six per cent as against Canada's 1.8 per cent. Unemployment rate in India is around eight per cent as against Canada's seven per cent. India's official currency is the Indian Rupee and Canada's is the Canadian Dollar. The Indian Rupee is not yet a freely convertible currency, whereas the Canadian Dollar is.

An equally quick look at the main political features of the two countries should be also instructive. India is a Republic with one of the longest Constitutions in the World, a Federation with a Parliamentary form of government and a successfully functioning vibrant democracy. Canada is a Constitutional Monarchy, a Dominion with a Federal system and a Parliamentary democracy. The Indian Federation comprises of twenty nine States and seven Union Territories. The Canadian Federation consists of ten Provinces and three Territories. At the time of independence on August 15, 1947 India too had dominion status. But once its Constitution was ready and adopted on January 26, 1950, the country proclaimed itself a Republic. India's Head of State is the President, the present incumbent (2014) being Pranab Mukherjee and the Head of Government (as of May, 2014) being Narendra Damodardas Modi. In Canada's case, the British Monarch is technically the Head of State with the Governor General, as the Monarch's representative, acting as the Head of State for all practical purposes, including receiving credentials of all diplomatic envoys to Canada. But it should be clarified in this context that the Letter of Accreditation from the Head of State of the envoy's sending State is addressed to the British Monarch with the Governor General receiving it on behalf of the Monarch. All this flows from Canada being a Dominion. The present (2014) Governor General of Canada is David Johnston. The country's Head of Government is the Prime Minister, presently (2014) Stephen Joseph Harper. Voting age in both India and Canada is 18 years. The term of Parliament too in both countries is the same, that is five years. Both India and Canada have a bi-cameral Parliament, the Lok Sabha (lower House) and the Rajya Sabha (upper House) with the total strength of both Houses being 790 in the case of India and the House of Commons (lower House) and the Senate (the upper House) with a total strength of 413 in Canada's case. Parliamentary seats held by women stand at 11 per cent in India and 24 per cent in Canada. Technically speaking, India has two National Days—August 15 as Independence Day and January 26 as Republic Day. Canada's National Day is July 01, known as Canada Day when the country acquired Dominion Status in 1867.

Annexure I: Text of the British North America Act of 1867

Preamble and Part I "Preliminary"

The Act begins with a preamble that declares that the three provinces New Brunswick, Nova Scotia and the Province of Canada (which would become Ontario and Quebec) have requested to form "one Dominion...with a Constitution similar in Principle to that of the United Kingdom".[2] This description of the Constitution has proven important in its interpretation. As Peter Hogg wrote in *Constitutional Law of Canada*, some have argued that since the United Kingdom had some freedom of expression in 1867, the preamble extended this right to Canada even before the enactment of the Canadian Charter of Rights and Freedoms in 1982; this was a supposed basis for the Implied Bill of Rights.[3] In *New Brunswick Broadcasting Co. v. Nova Scotia (Speaker of the House of Assembly)*,[4] the leading Canadian case on parliamentary privilege, the Supreme Court of Canada grounded its 1993 decision on the preamble. Moreover, since the UK had a tradition of judicial independence, the Supreme Court ruled in the *Provincial Judges Reference* of 1997 that the preamble shows judicial independence in Canada is constitutionally guaranteed. Political scientist Rand Dyck has criticized the preamble, saying it is "seriously out of date". He claims the Constitution Act, 1867 "lacks an inspirational introduction".[5]

The preamble to the Constitution Act, 1867 is not the Constitution of Canada's only preamble. The Charter also has a preamble.

Part I consists of just two sections. Section 1 gives the short title of the law as *The British North America Act, 1867*. Section 2 indicates that all references to the Queen (then Victoria) equally apply to all her heirs and successors.

Part II "Union"

The British North America Act, 1867 established the Dominion of Canada by fusing the North American British "Provinces" (colonies) of Canada, New Brunswick, and Nova Scotia. Section 3 establishes that the union would take effect within six months of passage of the Act, and Section 4 confirmed that "Canada" was the name of the new country (and the word "Canada" in the rest of act refers to new federation and not the old province).

Section 5 lists the four provinces of the new federation. These are formed by dividing the former Province of Canada, into two; its two subdivisions, Canada West and Canada East, were renamed Ontario and Quebec, respectively, and became full provinces in Section 6. Section 7 confirms that the boundaries of Nova Scotia and New Brunswick were not changed. And Section 8 provides that a national census of all provinces must be held every ten years.

Part III "Executive Power"

Section 9 confirms that all executive powers remain with the Crown, as represented by a governor general or an administrator of the government, as stated in Section 10. Section 11 creates the Queen's Privy Council for Canada. Section 12 states that the executive branches of the provinces continue to exist and their power is exercised through the lieutenant governors, and that the powers exercised by the federal government must be exercised through the governor general, either with the advice of the privy council or alone. Section 13 defines the Governor-General in Council as the governor-general acting with the advice of the Privy Council. Section 14 allows the governor general to appoint deputies to exercise his powers in various parts of Canada. The commander-in-chief of all naval armed forces in Canada continues with the Crown under Section 15. Section 16 declares Ottawa the capital of the new federation.

Part IV "Legislative Power"

The Parliament of Canada, composed of the Crown and two houses (the House of Commons of Canada and the Canadian Senate) is created by section 17. Section 18 defines the powers and privileges of the parliament as being no greater than those of the British parliament. Section 19 states that Parliament's first session must begin six months after the passage of the act, and Section 20 holds that Parliament must hold a legislative session at least once every twelve months.

Senate

At the time of the Union, there were 72 senators (Section 21), equally divided between three regions Ontario, Quebec, and the Maritime Provinces (Section 22). Section 23 lays out the qualifications to become a senator. Senators are appointed by the governor general under section Section 24, and the first group of senators was proclaimed under section 25. Section 26 allows the Crown to add three or six senators at a time to the Senate, divided among the three regions, but according to section 27 no more senators can then be appointed until, by death or retirement, the number of Senators drops below the regular limit. The maximum number of Senators was set at 78, in Section 28. Senators were appointed for life (at the time), under Section 29, though they can resign under Section 30 and Senators can be removed under the terms of section 31, in which case the vacancy can be filled by the governor general (Section 32). Section 33 gives the senate the power to rule on its own disputes over eligibility and vacancy. The speaker of the Senate is appointed and dismissed by Governor General under Section 34. Quorum for the Senate was initially set at 15 senators by Section 35, and voting procedures are set by Section 36.

House of Commons

The initial composition of the Commons, under Section 37, consisted of 181 members, 82 for Ontario, 65 for Quebec, 19 for Nova Scotia, and 15 for New Brunswick. It is summoned by the Governor General under Section 38. Section 39 forbids senators to sit in the Commons. Section 40 divides the provinces in electoral districts. Section 41 continues electoral laws and voting qualifications of the time, subject to later revision, and Section 42 gives the Governor General the power to issue writs of election for the first election. Section 43 allows for by-elections. Section 44 allows the house to elect its own Speaker, and allows the house to replace the Speaker in the case of death (Section 45) or prolonged absence (47). The Speaker is required to preside at all sittings of the house (46). Quorum for the house was set at 20 members, including the Speaker by Section 48. Section 49 says that the Speaker cannot vote except in the case of a tied vote. The maximum term for a house is five years between elections under Section 50. Section 51 sets out the rules by which seats of the Commons are to be redistributed following censuses, allowing for more seats to be added by section 52.

Money Votes and Royal Assent

"Money bills" (dealing with taxes or appropriation of funds) must originate in the Commons under section 53, and must be proposed by the Governor General (i.e. the government) under section 54. Section 55 specifies that all bills require royal assent. Sections 56 and 57 allowed the Governor General to "reserve" or the British government to "disallow" Canadian laws within three years of their passage.

Annexure

Part V "Provincial Constitutions"

The basic governing structures of the Canadian provinces are laid out in this part of the bill. Specific mentions are made to the four founding provinces, but the general pattern holds for all the provinces.

Executive Power

Each province must have a lieutenant governor (Section 58), who serves at the pleasure of the Governor General (Section 59), whose salary is paid by the federal parliament (Section 60), and who must swear an oath of allegiance (Section 61). The powers of a lieutenant governor can be substituted for by an administrator of government (Sections 62 and 66). All provinces also have an executive council (Sections 63 and 64). The lieutenant governor can exercise executive power alone or "in council" (Section 65). The capital cities of the first four provinces were established by Section 66, but the Section also allows those provinces to change their capitals.

Legislative Power

Ontario and Quebec

Sections 69 and 70 established the Legislature of Ontario, comprising the lieutenant governor and the Legislative Assembly of Ontario, and Sections 71 to 80 established the Parliament of Quebec, which at the time comprised the lieutenant governor, the Legislative Assembly of Quebec (renamed in 1968 to the National Assembly of Quebec), and the Legislative Council of Quebec (since abolished). The first sessions of both legislatures were set for six months after the passage of the bill (Section 81), and since that time they can regularly be summoned by the lieutenant governors (Section 82). Section 83 prohibits provincial civil servants (excluding cabinet ministers) from sitting in the provincial legislatures. Section 84 allows for existing election laws and voting requirements to continue after the Union. Section 85 sets the life of each legislature as no more than four years, with a session at least once each twelve months under Section 86. Section 87 extends the rules regarding speakers, by-elections, quorum, etc. as set for the federal House of Commons to the legislatures of Ontario and Quebec.

Nova Scotia and New Brunswick

Section 88 simply extends the pre-Union constitutions of those provinces into the post-Confederation era.

Other

Section 89 sets the times for the first provincial elections, and Section 90 extends the provisions regarding money votes, royal assent, reservation and disallowance, etc. as established for the federal parliament to the provincial legislatures.

Division of Powers

The powers of government are divided between the provinces and the federal government and are described in sections 91 to 95 of the Act. Sections 91 and 92 are of particular importance, as they enumerate the subjects for which each jurisdiction can enact law, with section 91 listing matters of federal jurisdiction and section 92 listing matters of provincial jurisdiction. Sections 92A and 93 are concerned with non-renewable natural resources and education, respectively (both are primarily provincial responsibilities). Section 94 leaves open a possible change to laws regarding property and civil rights, which so far has not been realized. Sections 94A and 95, meanwhile, address matters of shared jurisdiction, namely old age pensions (section 94A) and agriculture and immigration (section 95).

Peace, Order and Good Government

It shall be lawful for the Queen, by and with the Advice and Consent of the Senate and House of Commons, to make Laws for the Peace, Order, and good Government of Canada, in relation to all Matters not coming within the Classes of Subjects by this Act assigned exclusively to the Legislatures of the Provinces; and for greater Certainty, but not so as to restrict the Generality of the foregoing Terms of this Section, it is hereby declared that (notwithstanding anything in this Act) the exclusive Legislative Authority of the Parliament of Canada extends to all Matters coming within the Classes of Subjects next hereinafter enumerated:

Section 91 authorizes Parliament to "make laws for the peace, order, and good government of Canada, in relation to all matters not coming within the classes of subjects by this Act assigned exclusively to the Legislatures of the provinces".[6] Although the text of the Act appears to give Parliament residuary powers to enact laws in any area that has not been allocated to the provincial governments, subsequent Privy Council jurisprudence held that the "peace, order, and good government" power is, in fact, a delimited federal competency like those listed under section 91 (see e.g. *AG Canada v AG*

Ontario (Labour Conventions), [1937] AC 326 (PC)). Canada's constitution therefore lacks a residuary powers clause.

First Nations, Inuit and Metis

Section 91(24) of the Constitution Act, 1867 provides that the federal government has the legislative jurisdiction for "Indians and lands reserved for the Indians." (Constitution Act, 1867 (U.K.), 30 & 31 Vict., c. 3, reprinted in R.S.C. 1985, App. II, No. 5 [hereinafter Constitution Act, 1867].) [6]Aboriginal Affairs and Northern Development Canada (AANDC) formerly known as Indian and Northern Affairs Canada (INAC) [7] has been the main federal organization exercising this authority (OAG 2011-06-04 p. 4).[8][notes 1]

Criminal Law

Section 91 (27) gives Parliament the power to make law related to the "criminal law, except the constitution of courts of criminal jurisdiction, but including the procedure in criminal matters". It was on this authority that Parliament created the Criminal Code of Canada, and it is on this authority that Parliament amends the said Code.

However, under section 92 (14), the provinces are delegated the power to administer justice, "including the constitution, maintenance, and organization of provincial courts, both of civil and criminal jurisdictions, and including procedure in civil matters in both courts". This allows the provinces to prosecute offences under the Criminal Code and to create a provincial police force such as the OPP and the Sûreté du Québec (SQ).

Section 91(28) gives Parliament exclusive power over "penitentiaries" while section 92(6) gives the provinces power over the "prisons". This means that offenders sentenced to two years or more go to federal penitentiaries while those with lighter sentences go to provincial prisons.

Property and Civil Rights

Main article: Section 92(13) of the Constitution Act, 1867
Further information: Canadian property law and Human rights in Canada

Section 92(13) gives the provinces the exclusive power to make law related to "property and civil rights in the province". In practice, this power has been read broadly giving the provinces authority over numerous matters such as professional trades, labour relations, and consumer protection.

Marriage

Section 91(26) gives the federal government power over divorce and marriage. On this basis, Parliament can legislate on marriage and divorce. However, the provinces retain the power over the solemnization of marriage (section 92(12)).

There are also several instances of overlap in laws relating to marriage and divorce, which in most cases is solved through interjurisdictional immunity. For instance, the federal Divorce Act is valid legislation, even though the Divorce Act has some incidental effects on child custody, which is usually considered to be within the provincial jurisdictions of "civil rights" (s. 92(13)) and "matters of a private nature" (s. 92(16)).

Works and Undertakings

Main article: Section 92(10) of the Constitution Act, 1867

Section 92(10) allows the federal government to declare any "works or undertakings" to be of national importance, and therefore remove them from provincial jurisdiction.

Education (Section 93)

Main article: Education in Canada

Section 93 gives the provinces power over education, but with significant restrictions designed to protect minority religious rights during a time when there was significant controversy between Protestants and Catholics in Canada over whether schools should be parochial or non-denominational. 93(2) specifically extends all pre-existing denominational school rights into the post-Confederation era.

Section 94

Section 94 allows for the provinces that use the British-derived common law system, in effect all but Quebec, to unify their property and civil rights laws. This power has never been used.

Agriculture and Immigration (Section 95)

Under Section 95, the federal and provincial governments share power over agriculture and immigration. Either order of government can make laws in this area, but in the case of a conflict, federal law prevails.

Part VII "Judicature"

The authority over the judicial system in Canada is divided between Parliament and the provincial Legislatures.

Parliament's Power to Create Federal Courts

Section 101 gives Parliament power to create a "general court of appeal for Canada" and "additional Courts for the better Administration of the Laws of Canada". Parliament has used this power to create the Supreme Court of Canada and lower federal courts. It has created the Supreme Court under both branches of s. 101.[9] The lower federal courts, such as the Federal Court of Appeal, the Federal Court, the Tax Court of Canada and the Court Martial Appeal Court of Canada are all created under the second branch, i.e. as "additional Courts for the better Administration of the Laws of Canada".

Provincial Power to Create Courts

Section 92(14) gives the provincial legislatures the power over the "Constitution, Maintenance, and Organization of Provincial Courts, both of Civil and of Criminal Jurisdiction". This power includes the creation of both the superior courts, both of original jurisdiction and appeal, as well as inferior tribunals.

Superior courts are known as "courts of inherent jurisdiction", as they receive their constitutional authority from historical convention inherited from the United Kingdom.

Section 96 Courts

Section 96 authorizes the federal government to appoint judges for "the Superior, District, and County Courts in each Province". No provinces have district or county courts anymore, but all provinces have superior courts. Although the provinces pay for these courts and determine their jurisdiction and procedural rules, the federal government appoints and pays their judges.

Historically, this section has been interpreted as providing superior courts of inherent jurisdiction with the constitutional authority to hear cases. The "section 96 courts" are typically characterized as the "anchor" of the justice system around which the other courts must conform. As their jurisdiction is said to be "inherent", the courts have the authority to try all matters of law except where the jurisdiction has been taken away by another court. However, courts created by the federal government under section 101 or by the provincial government under 92(14) are generally not allowed to intrude on the core jurisdiction of a section 96 court.

The scope of the core jurisdiction of the section 96 courts has been a matter of considerable debate and litigation. When commencing litigation a court's jurisdiction may be challenged on the basis that it does not have jurisdiction. The issue is typically whether the statutory court created under section 101 or 92(14) has encroached upon the exclusive jurisdiction of a section 96 court.

To validate the jurisdiction of a federal or provincial tribunal it must satisfy a three-step inquiry first outlined in *Re Residential Tenancies Act, 1979* (1981). The tribunal must not touch upon what was historically intended as the jurisdiction of the superior court. The first stage of inquiry considers what matters were typically exclusive to the court at the time of Confederation in 1867. In *Sobeys Stores Ltd. v. Yeomans* (1989) the Supreme Court stated that the "nature of the disputes" historically heard by the superior courts, not just the historical remedies provided, must be read broadly. If the tribunal is found to intrude on the historical jurisdiction of the superior court, the inquiry must turn to the second stage which considers whether the function of the tribunal and whether it operates as an adjudicative body. The final step assesses the context of the tribunal's exercise of power and looks to see if there are any further considerations to justify its encroachment upon the superior court's jurisdiction.

Constitutional Jurisdiction

Not all courts and tribunals have jurisdiction to hear constitutional challenges. The court, at the very least, must have jurisdiction to apply the law. In *N.S. v. Martin; N.S. v. Laseur* (2003) the Supreme Court re-articulated the test for constitutional jurisdiction from *Cooper v. Canada (Human Rights Commission)*. The inquiry must begin by determining whether the enabling legislation gives explicit authority to apply the law. If so, then the court may apply the constitution. The second line of inquiry looks into whether there was implied authority to apply the law. This can be found by examining the text of the Act, its context, and the general nature and characteristics of the adjudicative body.

Part VIII "Revenues; Debts, Assets; Taxation"

This Part lays out the financial functioning of the government of Canada and the provincial governments. It establishes a fiscal union where the federal government is liable for the debts of the provinces (Sections 111-116). It established the tradition of the federal government supporting the provinces through fiscal transfers (Sections 118 and 119). It creates a customs union which prohibits internal tariffs between the provinces (Sections 121-124). Section 125 prevents one order of government from taxing the lands or assets of the other.

Part IX "Miscellaneous"

Section 127 forbids members of the provincial upper houses (which still existed at the time), to also serve as senators at the same time.

Section 132 gives the federal government the sole responsibility to makes treaties with other countries, either within or without the British Empire.

Section 133 establishes English and French as the official languages of the Parliament of Canada and the Parliament of Quebec. No provision was made for the official languages of other government bodies.

Part X "Intercolonial Railway"

This part has only one section, which obligates the federal government to construct a railway uniting all the four original provinces.

Part XI "Admission of Other Colonies"

Section 146 allows the federal government to negotiate the entry of new provinces into the Union without the need to seek the permission of the existing provinces. Section 147 establishes that Prince Edward Island and Newfoundland would have 4 senators each if they were to join Confederation.

Small Bill of Rights

Professor Peter Hogg lists rights within the Constitution Act, 1867, which he calls a "small bill of rights."

Aside from the theory of the Implied Bill of Rights, there is no actual written bill of rights in the Constitution Act, 1867. Still, there are narrow constitutional rights scattered throughout the document. Hogg has referred to them as the **"small bill of rights"**, though the Supreme Court in *Greater Montreal Protestant School Board v. Quebec* (1989) disliked that characterization in that rights in the Constitution Act, 1867 should not be interpreted as liberally as rights in the Charter. The rights Hogg identifies include language rights.

There are also denominational school rights under section 93 (reaffirmed by section 29 of the Charter), notwithstanding provincial jurisdiction over education in Canada. Section 99 establishes a right for judges to serve unless removed by the legislature. Democratic rights include the rule that Parliament and the legislatures of Ontario and Quebec must sit at least once a year under sections 20 and 86, and there must be a federal election at least once every five years under section 50. These are repeated in section 4 and section 5 of the Charter and section 20 of the Constitution Act, 1867 has been repealed. The Constitution Act, 1867 also guarantees representation by population. Finally, section 121 allows for people to carry goods across provincial borders at no charge, and section 125 exempts government from paying most taxes.

Language Rights

Although the 1867 Act did not establish English and French as Canada's official languages, it did provide some rights for the users of both languages in respect of some institutions of the federal and Quebec governments.

Section 133 allowed bilingualism in both the federal Parliament and the Quebec provincial legislature, allowed for records to be kept in both languages, and allowed bilingualism in federal and Quebec courts. Interpretation of this section has found that this provision requires that all statutes and delegated legislation be in both languages and be of equal force.[11] Likewise, it has been found that the meaning of "courts" in section 133 includes all federal and provincial courts as well as all tribunals that exercise an adjudicative function. [12]

These rights are duplicated in respect to the federal government, but not Quebec, and extended to New Brunswick, by section 17, section 18, and section 19 of the Charter of Rights; section 16 and section 20 of the Charter elaborate by declaring English and French to be the official languages and allowing for bilingual public services.

Annexure II: Text of the Constitution Act of 1982

The **Constitution Act, 1982** (Schedule B of the Canada Act 1982 (UK)) is a part of the Constitution of Canada. The act was introduced as part of Canada's process of patriating the constitution, introducing several amendments[1] to the British North America Act, 1867, and changing the latter's name in Canada to the Constitution Act, 1867. Elizabeth II, as Queen of Canada, brought the act into effect with a proclamation she signed in Ottawa on April 17, 1982.

The Canadian Charter of Rights and Freedoms forms the first thirty-five sections (counting Section 16.1 and not counting Section 35) of the Constitution Act, 1982.

As of 2013, the government of Quebec has never formally approved of the enactment of the act, though formal consent was never necessary[2] Nonetheless, it has remained a persistent political issue in Quebec. The Meech Lake and Charlottetown Accords were designed to secure approval from Quebec, but both efforts failed to do so.

Charter of Rights and Freedoms

The Canadian Charter of Rights and Freedoms is a bill of rights. The Charter is intended to protect certain political and civil rights of people in Canada from the policies and actions of all levels of government. It is also supposed to unify Canadians around a set of principles that embody those rights.[3][4] The Charter was preceded by the Canadian Bill of Rights, which was introduced by the government of John Diefenbaker in 1960. However, the Bill of Rights was only a federal statute, rather than a constitutional document. Therefore, it was limited in scope and was easily amendable. This motivated some within government to improve rights protections in Canada. The movement for human rights and freedoms that emerged after World War II also wanted to entrench the principles enunciated in the Universal Declaration of Human Rights.[5] Hence, the government of Prime Minister Pierre Trudeau enacted the Charter in 1982.

One of the most notable effects of the adoption of the Charter was to greatly expand the range of judicial review, because the Charter is more explicit with respect to the guarantee of rights and the role of judges in enforcing them than was the Bill of Rights. The courts, when confronted with violations of Charter rights, have struck down unconstitutional statutes or parts of statutes, as they did when Canadian case law was primarily concerned with resolving issues of federalism. However, the Charter granted new powers to the courts to enforce more creative remedies and to exclude more evidence in trials. These powers are greater than what was typical under the common law and under a system of government that, influenced by Canada's mother country the United Kingdom, was based upon Parliamentary supremacy.[6]

Aboriginal Rights Clause

Section 35 of the Constitution Act, 1982 "recognizes and affirms" the "existing" aboriginal and treaty rights in Canada. These aboriginal rights protect the activities, practice, or traditions that are integral to the distinct cultures of the aboriginal peoples. The treaty rights protect and enforce agreements between the crown and the aboriginal peoples. Section 35 also provides protection of aboriginal title which protects the use of land for traditional practices. These rights extend to Indian, Inuit, and Métis people.

Other sections of the Constitution Act, 1982 that address aboriginal rights include section 25 of the Charter and section 35.1, which sets expectations for aboriginal participation in the amendment of relevant constitutional provisions.

Equalization and Equal Opportunity

Section 36 enshrines in the Constitution a value on equal opportunity for the Canadian people, economic development to support that equality, and government services available for public consumption. Subsection 2 goes further in recognizing a "principle" that the federal government should ensure equalization payments.

Writing in 1982, Professor Peter Hogg expressed skepticism as to whether the courts could interpret and enforce this provision, noting its "political and moral, rather than legal" character.[7] Other scholars have noted section 36 is too vague. Since the courts would not be of much use in interpreting the section, the section was nearly amended in 1992 with the Charlottetown Accord to make it enforceable. The Accord never came into effect.[8]

Amending the Constitution

Section 52(3) of the Constitution Act, 1982 says that constitutional amendments can only be made in accordance with the rules laid out in the Constitution itself. The purpose of this section was to entrench constitutional supremacy and remove the ability of legislators to amend the constitution using simple legislation.

The rules for amending Canada's constitution are quite dense. They are laid out in Part V of the Constitution Act, 1982.

There are five different amendment formulas, each applicable to different types of amendments. These five formulas are:

1. The General Formula (the "7/50" procedure) - s. 38. The amendment must be passed by the House of Commons, the Senate, and at least two-thirds of the provincial legislatures representing at least 50% of the population. This covers any amendment procedure not covered more specifically in ss. 41, 43, 44 or 45. The general formula **must** be used for any of the six situations identified in s. 42.

2. The Unanimity Procedure - s. 41. The amendment must be passed by the House of Commons, Senate, and *all* provincial legislatures.

3. "Some-but-not-all Provinces" (or "bilateral" procedure) - s. 43. The amendment must be passed by the House of Commons, the Senate, and the legislative assemblies of those provinces that are affected by the amendment.

4. Federal Parliament Alone (or "federal unilateral" procedure) - s. 44. The amendment must only be passed by the House of Commons and the Senate.

5. Provincial Legislature Alone (or "provincial unilateral" procedure) - s. 45. The amendment must only be passed by the provincial legislature.

Various other sections of Part V lay out such things as compensation for opting out, when and how a province may opt out of a constitutional amendment, and time limits for achieving a constitutional amendment.

Supremacy Clause

Section 52 of the Constitution Act, 1982 provides that the Constitution of Canada is the "supreme law of Canada", and any law inconsistent with it is of no force or effect.[9] This gives Canadian courts the power to strike down legislation. Though such laws remain on the statute book until they are amended, after being struck down they cannot be enforced.

Before the 1982 Act came into effect, the British North America Act, 1867 (now known as the Constitution Act, 1867) had been the supreme law of Canada. The supremacy of the 1867 Act had originally been established by virtue of s. 2 of the Colonial Laws Validity Act,[10] a British Imperial statute declaring that no colonial law that violated an Imperial statute extending to a colony was valid. Since the British North America Act was an Imperial statute extending to Canada, any Canadian law violating the BNA Act was inoperative. Although there was no express provision giving the courts the power to decide that a Canadian law violated the BNA Act and was therefore inoperative, this power was implicit in s. 2 of the Colonial Laws Validity Act, which established the priority of statutes to be applied by the courts.

In 1931, the British Parliament enacted the Statute of Westminster, 1931. This Act provided that the Colonial Laws Validity Act no longer applied to the British Dominions, including Canada.[11] However, it provided that Canada could not amend the British North America Act,[12] which remained subject to amendment only by the British Parliament. This provision maintained the supremacy of the British North America Act in Canadian law until the enactment of the Constitution Act, 1982.

Definition of the Constitution

Section 52(2) of the Constitution Act, 1982 defines the "Constitution of Canada." The Constitution of Canada is said to include:

(a) the Canada Act 1982 (which includes the Constitution Act, 1982 in Schedule B),
(b) 30 Acts and Orders contained in the Schedule to the Constitution Act, 1982 (including, most significantly, the Constitution Act, 1867), and
(c) any amendments which may have been made to any of the instruments in the first two categories.

Section 52(2), in addition to containing many Imperial Statutes, contains eight Canadian statutes, three of which created provinces, and five of which were amendments to the Constitution Act, 1867.

The Canadian courts have reserved the right to add and entrench principles and conventions into the Constitution unilaterally. Although a court's ability to recognize human rights not explicitly stated in a constitution is not particularly unusual, the Canadian situation is unique in that this ability extends to procedural issues not related to human rights.

In particular, in *New Brunswick Broadcasting Co. v. Nova Scotia (Speaker of the House of Assembly)*, the Supreme Court of Canada said that s. 52(2) was not an exhaustive listing of all that comprised the Constitution. The Court reserved the right to add unwritten principles to the Constitution, thereby entrenching them and granting them constitutional supremacy (in this case, they added parliamentary privilege to the Constitution). The Court did note, however, that the list of written documents was static and could not be modified except for through the amending formulas.

General

Section 52 and the remaining sections of the Constitution Act, 1982 are located under the header "General."Section 56 of the Act states that the English and French versions of the Constitution are equal, and section 57 adds that the English and French versions of the Constitution Act, 1982 itself are equal. Legal experts compare this to section 18, which states that English and French versions of statutes are equal.[13]

Section 59 limits the application of section 23 of the Charter (minority language education) in Quebec. The section will not be fully valid in Quebec until the provincial government chooses to ratify it.

Section 60 states that the Act may be called the Constitution Act, 1982, and that the Constitution Acts can be collectively called the Constitution Acts, 1867 to 1982.

Annexure III: List of the Prime Ministers of Canada since 1867

1 Rt. Hon. Sir John A. Macdonald
   July 1, 1867 to Nov. 5, 1873   Liberal-Conservative

2 Hon. Alexander Mackenzie*
   Nov. 7, 1873 to Oct. 8, 1878   Liberal

3 Rt. Hon. Sir John A. Macdonald
   Oct. 17, 1878 to June 6, 1891   Liberal-Conservative

4 Hon. Sir John J.C. Abbott*
   June 16, 1891 to Nov. 24, 1892   Liberal-Conservative

5 Rt. Hon. Sir John S.D. Thompson
   Dec. 5, 1892 to Dec. 12, 1894   Liberal-Conservative

6 Hon. Sir Mackenzie Bowell*
   Dec. 21, 1894 to April 27, 1896   Conservative

7 Rt. Hon. Sir Charles Tupper* (Baronet)
   May 1, 1896 to July 8, 1896   Conservative

8 Rt. Hon. Sir Wilfrid Laurier
   July 11, 1896 to Oct. 6, 1911   Liberal

9 Rt. Hon. Sir Robert Laird Borden
   Oct. 10, 1911 to Oct. 12, 1917   Conservative

10 Rt. Hon. Sir Robert Laird Borden
   Oct. 12, 1917 to July 10, 1920   Conservative**

11 Rt. Hon. Arthur Meighen
   July 10, 1920 to Dec. 29, 1921   Conservative

12 Rt. Hon. William Lyon Mackenzie King
   Dec. 29, 1921 to June 28, 1926   Liberal

13 Rt. Hon. Arthur Meighen
   June 29, 1926 to Sept. 25, 1926   Conservative

14 Rt. Hon. William Lyon Mackenzie King
Sept. 25, 1926 to Aug. 7, 1930   Liberal

15 Rt. Hon. Richard Bedford Bennett
(became Viscount Bennett, 1941)
Aug. 7, 1930 to Oct. 23, 1935   Conservative

16 Rt. Hon. William Lyon Mackenzie King
Oct. 23, 1935 to Nov. 15, 1948   Liberal

17 Rt. Hon. Louis Stephen St-Laurent
Nov. 15, 1948 to June 21, 1957   Liberal

18 Rt. Hon. John George Diefenbaker
June 21, 1957 to Apr. 22, 1963   Progressive Conservative

19 Rt. Hon. Lester Bowles Pearson
Apr. 22, 1963 to Apr. 20, 1968   Liberal

20 Rt. Hon. Pierre Elliott Trudeau
Apr. 20, 1968 to June 4, 1979   Liberal

21 Rt. Hon. Charles Joseph Clark
June 4, 1979 to March 3, 1980   Progressive Conservative

22 Rt. Hon. Pierre Elliott Trudeau
March 3, 1980 to June 30, 1984   Liberal

23 Rt. Hon. John Napier Turner
June 30, 1984 to Sept. 17, 1984   Liberal

24 Rt. Hon. Martin Brian Mulroney
Sept. 17, 1984 to June 25, 1993   Progressive Conservative

25 Rt. Hon. A. Kim Campbell
June 25, 1993 to Nov. 4, 1993   Progressive Conservative

26 Rt. Hon. Jean Joseph Jacques Chrétien
Nov. 4, 1993 to Dec. 11, 2003   Liberal

27 Rt. Hon. Paul Edgar Philippe Martin
Dec. 12, 2003 to Feb. 5, 2006   Liberal

28 Rt. Hon. Stephen Joseph Harper
    Feb. 6, 2006 - Oct. 20, 2015   Conservative

29 Rt. Justin Trudeau
    Oct. 20, 2015 -   Liberal

* Prior to 1968, "Right Honourable" was accorded only to Prime Ministers, who had been sworn into the Privy Council for the U.K. Prime ministers Mackenzie, Abbott and Bowell were only members of the Canadian Privy Council and Prime Minister Tupper became a U.K. Privy Councillor after his term as Canada's prime minister.

** During his second period in office, Prime Minister Borden headed a coalition government.

Annexure IV: Bilateral Investment

The stock of two-way investment figures for the period 2000-2011 is as under:

Table 1: India-Canada Bilateral Foreign Direct Investment Stock During 2000-2011
[Figures in million C$]

Sr. No.	Year	Indian FDI in Canada	Canadian FDI in India
1	2000	NA	129
2	2001	29	145
3	2002	31	222
4	2003	59	204
5	2004	92	214
6	2005	171	319
7	2006	211	677
8	2007	1,988	506
9	2008	6,514	667
10	2009	6,217	520
11	2010	4,364	676
12	2011	4,396	587

[*Source:* Statistics Canada]

The cumulative foreign direct investment by India into Canada during 2000-2011 was C$ 4.396 billion as against Canadian FDIs of C$ 587 million during the same period. In 2011, India ranked 13 in terms of Indian FDIs into Canada and 40 in terms of Canadian FDIs abroad.

Table 2: Canadian Outward and Inward Foreign Direct Investment Stock During 2000-2011 [Figures in million C$]

Sr. No.	Year	FDI Outward	FDI Inward
1	2000	356,506	319,116
2	2001	399,253	340,429
3	2002	435,494	356,819
4	2003	412,217	373,685
5	2004	448,546	379,450
6	2005	452,195	397,828
7	2006	518,839	437,171
8	2007	515,294	512,266
9	2008	641,920	550,539
10	2009	629,717	572,842
11	2010	639,911	585,107
12	2011	684,496	607,497

[*Source:* Statistics Canada]

Indian investment in Canada has increased steadily in the recent years, especially in the information technology and software sectors. Indian companies with substantial operations in Canada include VSNL (Tata), Aditya Birla Group, Hindalco, Essar, Tata Consultancy Services, BFL Software, Patni Computer Systems, Satyam Computer Services, WIPRO and Infosys Technology. Two

Indian Banks, State Bank of India and ICICI Banks, have six branches each in Canada. Punjab National Bank and Bank of Baroda are in advanced stages of planning to enter Canada. Other areas of significant Indian investment in Canada are financial services and pharmaceuticals. Among the major Indian investments in Canada are the following:

- Aditya Birla Group – US$ 25 millions – Softwood and Hardwood Pulp – 1998

- Bikanervala Foods Pvt. Ltd. – US$ 5 million – Agriculture, Food and Beverages – 2003

- Aditya Birla Group – US$ 146 millions – Acquisition of St. Anne Nackawic Pulp Mill –

- 2005

- Piramla Healthcare Limited – US$ 6 millions – Biotechnology and drugs – 2005

- VSNL Limited – US$ 239 millions – Communications equipment – 2005

- Kavveri Telecom Products Ltd. – US$ 2.5 millions – Communications equipment – 2006

- Aditya Birla Group – US$ 125 millions – ICT; acquired Mincas Worldwide – 2006

- Carborundum Universal Limited – US$ 14 millions – Industrial Goods – 2006

- WF Limited – US$ 5 millions – Consumer Products and Sales – 2007

- Subex Azure Limited US$ 164.5 millions – Information-Communications and Technology – 2007

- Hindalco Limited – US$ 6000 millions – Mining – 2007 – Acquired Novelis

- Baltiboi Limited – US$ 7 millions – Engineering Services – 2007

- Essar Steel Limited – US$ 1850 millions – Iron & Steel – 2007

- Aditya Birla Group – US$ 15 millions – Conglomerate – 2007 – Investment in Atholville, New Brunswick

- Universal Power Transformers – US$ 7.2 millions – Electronic Instruments & Controls – 2007

- Kavveri Telecom Products Ltd. – US$ 7 million – Communications Equipment – 2008

- Jubilant Organosys Ltd. – US$ 255 millions – Biotechnology & Drugs – 2008

- Aditya Birla Group – US$ 9 millions – Conglomerate – 2008

- Essar Steel Limited – US$ 135 millions – Iron & Steel – 2009

- Tata Steel Limited – US$ 300 million – Misc. Fabricated Products – 2009

- Vedanta Resources Plc. – Mining - acquired 10 per cent shares in HudBay Minerals Inc.

- Hind High Vacuum Co. Ltd. – US$ 240 million – Renewable Energy – Solar – 2010

- Zylong Systems – US$ 35 million – Acquired Brainhunter Inc. - 2010

- Tata Steel purchased an additional 14,285,714 common shares in the New Millennium Capital Corp. raising its stake from 19.9 to 27.4 per cent - $ 20 million – June 2010

- Tata Steel Global Minerals Holdings Pte. Limited signs a binding heads of agreement (HOA) with New Millennium Capital Corporation for approximately worth $ 5 billion to develop the LabMag and KéMag iron ore deposits, known collectively as the Taconite Project –February 2011

- Aditya Birla Group - $ 110 million – acquired assets of Ontario-based Terrace Bay Pulp mill another $ 250 million to be invested in phased manner- July 2012

Canadian investments in India are present in energy, infrastructure, banking, insurance, oil and gas, transportation, etc. sectors, as also in engineering and consultancy services. The Indian economy has attracted many Canadian companies including SNC Lavalin, Bombardier, RIM, CAE Electronics, Sun Life, MDS Nordion, BCE, etc. Royal Bank of Canada and Scotia bank has branches in India. Canadian clean technology companies have also entered into joint ventures with Indian companies in India. Major investments from Canada in India are:

- SNC Lavalin has been active in India since 1960s in various sectors such as chemicals, petroleum, infrastructure, pharmaceutical, power, etc. It has about 150 completed and ongoing projects in India. It has acquired a number of Indian companies in various sectors.

- Quebec's Mediagrif Interactive Technologies Inc. acquired a 50% interest in Mumbai-based Centerac DMCC for US$1 million. (Feb. 2006) - Magna Powertrain, a division of Aurora-based Magna International that produces powertrain and drivetrain components, formed a 50-50 joint venture with its long-term parts supplier Amtek Auto of India. (2006)

- CAE Montreal – Helicopter Pilot Training Center in Bangalore – $ 55 million – 2007

- Bombardier – Metro rail coaches manufacturing plant in India - $ 41 million

- Marikon Inc purchased the remaining 51% of Matrikon-SoftDel India Private Limited for C$ 575,000 – 2009

- Export Development Canada (EDC), Canada's official export credit agency, as part of its program to encourage investment from Canada in India has encouraged following investments under its India Equity portfolio:

    * Avigo SME Fund II – US$ 7.5 million – August 2007

    * IDFC India Infrastructure Fund – US$ 1 billion

    * Kotak India Private Equity Co. Limited – US$ 250 million

- Urbana Corporation has taken a C$26.5 million interest in the Bombay Stock Exchange (BSE). This purchase was made indirectly by way of an investment in shares of Caldwell India Holdings Inc. (CIH) and was facilitated by Caldwell Asset Management Inc., Urbana's investment manager.

- The CIH acquisition of 308,888 BSE shares cost approximately C$43.5 million, with Urbana owning 60.9% of CIH's equity shares. Urbana is a Toronto-based investment company focused on buying seats and shares in private and public securities exchanges around the world. (2007)

- Montreal-based Alcan Inc. acquired 76% of the shares of Mumbai, India-based Alukbond India Private Ltd. The Indian company will be renamed Alcan Composites India Private Ltd., Alukbond's production facility currently manufactures the Alukbond brand of aluminium composite panels. (2007)

- Montreal-based CAE acquired Bangalore, India-based Macmet Technologies Limited for approximately C$5 million in cash. (2007)

- Hyderabad-based Matrix Group entered into a joint venture with Montreal-based Ethica Clinical Research Inc. to create a contract research company, Ethicamatrix Clinical Research Pvt. Ltd. Ethicamatrix will pursue clinical research on biologicals, natural health and drug products and be equally owned by the joint venture partners which plan to invest C$2.6 million to strengthen operations. (2007)

- Toronto-based CCL Industries Inc. announced its plans to invest $25 million over 2008 and 2009 to expand its CCL Label operations in Asia. A new start-up in Pune, India will focus on personal care and healthcare customers. (2008)

- Calgary-based Canoro Resources Ltd., finalized negotiations with Essar Oil Limited and Essar Energy Holdings Limited to obtain a 30% participating interest in two exploration production sharing contracts in northeast India. (2008)

- Quebec City-based H2O Innovation Inc. signed a joint venture agreement to create H2O Innovation India Limited. The new company will operate out of facilities located in Chembond's centre in Mumbai, and be dedicated to providing water treatment systems and maintenance services to the Indian industrial and commercial markets for the production of boiler feed and process water, for industrial wastewater reclamation and reuse, as well as for wastewater treatment. Chembond will own 51% of the shares of the joint venture and H2O Innovation will own the remaining 49%. (2010)

- Minaean Habitat India Pvt. Ltd. (), a wholly owned subsidiary of Vancouver-based Minaean International Corp secured a contract for the turnkey design and construction of the hostel and library covering a total area of 24,000 sq. feet for a new medical college campus in Valsad, Gujarat, India. (2010)

Recent Important Bilateral Investments/Tie-ups

- SpiceJet of Gurgaon, India has placed a firm order for 15 Q400 NextGen turboprop airliners with Bombardier Aerospace and has taken options on an additional 15 airliners. The order is valued at approximately US$446 million, and could increase to approximately US$915 million if all 15 options are converted to orders. (Dec. 2010)

- Calgary-based Poynt Corporation joined with Times Internet Limited in India to form TimesPoynt to make the Poynt applications available to mobile users in India. The services will be launched during the first quarter of 2011 (Dec. 2010).

- Tata Communications signed a sourcing agreement with Videotron, Quebec. Under this agreement, Videotron will route 100% of its international voice traffic through the Tata Communications network and Videotron will continue to be one of Tata Communications' key suppliers of telecommunication services in Canada (Dec. 2010).

- Montreal-based CAE Inc. has been awarded a series of military contracts to supply Advanced Integrated Magnetic Anomaly Detection (MAD) System for eight P-8I Poseidon aircraft to be operated by the Indian Navy. The total value of the new contracts is more than C$140 million. (Jan. 2011)

- CAE, a Montreal-based company sold one of its A320 full-flight simulators (FFS) to an undisclosed customer in India. (Jan. 2011)

- Tata Steel Global Minerals Holdings Pte. Limited and Montreal based New Millennium Capital Corporation signed a binding heads of agreement (HOA) worth $ 5 billion to develop the LabMag and KéMag iron ore deposits, known collectively as the Taconite Project. Under the Binding HOA, Tata Steel will participate in the development of a feasibility study of the Taconite Project and contribute towards 64% of the related costs. (Feb. 2011)

- Mississauga-based Magellan Aerospace Corporation and Hindustan Aeronautics Ltd. In Bangalore, India, signed an agreement for a new wire strike protection system including the design and development of the wire strike protection system by Magellan's Bristol division in Winnipeg for Hindustan Aeronautics' advanced light helicopter. (Feb. 2011)

- Wipro Technologies of India inaugurated a new office in Mississauga, Ontario as part of an expansion plan for its Canadian operations. The Mississauga office will serve as Wipro's Canadian headquarters. (Feb. 2011)

- Montreal-based CAE reported inauguration of its new aerospace and defense complex in Bangalore, India. The complex is the headquarters for CAE's operations in India. (Feb. 2011)

- Jigsee Inc., a Toronto-based provider of adaptive video streaming technology for wireless devices in developing countries, received Series-A funding from the Indian Angel Network. The Indian Angel Network is India's only national network of investors in start-ups. (Feb. 2011)

- Vancouver-based Maxtech Ventures Inc., will set up a camp in the Girar area of Uttar Pradesh Province, India to drill two-to-three diamond drill holes. The work will happen through the geological team of its subsidiary, Maxtech Resources Private Limited. The drilling is planned to intercept the auriferous Precambrian banded iron formation. (Feb. 2011)

- Toronto-based Brookfield Asset Management Inc. entered into a framework agreement with Japan-based Sumitomo Mitsui Banking Corporation and India- based Kotak Mahindra Group, to set up an India-focused infrastructure fund.

- Tata Communications of India selected Tranzeo Wireless Technologies Inc., Richmond, BC, to supply broadband wireless access equipment for network services to enterprise customers. Tata will be deploying Tranzeo's WiMAX and WiFi solutions in over 200 cities in India. (Feb. 2011)

- Clearford Industries Inc., an Ottawa-based developer of wastewater collection systems, signed an agreement with Lakepoint Builders Pvt Ltd, the owner and developer of The Villas at Devananhalli, Bangalore, India to build a sewerage collection and treatment system for The Villas using Clearford's small bore sewer (SBS) system. (April 2011)

- Quebec City based H2O Innovation Inc. announced that its Indian joint-venture, H2O Innovation India Ltd., Mumbai, opened its first manufacturing plant near Vadodara, India. H20 Innovation India has also secured C$4.2 million in bookings of water treatment systems and equipment for Indian industrial customers. (April 2011)

- Calgary-based Grand Power Logistics Group Inc., entered into an exclusive partnership with Necko Freight Forwarders Ltd. of India for the development of India-Hong Kong-Greater China airfreight and ocean freight markets. Grand Power Logistics signed the partnership contract through its subsidiary, Grand Power Express International Limited. Necko is a subsidiary of Budget Couriers Pvt. Ltd. (April 2011)

- CSA Group, Toronto, to collaborate with U.S.-based Wipro Technologies to provide localized testing and certification services in India. The agreement will enable Wipro and CSA Group to provide compliance testing and certification services to companies developing products in India for international markets in diverse fields, such as information technology, medical, test and measurement, laboratory, and industrial control equipment. (April 2011)

- Dantherm Power of Denmark, a subsidiary of Ballard Power Systems, a Vancouver-based clean energy fuel cell provider signed a collaboration agreement with Delta Power Solutions (India) Pvt. Ltd. to market clean energy fuel cell power solutions in the India telecommunications sector. Under the agreement, Dantherm Power and Delta will jointly work to deploy product field trials comprised of Dantherm's direct hydrogen 2-kilowatt (kW) DBX2000 fuel cell system and its 5kW DBX5000 fuel cell system, which will be integrated by Delta, along with its Site Management & Control System (SMCS), and deployed at telecom customer sites in India. (July 2011)

- Wind Works Power Corp of Ottawa concluded a contract with RE Power Systems SE, a Germanybased subsidiary of Suzlon Energy Limited of India for the delivery of 25 wind turbines for five wind farm projects in Ontario. The wind farms will generate more than 50 megawatts of power. The turbines are scheduled to be delivered in the spring of 2013 and put into operation the following summer. (August 2011)

- Canadian Solar Inc. of Kitchener, Ontario has signed a photovoltaic (PV) solar module sales agreement with Cirus Solar Systems Private Limited, a solar engineering, procurement and construction company based in Hyderabad, India. Under the terms of the agreement, Canadian Solar is expected to deliver 33 MW of solar modules in the third and fourth quarters of 2011. The modules will be utilized for solar PV projects that are designed, installed and commissioned by Cirus on behalf of two prominent Indian conglomerates. (August 2011)

- Bombardier Transportation, a subsidiary of Montreal-based Bombardier Inc received an order of 76 additional Bombardier MOVIA metro cars from Delhi Metro Rail Corporation Ltd. The contract is valued at approximately US$ 120 million and follows an earlier order for 114 vehicles announced in mid-2010. Delivery will commence in the third quarter of 2012 and is expected to end in early 2013. (September 2011)

- Montreal-based DataWind Ltd., a developer of wireless web products and services, has been awarded a contact with the Indian government to produce low-cost Aakash tablet computers which will be resold to university students. Datawind has opened a factory in India to make the tablets. (October 2011)

- Clearford Industries Inc., Ottawa-based developer of wastewater collection systems, has signed an agreement with Lakepoint Builders Pvt. Ltd. to implement Clearford's wastewater treatment unit in India. Lakepoint is a subsidiary of India's Hiranandani Group, a real estate development company. The unit will be installed at a luxury development in Bengaluru in southern India. This agreement covers the implementation of a wastewater collection and treatment system for Phase I of the development, which is approximately 25% of the planned project size. Development is expected to start in the final quarter of 2011 pending both parties entering a bindingconstruction agreement. (Oct. 2011)

- Ashok Piramal Group (APG), IDFC Project Equity Fund of India and SNV-Lavalin formed a Joint Venture to develop road and highway projects in a public-private partnership. Piramal Roads Infrastructure will own 51 per cent equity in the partnership, India Infrastructure Fund (IIF), managed by IDFC Project Equity, will hold 39 per cent stake, while SNC-Lavalin will own the remainder. The partnership will commit $ 250 million- $ 300 million in equity in a combined funder over the next 3 to 4 years. (November 2011)

- REpower Systems SE, a wholly-owned subsidiary of India-based Suzlon Energy Limited, has signed a framework contract with EDF EN Canada Inc., a Toronto- and Montreal-based subsidiary of EDF Energies Nouvelles, to supply 75 wind turbines in Québec. This is the third order from the framework agreement concluded between EDF Energies Nouvelles and REpower in November 2009. REpower will deliver the first turbines from early 2012, and will be responsible for maintaining the turbines. REpower develops produces and markets wind turbines and offers service and maintenance packages. (Nov.2011)

- Export Development Canada (EDC) announced that it has provided US$2.5 million in financing to Manjushree Technopack Limited, an India-based packaging solutions provider, to facilitate the purchase of equipment from Husky Injection Moulding (Husky) of Bolton, Ontario. Husky equipment is used to manufacture plastic products such as bottles and caps for beverages, containers for food, medical components and consumer electronic parts. (Nov. 2011)

- Eurocontrol Technics Group Inc. of Toronto has signed an exclusive distribution agreement with Aimil Ltd. of India through Xenemetrix Inc., its wholly-owned, Israel-based subsidiary. Eurocontrol Technics specializes in the acquisition, development and commercialization of authentication, verification and energy security technologies. Xenemetrix designs, manufactures and markets energy-dispersive X-ray fluorescence systems and components for a range of industries and applications. Aimil focuses on the instrumentation industry across the Indian subcontinent. According to the agreement, Aimil has been granted exclusive rights to promote and distribute Xenemetrix's products in India, Bangladesh and Sri Lanka. (Nov. 2011)

- Bombardier Inc's train unit received a contract worth USD 214.4 million (Rs.11,200 crore) to make railway equipment for Mumbai Railway Vikas Corp (MRVC). Bombardier Transportation will design, manufacture and test propulsion and control equipment for trains and other equipment including fans, compressors, passenger information systems and high voltage instruments, the delivery of which will start in the last quarter of 2012 and will be completed in the third quarter of 2014. The order relates to a total of 72 commuter trains of 12 cars each. (Nov. 2011)

- Stealth Ventures Ltd., an oil and gas development company based in Calgary, has signed a binding agreement to acquire a private company with working interests in producing oil and gas, assets coupled with exploration acreages, in India. Terms of the acquisition include a 30% working interest in producing oil and gas assets and a 10% working interest in oil and gas acreages. The transaction is valued at US$45 million and viewed as part of an arrangement that involves the acquisition of the entire equity shares of the target company. The purchase consideration will be settled with a split of US$20 million in cash and the equivalent of US$25 million in non-voting shares of the private company. The transaction will be completed after necessary approvals from the Government of India are received (Dec. 2011).

- Hammond Power Solutions Inc., a Guelph-based designer and manufacturer of dry-tape custom electrical engineered magnetics, electrical dry-type and cast coil transformers, has completed the acquisition of Pan-Electro Technic Enterprises Private Limited in

India. The acquisition supports HTS efforts to expand into the Indian, Asian and African markets with 70% equity ownership of Pan-Electro's power transformer business. (Feb. 2012)

- Vancouver-based Ballard Power Systems has announced that 30 fuel cell systems manufactured by Dantherm Power, its backup power company, are being deployed in the Idea Cellular wireless telecommunications network in India. Idea Cellular is part of the multinational Aditya Birla Group and is a major mobile services operator in India. Dantherm Power, a joint venture between Ballard Power Systems Inc. and Denmark's Danfoss A/S and Dantherm A/S, will work jointly with Delta Power Solutions of India to install Dantherm Power's DBX2000 systems into a hybrid powersolution at Idea Cellular sites and will then provide operational support for these systems under a 10-year service agreement with Idea Cellular. Ballard Power Systems provides clean energy fuel cell products enabling power systems for a range of applications. (Feb. 2012)

- Sensaas India, a subsidiary of Montreal-based Integrim, announced that it has signed an agreement with Global Clinical Research Services Private Limited, a clinical trial division of India-based Global Hospitals. Global Hospitals is a chain of specialty care and multi-organ transplantation facilities in India. Integrim will provide automated information recognition, clinical data management and statistical analysis services to Global Hospitals for its clinical trials. Integrim focuses on helping companies maximize efficiency and reduce costs by providing automated document processing solutions. (Feb. 2012)

- Export Development Canada (EDC) announced that it has provided US$100 million in financing to India's Tata Motors Limited (TML) to support procurement from Canadian companies within the greater TML family of companies. EDC is Canada's export credit agency, offering commercial solutions to help Canadian exporters and investors expand their international business. (Feb. 2012)

- Toronto-based Montero Mining and Exploration Ltd. announced that it has signed a non-binding Memorandum of Understanding (MOU) with Star Earth Minerals (Pvt) Limited, a rare earth chemical company based in Mumbai, India. The MOU's primary purpose is to lay out the basis of cooperation between Montero and Star Earth Minerals, with the aim of reaching an off-take agreement for Star to buy cerium carbonate and mixed rare earth from Montero. (March 2012)

- CAE Inc., a Montreal-based company focused on modelling, simulation and training for civil aviation and defence, announced that it has been awarded contract by a customer in India. CAE sold two Airbus A320 FFSs for the new Interglobe-CAE joint venture airline training centre in Delhi, India, In addition, CAE sold an A320 Airbus Procedures Trainer (APT) for the Delhi training centre. The FFSs and the APT will be ready for training by the end of 2012 at the new training centre in the National Capital Region, Delhi. (April 2012)

- East West Petroleum Corp., a Vancouver-based TSX Venture exchange-listed company focused on investing in emerging international unconventional resource plays, has signed a production sharing contract (PSC) with the Directorate General of Hydrocarbons of India. Partners in this NELP IX bid are Oil India Ltd. (operator, 40%), Oil and Natural Gas Corporation of India (30%), and Gas Authority of India Ltd. (20%) and East West Petroleum (10%). The exploration block lies in the Assam-Arakan Basin oil producing region of northeast India. Under the terms of the PSC work program commitment, the partnership will acquire 395 sq km of 3D seismic data and drill two wells, at an estimated cost of $2.8 million. (April 2012)

- Montreal-based Bombardier Aerospace announced the official inauguration of its Engineering Service Office in Bangalore, India. The new office, which will house approximately 50 aerospace engineers by the end of 2013, will support Bombardier Aerospace's in-production and in-development aircraft programs by providing assistance to both the company and the more than 400 engineers at its partners' offices in the areas of complex engineering structure design, advanced stress analysis and project management services. Bombardier is a manufacturer of transportation solutions, from commercial aircraft and business jets to rail transportation equipment, systems and services. (April 2012)

- Ultra Electronics, TCS, a tactical communications system company based in Montreal, has been awarded an order for Electronic Warfare (EW) equipment totalling C$3.4 million. The system will be delivered to the Defence Avionics Research Establishment (DARE) in Bangalore, India. Ultra TCS will supply a shelter-based, mobile simulator system. The complete system will be used in a test environment to evaluate aircraft EW radar capability and provide an opportunity for pilots to assess the equipment's functionality, specifically the effectiveness of countermeasure techniques. (April 2012)

Annexure V: Bilateral Mechanisms

To further expand bilateral relations both in terms of quality and quantity, the two countries have established various mechanisms to interact on an annualized basis in areas of mutual interest. These are:

- Foreign Office Consultations
- Strategic Dialogue
- Joint Working Group on Counter Terrorism
- Trade Policy Consultations
- Science & Technology Joint Committee
- Environment Forum
- Energy Forum
- Joint Working Group on Agriculture
- Steering Committee on Mining
- Health Steering Committee

Bilateral Agreements

- Reciprocal Protection of the Priority of Patents of Invention (1956)
- Air Services Agreement (1982)
- Extradition Treaty (1987)
- Treaty on Mutual Legal Assistant in Criminal Matters (1994).
- Avoidance of Double Taxation and the Prevention of Fiscal Evasion with respect to Taxes on Income and on Capital (1996)
- Memorandum of Understanding between the Ministry of Mines, Government of the Republic of India and the Department of Natural Resources (represented by the Earth Sciences Sector), Government of Canada concerned cooperation in the Geosciences (April 2003)
- Memorandum of Understanding between the Indian Council of Medical Research (ICMR), New Delhi, India and the Canadian Institute of Health Research (CIHR), Ottawa, Canada (January 2005)

- Agreement for Scientific and Technological Cooperation between the Government of the Republic of India and the Government of Canada (November 2005)

- India-Canada Forum for Environmental Cooperation (September 2007)

- Letter of Agreement – Joint Collaborative Projects in Plant Biotechnology, Department of

- Biotechnology, Government of India and National Research Council of Canada, Plant

- Biotechnology Institute (September 2007)

- Programme of Cooperation between National Institute of Plant Genome Research, New Delhi and University of Saskatchewan, Canada and Department of Biotechnology, Ministry of Science and Technology, Government of India (March 2008)

- Memorandum of Understanding – Cooperation Agreement between the Council of Scientific and Industrial Research, New Delhi, India represented by the National Aerospace Laboratories, Bangalore, India and the Consortium for Research and Innovation in Aerospace in Quebec, Canada (April 2008)

- Memorandum of Understanding between the Department of Agriculture and Agri-Food Canada and the Ministry of Agriculture of the Republic of India on cooperation in the field of Agriculture and Allied Sectors (January 2009)

- Memorandum of Understanding between the Chennai Port, India and the Halifax Port (January 2009)

- MoU between the Ministry of Mines, India and the Ministry of Northern Development, Mines and Forestry, Ontario Province, Canada in July 2009.

- MoU between the Department of Natural Resources of Canada and the Ministry of Science and Technology of the Republic of India concerning Cooperation in Science and Technology related to Geospatial Information (November 2009).

- MoU between the Department of Natural Resources of Canada and the Ministry of Power, Government of India concerning Cooperation in the field of Energy (November 2009)

- Agreement between India and Canada for Cooperation in Peaceful Uses of Nuclear Energy signed (27 June 2010).

- Memorandum of Understanding between the Ministry of Mines, Government of the Republic of India and the Department of Natural Resources, Government of Canada, concerning cooperation in the field of Earth Sciences and Mining signed (27 June 2010).

- Memorandum of Understanding between India and Canada concerning Cooperation in Higher Education signed (27 June 2010).

- Memorandum of Understanding between the Ministry of Culture, India and the department of Canadian Heritage on Cultural Cooperation signed (27 June 2010).

- MoU between the College of Surgeons of India (CSI) and the Royal College of Physicians and Surgeons of Canada (RCPSC) signed a Memorandum of Understanding in Ottawa to build a strong relationship to establish the CSI for the development and evolution of an educational partnership between the RCPSC and CSI with a view to advancement of surgical residency education in India on 11 January 2011.

- A Memorandum of Understanding for establishing Canada-India Centre for Excellence in Science, Technology, Trade and Policy was signed at the Carleton University on 24 January 2011.

- MoU between Carleton University and the University of Petroleum and Energy Studies in Delhi on renewable energy and aerospace engineering in February 2011.

- MoU between Carleton University and Jindal Global University on business management in February 2011.

- MoU between the Institute of Chartered Accountants of India and the Canadian Institute of Chartered Accountants on Reciprocal Membership Arrangements on 7 February 2011.

- MoU between the Union Public Service Commission (UPSC) and the Public Service Commission of Canada (PSCC) in New Delhi today regarding cooperation to promote best practices on 15 March 2011. On 17 March 2011. MoU between the Ministry of Mines,

India and the Ministry of Energy and Resources, Saskatchewan Province, Canada regarding cooperation in the field of Geology and Mineral Sources on 15 March 2011.

- MoU between the Indian Council of Medical Research (ICMR) and the Canadian Institute of Health Research (CIHR) to establish new and/or strengthen existing collaborations in special health related fields of research on 17 March 2011.

- Agreement between the Ministry of Mines, India and the Ministry of Natural Resourcesand Wildlife and the Ministry of Economic Development, Innovation and Export Trade, Saskatchewan Province, Canada regarding cooperation in the field of Mineral Sources on 24 May 2011.

- Agreement between Ministry of Mines, India and Quebec Minister of Natural Resources

- and Wildlife and the Quebec Minister of Economic Development, Innovation and Export Trade for cooperation in the field of Mineral Resources on May 24, 2012

- MoU between Ministry for Roads and Highways, India and the Canadian Ministry of Transport, Infrastructure to enhance cooperation in road transportation on June 11, 2012

Other agreements under negotiation are:

- Bilateral Investment Promotion and Protection Agreement (FIPA/BIPA)

- Comprehensive Economic Partnership Agreement (CEPA)

- Social Security Agreement (SSA) – concluded

- Audio-Visual Co-Production Agreement

- MoU with DRDO

- MoU on Traditional Medicines

Annexure VI: High Commissioners of India to Canada-1947-2015

1.	H.S. Malik	September, 1947 to August, 1949
2.	S.K. Kriplani	October, 1949 to March, 1951
3.	R.R. Saksena	June, 1951 to September, 1954
4.	Dr. M.A. Rauf	October, 1954 to August, 1958
5.	C.S. Venkatachar	August, 1958 to October, 1960
6.	B.N. Chakravarty	October, 1960 to July, 1962
7.	C.S. Jha	July, 1962 to January, 1964
8.	B.K. Acharya	May, 1964 to July, 1966
9.	General J.N. Chaudhuri	July, 1966 to August, 1969
10.	A.B. Bhadkamkar	December, 1969 to October, 1972
11.	U.S. Bajpai	October, 1972 to April, 1977
12.	Mahboob Ahmed	April, 1977 to September, 1978
13.	General T.N. Raina	February, 1979 to May, 1980
14.	G.S. Dhillon	September, 1980 to August, 1982
15.	M.R. Sivaramakrishnan	October, 1982 to May, 1984
16.	S.J.S.Chhatwal	June, 1985 to March, 1990
17.	G.N. Mehra	June, 1990 to June, 1992
18.	Prem K. Budhwar	November, 1992 to September, 1997
19.	Rajnikanta Verma	December, 1997 to June, 2002
20.	Shashi Uban Tripathi	August, 2002 to August, 2004
21.	Shyamala B. Cowsik	December, 2004 to February, 2007

22.	R.L. Narayan	March, 2007 to September, 2008
23.	Shashishekhar M. Gavai	November, 2008 to August, 2012
24.	Admiral Nirmal Kumar Verma	November, 2012 to Nov, 2014
25.	Vishnu Prakash	March, 2015 to date

Annexure VII: High Commissioners of Canada to India

Head Of Post	Title	Career	Appointment Date	Presentation of credentials	Termination of mission
Kearney, John Doherty	HC	NC	1946/12/23	1947/04/27	
Chipman, Warwick Fielding	HC	NC	1949/03/31	1949/12/16	
Reid, Escott Meredith	HC	C	1952/07/31	1952/11/21	1957/05/04
Ronning, Chester Alvin	HC	C	1957/03/07		1964
Rettie, Edward Rose	A/HC	C	1964		1964/09/07
Michener, Hon. Daniel Roland	HC	NC	1964/07/09	1964/09/07	1967/04/12
Hicks, Douglas Barcham	A/HC	C	1967/04/12		1967/10/21
George, James	HC	C	1967/07/17	1967/10/21	1972/08/20
Williams, Bruce MacGillivray	HC	C	1972/06/08	1972/09/23	1974/07/02
Maybee, John Ryerson	HC	C	1974/06/13	1974/09/26	1977/05/31
Rogers, Robert Louis	HC	C	1977/07/14	1977/09/24	1979/08/23
Hadwen, John Gaylard	HC	C	1979/04/04	1979/10/26	1973/08/25
Warden, William Thomas	HC	C	1983/10/13		1986/08/00
Harris, James Gordon	HC	C	1986/07/23	1986/10/09	1991/10/07
Paynter, John Lawrence	HC	C	1991/01/03		

Head Of Post	Title	Career	Appointment Date	Presentation of credentials	Termination of mission
Gooch, Stanley Edward	HC	C	1994/08/16	1994/10/04	1997/09/00
Walker, Peter F.	HC	C	1997/10/30	1997/11/27	2000/08/22
Sutherland, Peter	HC	C	2000/09/22	2000/10/23	2003
Edwards, Lucie Geneviève	HC	C	2003/07/31	2003/11/24	2006/08/02
Malone, David	HC	C	2006/07/13	2006/09/12	
Caron, Joseph	HC	C	2008/09/02	2008/11/10	
Beck, Stewart	HC	C	2010/09/20	2010/12/08	
Patel, Nadir	HC	C	2014/10/03	2015/01/16	

Annexure VIII: Map of India in Colour

Source: http://2.bp.blogspot.com/-cLP_y9bdjBw/VcGFbnr6YrI/AAAAAAAADAc/
FA0gSwdY5r0/s1600/india_state_map.png

Annexure IX: Map of Canada in Colour

Source: http://www.worldofmaps.com/images/map-canada.gif

Annexure

Annexure X: Map of the World in Colour

WORLD MAP

Copyright ©2011 www.whereig.com

Bibliography

1. Archie Hobson (ed.). *The Cambridge Gazetteer of the United States and Canada*, (New York: Cambridge University Press, 1995).

2. Brian Moore. *Canada* (Life World Library), (New York: Time, Inc., 1963).

3. "Canada North", Report of the Department of Northern Affairs, Government of Canada, Ottawa. (1994).

4. Michael Spencer and Suzan Ayscough. *Hollywood North: Creating the Canadian Motion Picture Industry*, (Montreal: Cantos International Publishing Inc., 2003).

5. Bhausaheb Ubale. *Politics of Exclusion: Multiculturalism or Ghettoism*, (City of North York, Ontario: Ampri Enterprises, 1992).

6. Inuit Masterworks—The Inuit Gallery of Vancouver (1990).

7. Sarjeet Singh Jagpaal. *Becoming Canadians: Pioneer Sikhs in Their Own Words*. (Vancouver, British Columbia: Harbour Publishing, 1994).

8. Neil Bissoondath. *Selling Illusions: The Cult of Multiculturalism in Canada*. (Ontario: Penguin Books Ltd, 1994).

9. Milton Israel. In the Further Soil: A Social History of Indo-Canadians in Ontario. (Toronto: University of Toronto Press Inc. 1994).

10. Escott Reid. *Envoy to Nehru*. (Delhi and Toronto: Oxford University Press 1981).

11. Clyde Sanger (ed.). Travels with a Laptop: Canadian Journalists Head South – An Anthology. (Ottawa: The North-South Institute, 1994).

12. J.S Grewal and Hugh Johnston (eds.). The India-Canada Relationship: Exploring the Political, Economic and Cultural Dimensions. (New Delhi/Thousand Oaks/London: Sage Publications, 1994).

13. Dave McIntosh. *Ottawa Unbuttoned or Who Is Running This Country Anyway?* (North York, Ontario: Stoddart Publishing Company Ltd., 1987).

14. Ron Graham. *One Eyed Kings: Promises and Illusion in Canadian Politics.* (Ontario: Collins Publishers, 1986).

15. Insight Guides. *Canada.* (Hong Kong: APA Publications Ltd., 1990).

16. Robert V. Bruce. *Bell: Alexander Graham Bell and the Conquest of Solitude.* (New York: Cornell University Press, 1990).

17. Alex Macdonald. *Alex in Wonderland.* (Vancouver: New Star Books, 1993).

18. Wikipedia Contributors. "Canada," Wikipedia, The Free Encyclopedia, http://en.wikipedia.org/w/index.php?title=Canada&oldid=661206405.

19. Statistics Canada. Canada's National Statistical Agency, www.statcan.gc.ca/start-debut-eng.html, (accessed ?).

20. Wikipedia Contributors, "Canada–India Relations," Wikipedia, The Free Encyclopedia, http://en.wikipedia.org/w/index.php?title=Canada%E2%80%93India_relations&oldid=657153918.

21. Canada vs India: Economy Stats Compared, *www.nationmaster.com/country-info/compare/Canada/India/Economy*

22. High Commission of India, Ottawa (Canada), *www.hciottawa.ca/*

23. High Commission of Canada in India: Canada International *www.canadainternational.gc.ca/india-inde/index.aspx?lang=eng*

24. Wikipedia Contributors, "Cinema of Canada," Wikipedia, The Free Encyclopedia, http://en.wikipedia.org/w/index.php?title=Cinema_of_Canada&oldid=655121598.

Index

Komagata Maru 135, 136, 137, 149

Korean War 21, 74, 111

Kosovo conflict 74

L

Lake Champlain 14

League of Nations 19, 71

Liquefied Natural Gas xiv, 79, 123, 126

Louis Joseph Papineau 15

M

Massey Commission 86

McMaster University 50

Meech Lake Accord 64

Mexican-US War 54

Montreal 9, 10, 17, 23, 26, 35, 39, 40, 41, 46, 76, 83, 84, 85, 86, 87, 88, 89, 96, 97, 102, 115, 139, 142, 171, 185, 186, 187, 188, 190, 191, 193, 194, 195, 209

N

Napoleonic wars 39, 84

Narendra Modi 117, 118

National Democratic Party xiv, 65, 67

National Film Board of Canada xiv, 89

National Parks

Cape Spear National Park 93

Gros Morne National Park 93

Signal Hill Park 93

Terra Nova National Park 93

Natural History Museum of Denmark's Centre for Geo Genetics 3

New France 8, 9, 10, 12, 33, 38, 53, 82, 83

Niagara Falls 89, 95

Non-Proliferation Treaty xiv, 116

Nootka Convention 69

North American Aerospace Defense Command xiv, 21, 74

North American Free Trade Agreement xiv, 49, 76, 152

North Atlantic Treaty Organization xiv, 21, 74, 76, 78, 108, 111, 120, 150

Northern Shipping Route xiv, 78, 79

North Pole viii, 25, 77, 78, 100, 102, 159

O

Old Crow basin 3

Ontario 13, 14, 15, 16, 17, 20, 23, 26, 41, 45, 47, 48, 53, 54, 58, 67, 76, 84, 85, 88, 89, 95, 96, 97, 139, 143, 162, 163, 164, 165, 167, 172, 184, 188, 190, 191, 197, 209, 210

Oregon Treaty 25, 69

Organization for Economic Co-operation and Development xiv, 45, 49, 76